D. E. Harding

. . .

The Trial of the Man Who Said He was God

With illustrations by the author

The Shollond Trust

Published by The Shollond Trust
87B Cazenove Road
London N16 6BB
England

headexchange@gn.apc.org
www.headless.org

The Shollond Trust is a UK charity reg. no 1059551

Copyright © The Shollond Trust 2019
Layout by rangsgraphics.com

All rights reserved. No part of this book may be reproduced or utilized in any form or by any means, electronic or mechanical, without prior permission in writing from the publishers.

This book was put into digital format by the following wonderful volunteers: George Mercadante, Jose Ruiz, Michael Adamson, Stephanie Klauser. OCR Scanning was done by Cathy Christian.

ISBN 978-1-908774-66-8

To Chris and Annie Harper, with love.

CONTENTS

Prologue	1
THE POLICE OFFICER	17
THE HUMANIST	29
THE SCHOOLGIRL	39
THE LAVATORY ATTENDANT	51
THE PASSENGER	65
THE HAIRDRESSER	77
THE OSTEOPATH	85
THE NEUROSURGEON	101
THE PSYCHOTHERAPIST	119
THE SOCIAL WORKER	133
THE OCCASIONAL BARMAID	149
THE STORE MANAGER	165
THE CANADIAN WIDOW	181
THE PSYCHIATRIST	195
THE NEW APOCALYPTIC	215
THE SUFFRAGAN BISHOP	229
THE ATHEIST	243
THE DEVOTEE	263
The Judge in Camera with Counsel and Accused	273
THE VENERABLE BHIKKHU	277
THE BODY WORKER	295
THE EX-SANYASSIN	307
THE ZOOLOGIST	319

THE MULLAH	337
THE REGISTRAR	353
THE MAN OF BUSINESS	371
THE COUNSELLOR	387
THE BORN-AGAIN CHRISTIAN	403
Prosecution Summing-up	423
Defence Summing-up	431
Judge's Directions to the Jury	451
The Verdict	455
Epilogue	459
The 8 x 8-fold Plebeian Path	473
Autobiographical Postscript	476

Prologue

My name is John a-Nokes, Jack to my friends.

The year is 2003 CE. Or, as I prefer to put it, 2003 AD.

I'm writing this in a prison cell, while I await the outcome of my Trial for the capital offence of BEING WHO I AM. OF BEING MYSELF, instead of what people tell me I am.

Of course that's not the official name of the crime I was charged with. Far from it! No, I was charged with blasphemy under the Blasphemy Act of 2002. Blasphemy, if you please! In fact, all I did was stop pretending I was someone else. I dared to start all over again and look at myself for myself—at what it's like being me. And to enthuse about my altogether unexpected findings—findings that (as you will presently see) were at least as sobering as they were exalting, sometimes hilarious, often beautiful and always practical. And not so hard to live by as you might think.

If that's blasphemy, I'll be damned! If that's blasphemy, God help us all!

This cell isn't the ideal writer's study, but it will do. The chair I'm sitting on is chair-shaped; the numbing effect no doubt arises from the fact that it's made of and upholstered with case-hardened cast iron. The table I'm sitting at is sufficiently supplied with mole-grey recycled writing-paper and ball-point pens that write as if they too have been recycled. The view from here is of an interestingly crazed WC pan and a cracked wash-basin set against shining grey graffiti-proof tile walls. High in the wall ahead is a window more heavily barred than it need be, seeing that only a ten-foot prisoner could possibly reach it; and certainly smaller than it should be, seeing that the light it admits seems to have been filtered through grey flannel underwear. The smell, which is of that underwear repeatedly but insufficiently dosed with disinfectant, leaves me gasping occasionally like a stranded but resigned trout.

I'm filling in the time by writing up this account of the Trial, based on the notes I made in the course of it and my present recollection of what happened. Though I shall be doing my best to be truthful, and in particular to be fair to the case for the Prosecution, I can't pretend to perfect impartiality. How could I? Heretics take a dim view of their inquisitors. In any event, this is not going to be a verbatim account of the proceedings, but (let's say) a fairly detailed record of my impressions—a layman's impressions, because I'm no lawyer. Much of the inconsequential to-and-fro between the parties will be left out. It's possible, of course, that there were things of substance said that I don't remember because I wish to forget them.

What I can promise you, my Reader (I've reason to hope that these pages will be got out of here and find their way to those they are meant for), is that you will get a clear picture of what I'm up to and why, and will be well able to decide for yourself whether or not I'm guilty as charged. In fact, I hereby warn you that my aim is conspiratorial: it isn't so much to defend myself (it's a bit late for that) as to involve you in the criminal adventure which led to my arrest and trial. If I can win you over to my side in this affair, I shall be satisfied. And all the more so if, less rash and vociferous than I am, you're able to keep your nose fairly clean—I mean, stay sufficiently quiet about your discoveries—and so avoid arrest and prosecution, with the risk of a death sentence

Yes, you do run a certain risk in reading this book. If this worries you, read no more, but pass it on to a friend who doesn't mind living dangerously. Living dangerously (I should add) for the sake of the Ultimate Safety.

Before getting down to the Trial itself you will need to be reminded of its historical background, of what led up to it.

The history of the social upheavals that gave rise to the passing of the Blasphemy Act of 2002 CE is too complicated to go into at all thoroughly here; to summarize will do. They began with the death sentence pronounced on Salman Rushdie by the Ayatollah, and the notorious outcome of that international scandal. They built up to the Fundamentalist Disturbances of 1999-2000, when a newspaper cartoonist, a popular comedian and a modernist bishop were kidnapped and burned at the stake for ridiculing the Second Coming of Christ promised (as millions believed) for 1 January 2000. They culminated in the widespread communal riots of the year 2001 in which hundreds died in Great Britain alone—many of them subjected to the farce of trial by kangaroo courts set up by sects claiming to represent the heart and soul of one or another of the great Western religions, and dedicated to rooting out blasphemy whatever the cost. After which, Parliament decided that the lesser evil would be to institute special courts to try charges of blasphemy in accordance with the law of the land. And so the old common law was updated and made statute law and given teeth. Teeth—following the reintroduction of the death penalty at the turn of the century—that could kill.

The new anti-blasphemy legislation of the year 2002 has been widely condemned as servile surrender to bigotry and superstition, and as a very serious curtailment of human rights. Many have talked of a revival of the Holy Inquisition. But at least it has, so far and touch wood, done something to calm the more excitable zealots and dissuade them from taking the law into their own hands. The large and growing 'conscience drain' (dubbed the 'blasphemy sewer' by certain fundamentalists) from the West to the Far East—where the concept of blasphemy is little understood—is reckoned a small price to pay for ending what had begun to look like civil war.

Why (you may well ask) this upsurge of religious fanaticism, throughout the Western world, at the very time when political fanaticism seems to be abating? Is it that people must have a scapegoat to vent their guilt on, or a bête noire to vent their anger on, no matter how unjustified by the facts? A plausible explanation, but not one that's easy to test. And not one to give any satisfaction or guidance to a government desperate to contain and reduce fundamentalist violence.

And certainly not one to give any comfort to me, at the receiving end of the violence.

As for the provisions of the Blasphemy Act—a long-winded document drafted in standard legal jargon—a note of some of the main points will be enough for our purpose here.

The Act is directed against anyone who disturbs public order by giving offence to religious communities, no matter what medium is used. It may be by means of the printed word or in public meetings or TV and radio broadcasts, or simply by going around and buttonholing strangers and stirring them up. Privately held opinions, expressed in the family and among friends and in peaceable meetings of scholars or like-minded persons, don't come under the Act. Nor does the occasional and accidental outburst: the offence must be sustained. Blasphemy is defined as the use in public of insulting words and behaviour aimed at any Being or Person or Object whatsoever that's held to be sacred by an appreciable number of the population. Notably it includes claiming to be one or another of the sacred Entities, but just about any behaviour that gravely upsets their devotees and worshippers is treated as criminal. In fact, it's difficult to see how anyone who isn't spiritually moribund could remain, all through his or her life, perfectly innocent of this offence. There's a good deal of agreement that the Act, as a result of having been drafted in haste and passed in panic, is exceptionally vague and hard to implement. And, what's much worse, that it's a bad case of the very disease it aims to treat—the disease of heresy-hunting carried to the point of terrorism. You, my Reader, will soon be well placed for checking how far these criticisms are justified.

Four or five much-publicized arrests have been made, and preparations for the trials of the alleged offenders have reached various stages. My own case is the first to be heard under the Act— which makes it the test case, calculated to bring to light (if doing little to solve) the problems of what promises to be a new and deplorable chapter in the history of jurisprudence. For this reason—and perhaps also because I conducted my own Defence in a way unheard of in the courts—it has become known to the press as the Great Blasphemy Trial. Ignorance of how to behave myself wasn't bliss, and I'm not sure how it went down with the Jury, but it helped me to extract what entertainment I could from all that pomp and circumstance.

Anyway, it follows from the provisions of the Act, and the special nature of the crime it's concerned with, that customs which have become sacrosanct in criminal trials can't be followed here. New and looser procedures are being developed and tried out. Thus in my own Trial the Prosecution was given a remarkably free hand, and the rules about what is and what isn't admissible evidence were much relaxed. Hearsay, and the opinions of non-expert witnesses, were to a large degree permitted by the Judge. So was the leading of witnesses. Throughout, Counsel and I frequently found ourselves addressing each other directly, in a brisk ding-dong—a gross irregularity which the judge was (apparently) quite happy about.

As a gesture of even-handedness, the Judge made two concessions to the Defence. The first arose from the large number of witnesses called by the Prosecution and the varied nature of their evidence. It was ruled that I should be free to defend myself against each witness's testimony in turn, as soon as it was given—the reason being that, if my Defence were left to the end, the Jury (and I) would have forgotten what it was all about. Thus I was able to contest the Prosecution's arguments as they came up and were fresh in all our minds. Counsel for the Crown agreed to this arrangement on the condition that he could at any time (within reason) interrupt my Defence in order to point out its weaknesses to the Jury.

The second concession arose from the difficulty that my witnesses, though far outnumbering the Prosecution's and far out weighing them in prestige, couldn't be subpoenaed to appear in court. The difficulty was that they were dead. Fortunately so, let me add: if they had been around and saying now what I'm quoting them as having said, many would have exposed themselves to prosecution under the Act. All the more reason for seeking leave to cite in my Defence the recorded testimony of these people who, though dead, were (say I) among the best that ever lived; and who, in a sense, live on, more alive than ever. Quite reasonably, the Prosecution objected that their so-called evidence was inadmissible, seeing that they couldn't be sworn and examined and cross-examined, and moreover seeing that (as everyone knows) the sayings attributed to the famous are often garbled and occasionally spurious. After some argument the Judge ruled that such material might, with discretion, be produced in court, but only as illustrations for giving shape and colour to my case and by no means as testimony for proving it. I expressed my satisfaction, inasmuch as I never dreamed of founding my case on what these or any other pundits say, but upon the experiments and practical demonstrations (helped out by visual aids) which test what they say. I pointed out to the Judge that it wasn't belief but doubt—my daring to question dogmas and assumptions that are rarely challenged—that had landed me in the dock. My unbridled scepticism is what some of my critics call it. They're about right.

The visual aids consisted of diagrams and sketches I had made in advance—for clarifying my case in detail—bound together in a booklet with a mirror mounted on the cover. The Judge, the Jury members and the Prosecution lawyers were each furnished with a copy. The importance of its role in the Defence can scarcely be exaggerated. I'm obliged to the authorities for their co-operation in the preparation of the booklet, and its use throughout the Trial.

The overall effect of these legal irregularities and concessions was to turn the court—Court One in London's New Bailey—into something like a superior debating-chamber, tricked out with all the pageantry of the law. A debating-chamber which nevertheless retained full powers of determining guilt and passing the severest of sentences.

The ultimate penalty prescribed by the Act is death—death by beheading, of course, since the reintroduction of the death penalty. The sentence may, however, be reduced to imprisonment and fine if the offender publicly recants and apologizes to the outraged parties, in terms and circumstances to be decided by the Judge. The impression one is left with is that the last thing the politicians who brought in the Act wanted was a line of martyrs whose bleeding but haloed heads could be laid at their door.

Two or three more points before we get down to business.

A thing that puzzled me at the time, and may well puzzle you as you read on, is what I can only call the patchy and enigmatical performance of Sir Gerald Wilberforce, the Crown Counsel. He has a reputation for knowledge in fields that top lawyers rarely have time to cultivate, and for skill in applying it. No doubt that's why he was chosen to prosecute. His versatility did indeed come out in the Trial. But so, mysteriously, did lost opportunities to press and follow through points that emerged to the Prosecution's advantage, or to the Defence's discomfiture. Not infrequently, he seemed to play into my hands. Again, though he generally put up the obligatory show of forensic vigour and aggression (and sometimes overdid it), there were occasions when he seemed to stray from his brief—to the extent of forgetting his role and the terms of the charge against me. At such times he slipped into the urbane and discursive polemic of the lecture theatre, instead of sticking to the tighter polemic of the lawcourt. It was as if Sir Gerald wasn't sure whether he was wearing his doctoral hood or his tie-wig. The question remains: was his peculiarly mixed performance incidental; or was it deliberate, arising from a secret brief behind his brief?

The other thing that puzzled me is the trouble the Prosecution took to call witness upon witness till there were twenty-seven of them, when it could have made its case with half that number. If it had known in advance how vulnerable many of them were to prove, it would no doubt have reduced them to a carefully selected dozen. But it's easy to be wise after a Trial without precedent. And having, of course, supplied the Defence in advance with abstracts of the testimonies of all twenty-seven, the Prosecution was committed to calling most if not all of them. Nevertheless we're left with the question: why so many in the first place? And again the bigger question: what was the Prosecution really up to?

Even now I'm not at all sure of the answer to these two conundrums. But whatever it is, I think it belongs at the end of this write-up of the proceedings. By then, your guess will be as good as mine.

The Trial

Nobody can be said to have attained to the pinnacle of truth until a thousand sincere people have denounced him for blasphemy.

Anthony de Mello, SJ

All great truths begin as blasphemies.

George Bernard Shaw

The Charge and the Plea

COUNSEL: Your Honour, I am Gerald Wilberforce, King's Counsellor, and I lead on behalf of the Crown in this case. My Junior at the Bar is Herbert Atkinson of the Inner Temple.

The Accused, John a-Nokes, is charged under the Act of 2002 CE with the crime of blasphemy.

I shall be calling some twenty-seven witnesses, each of whom will testify to one or more of the following essential matters—I say, matters of fact:

First, the blasphemy. In all manner of ways John a-Nokes has insulted and brought into contempt One whom many people perceive as divine.

Second, its extreme form. In John a-Nokes the offence peaks: for he falsely claims that he is none other than the Unique Being whom ordinary humans worship as the highest and the holiest.

Third, its dissemination. To gain publicity for his blasphemous beliefs, he has persistently used all available means, including radio and television broadcasts, books, magazine articles and public lectures.

Fourth, the reaction. His teachings have so outraged religious people that they have repeatedly committed such breaches of the peace as riotous assembly, arson, unlawful killings—and prima facie murder.

In applying these four criteria, Your Honour, the Prosecution sets out to prove the Accused guilty of the crime of blasphemy as defined in the Act, Sections 4, 7c, 12, and 13b.

JUDGE: How do you plead, John a-Nokes? Guilty or Not Guilty?

MYSELF: Not Guilty, Your Honour.

JUDGE: I understand that you wish to conduct your own Defence. Indeed I see that the dock has already been fitted with shelves for your books and papers. However, it's my duty to warn you of the risk that your inexperience may hamper the presentation of your case to the Jury. Are you sure you can do justice to the evidence and the arguments that are in your favour, and can do battle with those that are not? Even at this late hour you may change your mind. There is in court a learned and able King's Counsellor who is well prepared to take on your Defence.

MYSELF: While I'm much obliged to Your Honour, I've decided to defend myself, notwithstanding the risks. But I do seek Your Honour's indulgence when, due to ignorance of court procedure and etiquette, I fail to conduct myself properly.

JUDGE: Have no fear on that score: I shall keep you in order.

MYSELF: My Defence, Your Honour, I summarize like this:

None of the four components of the Prosecution's case against me—what Counsel calls my blasphemy, the extreme form it takes, its dissemination and the public's reaction—none of these is resisted in principle. I'll go along with all four once they are stripped of pejorative and prejudicial language. My Defence doesn't consist so much in combating as in reinterpreting them, in the light of two considerations.

The first and comparatively unimportant one is that the outrage I have undoubtedly given rise to was unintentional. So far from being deliberate, it was and is much regretted. Alas, it is unavoidable if the truths I publicize are at all important—and I say they are supremely important, indeed critical, for the health and even the survival of our species. Though the Act, as I read it, does little to distinguish between offence that's given inadvertently and offence that's given deliberately, it's hardly a difference which the Judge and the Jury can ignore.

The second and crucial Defence argument—the pith and substance of my case—I state baldly here. Baldly, but without rancour or complacency. Full supporting evidence will come out in the course of the Trial.

Here it is: I am the only one in court who is not guilty of blasphemy! *I accuse my accusers of this most serious crime!*

It's you who stand in the dock today!

The Prosecution Witnesses and the Defence Rebuttal

Prosecution Witness No. 1

THE POLICE OFFICER

Preliminaries over, all is now set in court for the Trial to proceed. Counsel for the Prosecution calls his first witness, a police officer in uniform. Prompted by Counsel, he gives evidence of arrest. He testifies how, armed with a warrant, he went to my home, where he cautioned me that anything I said was liable to be taken down and used in evidence.

COUNSEL: What was the Accused's reaction?

OFFICER, consulting his notebook: Paying no attention to my warning, he kept bragging it was impossible to arrest him. He was a sight too big and slippery (vac... vacous? and tenous? are words I've got down here) for any officer of the law to handle. Apprehending this suspect would be like taking the West Wind into custody, he told me.

COUNSEL: You proved him wrong?

OFFICER: I surely did, sir. He came along quietly, and there was no trouble on the way to the police station. There, he started up again. He kept boasting that no cell was strong enough to hold him, and promised to smash down at least one wall and break out of the building. There was something I didn't get, about taking off into space.

COUNSEL: Was he claiming to be an unusually clever magician, or perhaps a second Houdini, an escape artist of the sort you see on the stage?

OFFICER: Not really. The impression I got was that he was rather mad, and convinced he wielded some kind of divine power.

COUNSEL, to Jury: Note the words 'divine power'. You might suppose that the Accused, content with announcing his divinity to the world in season and out of season, would let up a little in prison. But not so. Here we have indeed a blasphemer for all seasons!

[To Witness] So you decided to see whether handcuffs would curb this marvellous power?

OFFICER: That's right, just to make sure. It seems they did. Either the power he packed wasn't Godlike enough to unlock an ordinary pair of darbies (let alone smash walls) or else it didn't exist at all.

COUNSEL: So what happened in the end?

OFFICER: Nothing special at all. The handcuffs soon came off, and John a-Nokes turned out to be a quite normal prisoner. Rather better behaved, I reckon, than most. But every bit as human. That stuff was just talk.

COUNSEL: There you have it all, Jury. A small man talking bigger than big.

That's all, Officer. But stay in the box: I think he has some questions to put to you.

The Police Officer

Defence: **My Let-out and My Let-in**

MYSELF: Officer, was my conversation with you abrasive, or humorous?

OFFICER: More humorous, I'd say. Funny stuff—with an edge to it.

MYSELF: And casual too, as if something perfectly obvious were being pointed out?

OFFICER: Well, yes, in a way.

MYSELF: What made you change your mind and decide to give the impression in your testimony that I was a wild and aggressive prisoner, if not actually raving mad?

OFFICER: Well, I don't know... I wasn't concerned with giving impressions, one way or another, but just answering Counsel's questions. I didn't say you *were* wild and aggressive. Only that you talked that way.

MYSELF: Thank you. No more questions from me. [The Witness stands down.]

Ladies and gentlemen of the Jury, let me tell you about a very significant thing that happened in that prison. After the Officer had satisfied himself that I would give no trouble, he took my handcuffs off—as you've just heard. Also, at my request, he gave me drawing materials. I wanted to verify how impossible it was to make a sketch of myself from *inside* that cell.

If you will please turn to Diagram No. 1 in the pamphlet which the Defence has supplied each of you with, you'll find a copy of my sketch.

The 'cell' wasn't a *cell* (the rear wall was missing) and I wasn't in what there was of it. All I found of myself was the odd arm and leg thrust in from outside. I was no more held in that cell than in that cracked basin while washing my hands. The truth is that I peek and prod into rooms, advancing a tentative feeler or two, but never O never—like other people—venture inside. You'll not catch *me* in one of your mantraps! Not nowadays you won't!

What happened to me was this. Having been told from an early age that the word 'cell'—or room, or compartment, or chamber, or courtroom—means a space closed in on *all* sides, I tailored my experience to the language. I hallucinated to order. And was everywhere a jailbird. But one day—O happy day!—I noticed that the poet Lovelace, writing from jail, said truly:

Stone walls do not a prison make

Nor iron bars a cage.

I came to my senses, and saw my way back to freedom. Not just figuratively but literally, saw my way back to freedom...

The business of this court is to go by the evidence that is clearly presented within its four walls. Correction: *three* walls. All I ask of you members of the Jury is to look at what's being displayed at this moment, what's clearly on show—not what's imagined, believed, thought up, cooked up, faked up, but actually seen. Namely, *three* walls—at most. Another glance at my picture may help you to see the *given* shape of the shapes around you.

The Police Officer

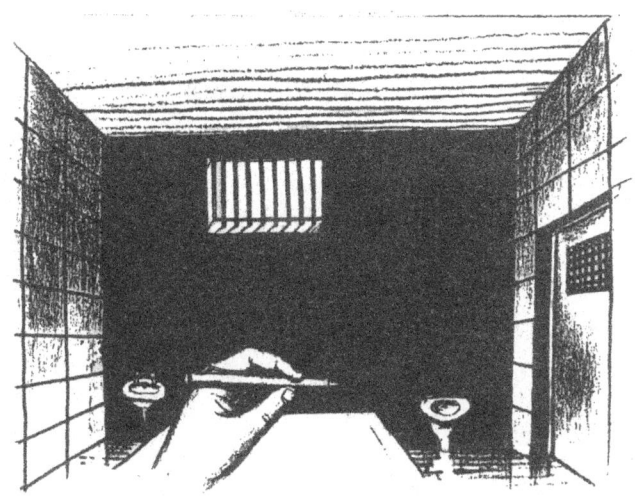

Diagram No. 1

Look! Ahead of you is the now-empty witness-box, with its telescreen for long-distance witnesses, and you see that it has for background an approximately *rectangular* wall. On your right, His Honour the Judge sitting there on his bench, and below him the Clerk to the Court, have a *wedge-shaped* wall background; and the thick end of the wedge—your end—is fuzzy. It fades out, On your left, the dock—with me in it—has a second wedge-shaped wall for background, fading out as before. Now can you honestly tell me that, on present evidence, these two wedges join up to make a fourth wall? Or that *you* have any background at all? Come on! Have you ever, even in the Underground during the rush hour, found yourself hemmed in *all* round? Aren't you always, *for yourself,* wide open at the rear, unconfined, at large, deeper than deep, immense?

In this direction the risk, if there were any, would surely be agoraphobia and not claustrophobia.

COUNSEL: I must protest, Your Honour! Is this a Trial for blasphemy? Or a seminar on perspective? Or—heaven help us!—a game for four-year-olds? The Accused is wasting the court's time.

JUDGE: I think he may be coming to the point.

MYSELF: I'm right there, Your Honour.

If you and the Jury will please turn to Diagram No. 2 in the booklet, it may help to bring out my meaning.

When overlooked and avoided, this Missing Wall or Rear Gap or Absence reads as useless and boring, the shadow of a shadow, a dead loss. Or worse: as more terrifying than any ghost or devil. When taken in and taken on, however, it becomes the Presence that is my

Diagram No. 2

treasure. This despised No-thing at my back turns out to be far more real than any of the things in front of me. This neglected Place is a truer one than any on the map for, in contrast to them, it's infinitely wide and deep, uniformly itself through and through, all on show at once, always accessible, unchanging and—ah!—my Native Land. The Big Country. the Country of Everlasting Clearness. This is what I see it is, not what I imagine it is. Above all, it's vividly *aware* of itself as all this, and free from every limitation. Described negatively, it's my way out of the tightest spot, my escape route from the most secure of prisons. Described positively, it's my way in to the absolute Liberty that I am. It didn't forsake me when the Officer thought he had me cooped up in his cell. It doesn't forsake me now in this sombre courtroom, of which it is the fourth side—the bright side which is God's side.

Yes! Every room—every place I am ever supposed to be 'in'—has its God's side. Which is my side. My let-out from the world, and my let-in to its Source. Here's the silver lining to the darkest cloud that ever gathered.

For thousands of years the wise have been siding with God and taking this way Home; and recommending, with all the eloquence at their command, this royal road from human bondage back to divine freedom. Now, at last, instead of being told about it by experts, we are being shown it. We are invited to see our own way through to God's own country. The Clear Country we're coming from and returning to.

COUNSEL, slicing the air with his brief: Did you hear what he said, members of the Jury? Graciously, Mr John a-Nokes takes God's side! Not, as you might think, out of need or reverence, but because of Who he thinks he is, because it's naturally his side. This, you'll agree, is blasphemy without qualms, the laid-back sort. And stupid: to find all four walls at once, he has only to mount a pair of steps and look down from the ceiling.

MYSELF: And then the room is ceilingless. There, on high this time, is his let-out from man's world into God's. In drawing plans of four-walled rooms open to the sky, the architect sides with the Architect of the Universe.

For God's sake let's come to our senses and give ourselves a break. We're all in business, the difficult business of living. What's the use of being upfront if our rear's in disarray, if our pants are down? Our success, our very survival depends ultimately on the Backup our enterprise draws on. Is it some mushroom corporation, with a confidence-inspiring logo and title and address in the City, sprung up overnight in the financial jungle? Or a half-hardy perennial like our High Street Barclays? Truly there's only one Bank I can always bank on, only one Firm that stays firm through all crises, only one Underwriter that never comes out from under, only one Resource that's infinitely resourceful. That's the one I have for backing, right now. I can count on this Thing because it isn't a thing at all, but the Origin and Receptacle of all things, the Source of all resources. Itself free from everything, its ability to come up with the things that are needed (including this description of itself right now) is astounding. It has a knack. My God, what a knack!

Call It what you like. The Void, Essence, Spirit, Awareness, Reality, the Treasury of the Kingdom of Heaven: or the true Banco di Santo Spirito. Only don't go on overlooking It. Look back without looking round. There's Nothing to It, It's that easy to appeal to and draw upon. And Everything's from It, It's that generous. Here's a Pocket infinitely deep and well-lined and perfect for picking. Our Source isn't playing hard to get. It's begging to be noticed and taken advantage of and cashed in on, positively tearing the courtroom apart in the effort. Tell me now, what more could It do to announce Itself?

COUNSEL, with a sneer: And these huge advances are quite interest-free to the great Mr Nokes, the divine bank customer, no doubt.

MYSELF: Certainly not. Backing like this invariably costs something. Interest has to be disbursed, attention has to be paid. I draw on the Bank's unlimited reserves to the extent that I'm awake to Its presence, and to the central position It occupies in my life. To be genuinely intrigued, to stick with It because I want to and not because I'm told to do so, is to cash in on It, to tap Its power, to be It. And just now It's revealing Itself as the Gap between the wedge-shaped walls of this courtroom. How vast and deep this Rear Gap is, how clean, how appreciative of Itself! Wonder-struck and delighted, I would say. The Gap is *agape!*

There are two pronunciations and two meanings of this word— the adjective 'agape' and the noun 'agapë', or love-feast—and both apply here. This wide-open-mouthed Appetite for the world is what I AM right here and right now, and It is infinitely mysterious. Truly

I can't say *what* It is but only *that* It is. Here is not a case of *I am this or that or the other*, but plain I AM. And, back of the I AM, the I AM NOT from which It arises without reason and without stint. A case of Being, without being someone or something. By contrast and with respect, I've only to glance across at Counsel to see what it's like being someone—an object which isn't backed by the Source of the world, or even by the world, but by a tiny bit of it. A man-shaped patch of courtroom.

What a relief to be backed by the One whose name is I AM, the name that precedes and introduces every other name! What a relief to merge into and be upheld by the Unlimited. In that police cell, in the dock of this court, in the condemned cell if you send me there, I find at my back only the Everlasting Freedom and the Incomparable Safety. For I am in none of those dim and poky places. They are in me who am Brightness itself, and I can take them.

God is my let-out.

My let-out into what place? My witnesses speak for me:

Into what place? Into the Place where place itself finds no admittance, where nothing exists save the lightning-flash of the Moon of Allah. It is far beyond all conception and imagination. It is the Light of light of light of light of light of light.

Rumi

True places are not found on maps.

Herman Melville

The lover has no back... He receives everything clean from Him.

Rumi

Let us be backed with God.

Shakespeare: Henry VI, Part 3

Bodhisattvas have their minds set to working without anything behind them... The Bodhisattva floats like a cloud in the sky without anything at its back.

D. T. Suzuki

The Sage all the time sees and hears no more than a young child sees and hears.

Tao Te Ching

I thank thee, O Father, Lord of heaven and earth, that thou hast hid these things from the wise and prudent, and hast revealed them unto babes.

Jesus

Prosecution Witness No. 2

THE HUMANIST

COUNSEL: The court would like to hear about your relationship with the Accused, in so far as it bears on the crime he stands accused of.

WITNESS: I'm a University Lecturer in Philosophy, and my special interest is the history of humanism. Some twenty years ago John a-Nokes attended a course of lectures I was giving on the ideas behind the French Revolution. I knew him vaguely as some kind of mystical freethinker, with a lively mind much given to enthusiasms. An oddball, you could say, if not a screwball. Since then we've bumped—and I mean bumped—into each other occasionally. From early days it was clear that we had little in common. Whenever our paths crossed, we crossed swords. This only resulted in our positions hardening and drifting even further apart. Gradually it dawned on me that he wasn't just ordinary religious, or Bible-thumping prayer-meeting religious, but what I can only call God-awful religious. I read as much of his stuff as I could take, which was very little. I listened to rather more than I could take on the subject of Who He Really Is. I concluded that we don't live in the same universe. We're mutually out of earshot. This deification syndrome, with its delusions of grandeur, leave me numb and practically speechless anyway.

COUNSEL: 'Deification syndrome', you say. Can you enlarge on that?

WITNESS: He's got so far above himself that he's out of my reach. If I could get to the man, I would challenge him to produce anyone who seriously regards him as divine. Why can't he see that his true dignity is to accept the world's view of him as only human after all? I'd like to see him stop posturing and, with Alexander Pope, admit his limitations:

Know then thyself, presume not God to scan,
The proper study of mankind is man.

Defence: **The Divinist**

MYSELF, to the Witness: This is ridiculous! It just isn't true that everyone says I'm essentially human. You must know about the Perennial Philosophy, according to which you and I are essentially divine—like it or lump it.

WITNESS: Well, there are all sorts of fantastic philosophical systems. I've forgotten (if ever I knew) most of what the so-called Perennial Philosophy teaches. Apparently it wasn't worth remembering.

MYSELF: Then let me remind you. It's to be found, more or less concealed, at the heart of all the great spiritual traditions. It insists that, really and truly, I am the One Self—alias Atman-Brahman, the Buddha Nature, Tao, Spirit, Being, God, the Aware No-thing that embraces All things. And that the whole reason for living is to realize that at core I am This and This Alone.

In that case my true dignity consists in my *denial* that I'm only human after all. A dignity arising out of lies isn't anything of the sort.

It's disgraceful and shaming and due for a tumble.

You appeal to popular opinion, that many-headed monster. Since when has philosophy subscribed to the dictum *Vox populi, vox Dei?* Rather it says *Vox populi, pox Dei!* Your common sense is nonsense, till the Perennial Philosophy brings you to your senses.

WITNESS: Why has this *soi-disant* Perennial Philosophy won for itself virtually no place in the history of philosophy? Because it makes horrible jokes? There must be a good reason why it doesn't figure in serious textbooks. I, who teach philosophy, know as much about it as I know about astrology. I suggest it's obscure because it deserves to be obscure.

MYSELF: In the East it has obscured all other philosophies for twenty-five centuries. Here in the West, it's the *only* philosophy that has survived intact down the ages, and is now more vigorous than ever. It doesn't date. Many a passage from the *Tao Te Ching* of 300 BCE reads as freshly today, and rings as true, as on the bright morning of its composition. No other body of doctrine is so free of historical and geographical discoloration, so practical no matter what the cultural constraints, so simple and self-evident and yet so deep. No other has stood half so well the test of time and of day-to-day experience. And yet no other is so wild, so daring, so madly and gloriously *happy!*

WITNESS: I wonder—

COUNSEL: Your Honour, what's going on in this lawcourt? Is a Witness being cross-examined? Or are two old sparring partners enjoying a knockabout at the Crown's expense?

JUDGE: It's all most irregular. But I think the outcome of the bout may have a bearing on the case, and that's what matters... The Accused may proceed, provided he's not much longer coming to the point.

MYSELF: I've arrived, Your Honour. I don't know about the Witness...

WITNESS: The trouble with dogmatic and speculative systems like this is that there's no way of testing them. Give me the full address with area code of this blessed deity of yours, tell me what time he's at home, and how to plant my foot in his door and how to recognize him when I get inside—and I'll take you and him seriously. Make this information so precise that anyone anywhere can track him down and find exactly the same blessed what's-it, and I'm your disciple—grovelling at your lotus-feet.

MYSELF: Done! I'll hold you to that! So far from being speculative or vague, the Perennial Philosophy tells you precisely:

(1) *Where* to find God: namely, right where you are. Which is in the witness-box of Court One, the New Bailey, Holborn, London EC4 England, Great Britain, Europe...

(2) *When* to find God: namely, right now. Which is 11.37 Greenwich Mean Time.

(3) *How* to find God: namely, by turning the arrow of your attention round 180° and looking inwards—looking in at what you're looking out of. And with childlike sincerity taking what you find there.

(4) *What to look for:* namely, that which has no form, features, colour or limits, but is like light or air or clear water or space. Great space, filled to capacity with what's on show. Which is Judge and Jury and

Accused and all the rest, with the sole exception of yourself. Great Space, *aware* of itself as thus empty and thus full.

The Perennial Philosophy has consistently and persistently put forward a hypothesis so amazing and so delectable—one's essential Godhood, no less—that it cries out to be tested by every available means, just in case it should turn out to be true. For good measure, as we've seen, it comes up with just the right tools for the job. *Precisely the four tests you listed, as it happens.* Precisely—in terms of feet and inches, of hours and minutes and seconds, of degrees of the compass. And to blazes with all spiritual-metaphysical waffle and cotton wool!

Tennyson said that God's nearer than my hands and my feet and my breathing, Muhammad that He's nearer than my jugular vein. Well then, let me see if they knew what they were talking about. Following those four guidelines we are agreed on: (1) I point, with both forefingers, at this nearest of places, the place I'm looking out of; (2) I do so now; (3) I do so in the spirit of a little child who takes what he gets; and (4) I notice whether what I'm pointing at is face-like or space-like, human or non-human, a thing or no-thing, small and bounded or limitless, dead to itself or alive—alive to Itself, in all Its blazing obviousness and uniqueness and—yes!—power. It looks as if Eckhart got it right: 'When the soul enters into her Ground, into the innermost regions of her Being, divine power suddenly pours into her.'

COUNSEL: First, members of the Jury, we were regaled with the spectacle of a fairly friendly punch-up. Now we have the winner positively exploding with admiration at himself—at the divine power he wields. But of course! He worships the ground he walks on- all the way to the dock today for sure. All the way to the scaffold tomorrow, it may be.

MYSELF: I appeal to His Honour and to each member of the Jury to ignore Counsel's blatant attempt to whip up prejudice against me and to *test* with an open mind what I'm saying. Just to watch and listen to me carrying out this crucial experiment would be worse than useless. What have you and I to fear from the truth? I beg you to follow my example, point right now—repeat, *right now*—to the Spot that's nearer than *your* breathing, and see *for yourself* what I'm going on about. Don't be nervous! Even if your mother (like mine) told you it was rude to point at anyone, I tell you it's all right to point at this One. He loves it! O how He loves it!

What is it like right where *you* are? What, on present evidence, are *you* looking out of? Who lives at the Centre of *your* universe? Only *you* are in a position to see and to say.

Till you have addressed—let alone settled—the question of your own identity, how can you settle mine? Wouldn't it be absurd and unjust to condemn me for claiming to be Someone, without looking to see whether *you* are that very same Someone? That incredible Someone?

I ask you: looking *in* now at what your two forefingers are pointing at, isn't it Aware Capacity for them and for the scene that lies between—namely, those little feet and those foreshortened legs, and those thighs, and the lower part of your trunk? Doesn't Diagram No. 3 (which I ask you to turn to) give a fair representation of what you're experiencing?

Diagram No. 3

Just what name do you propose to give to this Immensity that's nearer to you than your hands and your feet and your breathing, to the Radiance here that is the Light and all It lights up? To call It Mary Smith or William Brown or Gerald Wilberforce or John a-Nokes would be as perverse as to call it Little Green Apples. It's precisely the opposite and the absence of those persons. Here is the one place in my world that's clean of John a-Nokes, where I'm let off being that little fellow, so opaque and unluminous. Here, at my Centre, is the one place where there shines the Light that lights up the light. This is the Light which, according to Dante, 'makes visible the Creator Himself to His creature, who finds his peace in seeing Him'.

To put Jack here at the Centre of his world isn't just diabolical pride and blasphemy: it's being horrible to myself. It's playing Bottom the Weaver, and mounting a jackass's head on these shoulders. It's unbelievably stupid. The third person's not for divinizing, the First Person's not for humanizing. True humanism *there* is true divinism *here*. The very best I can do for Jack is to keep seeing him off, and God in.

In so far as I am, I am Him. As Rumi explains:

'I am God' is an expression of great humility. The man who says 'I am the slave of God' affirms two existences, his own and God's, but he that says 'I am God' has made himself non-existent and has given himself up... He says 'I am naught, He is all: there is no being but God's.' This is extreme humility and abasement.

Out of the scores of further witnesses I have lined up, these are the ones I have chosen:

In appearance a man, in reality God.

Chuang-tzu

Jesus said: What I now seem to be, that am I not... And so speak I, separating off the manhood.

Acts of John

They saw the body, and supposed he was a man.

Rumi

Man is not, he becomes: he is neither limited being nor unlimited, but the passage of limited being into unlimited; a search for his own perfection, which lies beyond him and is not himself but God... The stirring of religion is the feeling that my only true self is God.

A. C Bradley

No matter how often he thinks of God or goes to church, or how much he believes in religious ideas, if he, the whole man, is deaf to the question of existence, if he does not have an answer to it, he is marking time, and he lives and dies like one of the million things he produces. He thinks of God, instead of experiencing being God.

Erich Fromm

God is alive and well—and living guess where.

Graffito in a lavatory

Prosecution Witness No. 3

THE SCHOOLGIRL

COUNSEL: Your Honour, in the public gallery there's a class of schoolchildren aged between ten and twelve. They are here as part of their education in citizenship. I'm told by their teacher that any one of them whom the Accused may choose is willing to take the stand and give evidence. Provided, of course, Your Honour and the Accused agree.

The peculiar nature of the offence, and the informality of these proceedings, encourage me to make this proposal. The reason for making it is that the Accused, in books and lectures and now here in court, insists that the children are on his side, and that if only we become like them we shall see eye to eye with him. Well, the Prosecution wishes to co-operate with the Defence to arrive at the truth. Let it not be said that the Crown is unfair. Have I Your Honour's permission to take the evidence of one of these children?

JUDGE: You do. Provided the Accused is willing—

MYSELF: I am, Your Honour.

JUDGE:— and provided the child hasn't been biased by parents or teachers against the Accused. Or, too strongly, for him.

COUNSEL: I'm assured that what little prejudice there may be is in favour of the Accused.

JUDGE *addressing me*: So you agree that the Prosecution goes ahead?

MYSELF: Certainly, Your Honour. As for which child testifies, let's say the youngest…

The teacher brings one of the children down from the gallery, and takes her to a chair placed in front of the witness-box.

COUNSEL, to Witness: Will you please tell us your name and how old you are.

WITNESS: I'm Mary. I'm ten.

COUNSEL: Mary, what do you know about Mr John a-Nokes there in the dock?

WITNESS: Our teacher told us he asks funny questions about himself. Like, is he *really* Mr Nokes?

COUNSEL: What do you say about that, Mary?

WITNESS: I think he's being silly. All he's got to do is look in the mirror.

COUNSEL: Will you please repeat that a little louder for the benefit of the Jury?

WITNESS: I feel sorry for him. All he's got to do is look in the mirror.

COUNSEL: Thank you, Mary. Now, Mr Nokes will ask you some questions.

MYSELF: Mary, do you have any brothers and sisters?

WITNESS: I've got a brother. His name is Dick. He's eighteen months old.

MYSELF: How does he react to what he sees in the mirror?

WITNESS: When he was very little he didn't take any notice. Now he's started making noises at the baby behind the glass and playing with him. Of course he's too young to realise it's himself. He's like a robin I saw who started pecking at his own reflection in a windowpane.

MYSELF: Mary, I know a little girl called Madge. She made up her face with her mother's lipstick—applying it to the bathroom mirror.

WITNESS: That's silly! She'll soon grow up.

MYSELF: That's all, Mary. Thank you for being so helpful and answering our questions. Please go back to your class now.

COUNSEL, to Jury: In the course of his Defence against the previous Witness—the Humanist, you'll remember—the Accused said two things that I want to draw your attention to now: first, that to see the truth about himself he must become childlike; and second, that when he does so he loses his human face and takes on a divine one. Or words to that effect.

Well, I should be surprised if Mary's testimony hasn't shaken his monolithic complacency somewhat.

We shall see what this asker of silly questions (I'm using Mary's language) has to say for himself.

Defence: The Tenfold Unmasking

MYSELF: Every important discovery began by asking a silly question. Ladies and gentlemen of the Jury, I don't feel quite as chastened as Counsel thinks I should. Not at all. Mary's testimony provides the perfect introduction to the story I have to tell.

Like all convincing stories, it comes in three parts. She supplied and illustrated the first two. It will be up to an adult—a truly grown-up grown-up—to supply the third.

COUNSEL, oozing irony, to the Jury: And we all know *who* that is, don't we?

MYSELF: The whole tale runs like this:

(1) The animal and the infant, in their direct experience of themselves, are faceless. Unconsciously they are living from Who they really, really are—from the Clear-faced One at the Centre of their universe. None is so deluded (and so blasphemous) as to superimpose on this central Clarity or No-thing any features of their own. Every one of them, from Mary's little brother in his play-pen down to the barely visible insect on the nursery window, and beyond, is *for itself* as immense and wide open as the cloudless sky. I think we should all go down on our knees to beg forgiveness for having despised these humble but majestic ones who—unlike all us humans—have never for a moment been guilty of blasphemy. And go on to recite Blake's lines:

> Seest thou the little winged fly, smaller than a grain of sand?...
> Withinside wondrous and expansive: its gates are not clos'd:
> I hope thine are not.

(2) But the infant grows into the child. Mary pays her literally immense subscription to the human club—namely, her Mary-free wide-openness—and gets in acknowledgement and exchange her card of identity and membership, her Mary-face. Finding herself in the mirror, she shrinks almost overnight from boundless Capacity for all things to just that one thing. No discredit to Mary. It's a stage we all have to go through.

(3) But now let's look forward to the day—that rebirthday —when Mary decides that her subscription to the human club is far too high. Accordingly she withholds it, secretly cancelling her standing order, yet without ceasing to enjoy the club's innumerable amenities. She reclaims her true Face, absolutely clear and immense and non-human, but is careful to hang on to her club membership card with its picture of that little human face—keeping it in that glass-fronted showcase over there. She again takes on her Original Face, and makes sure that acquired face stays where it belongs, a yard or so away. Now she looks in that showcase—which is her mirror—to see what she *isn't* like! She's herSelf again.

Your Honour and members of the Jury, you will have noticed the mirror stuck on the front of the booklet of diagrams that each of you has been given. Will you please now look in that mirror, as if for the first time, and without prejudgement take what you find, where you find it. No—don't look at me. Look steadily into your mirror—to see, for a change, not yourself but a close friend. Close, but not too close. A friend, but not too friendly.

COUNSEL: This is farcical! John a-Nokes, I see you've got one of those mirror-covered booklets of yours. I challenge you to look in that glass right now and tell the court in all seriousness that it's not your face that you see.

MYSELF, complying carefully with Counsel's request: No! that's not my face!

COUNSEL: Then for heaven's sake *whose* face is it?

MYSELF: Good question! I can truthfully tell you it doesn't belong to me

COUNSEL: I can't believe my ears! Just give me one reason why that face you're looking at isn't yours.

MYSELF: I'll give you *ten!*

COUNSEL: Funny man!

MYSELF: Your Honour and members of the Jury, let's address

this very funny and very serious matter together, very carefully. And very humbly, prepared to follow whithersoever the facts lead us. I'm asking you not to look at me when I go through these ten reasons, but look in your mirror and check up whether what I'm saying about me is true also of you.

That face is *not* my face, because:

(1) It's the wrong way round—faces inwards instead of outwards.

(2) It's the wrong size—a miserable three inches across.

(3) It's in the wrong place—off-centre by upwards of ten inches.

(4) It's all over the shop—liable to come at me from any angle, incapable of getting its act together.

(5) Appropriately, it haunts crazy rooms, where clocks go anti-clockwise and printing reads back to front.

(6) It's locked in one direction, unable to glance up or down or sideways.

(7) It's intangible.

(8) In these and all other respects it's the opposite of what I find on these shoulders, and therefore not my face but someone else's.

(9) A conclusion I check by slowly bringing the mirror right up to me. On the way here, I try to catch hold of that face, turn it round, enlarge it to full size, and plant it on these shoulders—thereby setting John a-Nokes up at the centre of my world . . . I can't. This place won't take it. Anyway, it vanishes without trace just before arrival.

(10) And if, instead of this mirror, a friend's camera makes the same journey, it comes up with the same pictures. Out there it registers that face. On the way here, parts of it. Here, none of it.

Ten reasons why that face is not my face. How many would you like, Sir Gerald? There are lots more, but perhaps ten's enough to be getting on with.

COUNSEL: *Whose* face is it then, for God's sake?

MYSELF: John a-Nokes's, of course. The face of a fairly close pal of mine. One whose charm is that he's about as different from me as he could be. It's often that way with friends, you know.

COUNSEL: Specious stuff, members of the Jury! But what does it boil down to? To this: we adults are wrong, the children are wrong, and only infants and Mr Nokes are right. So let's all go infantile. Back to the cradle! This isn't the way to be taken seriously in a lawcourt, which of all places on earth is reserved for grown-ups.

MYSELF: I'm not saying 'back to infancy' but 'forward to sanity, to true adulthood, to sagehood, to the wisdom of God which is foolishness with men'—in a word, to Godhood.

COUNSEL, flourishing his brief wildly, shouts: To blasphemy!

MYSELF: To truthfulness! It's all so very simple and sensible. To find out who you are—whether you are George or Henry or Marmaduke or Lady Godiva or whoever—I look at your face. *To find out who I am—whether I'm Jack or Jill or the Elephant Man or whoever—I look at my face.* How else, for goodness' sake? I look at my true and present and naked Original Face, instead of at that acquired face over there in its glass case, with its tenfold disclaimer, its tenfold denial that it's mine. I look at the bright and charming Face of the One I really, really, really am.

However did I come to trade This for that, to disfigure myself so? Wasn't my Original Face attractive enough, its complexion clear enough? Was it losing the bloom of youth? Did looking myself in the Face suddenly become—absurd, wicked, impossible?

Between Dick's age and Mary's, I learned the art of self-dodging, of deliberately looking for myself *in the wrong direction*—as if were now to seek myself on the Judge's bench instead of in the dock! I looked *there* in the glass—in that glass case—to see myself *here* in God's fresh air! But now I look in it to see my buddy, my mate, my opposite number. I used to say to myself, 'That's me!' Now I say, 'Hello there! I like you because I'm unlike you!' The very same gadget which tricked me into hallucinating a small, coloured, opaque, tightly packed, complex, dying LUMP of a fellow at the Centre of my world now relieves me of him. Taking him clean off me, I'm left free here to be—Myself. And the fellow who was my enemy here is now my faithful companion there, at home in his stuffy glass-fronted house, my good neighbour. A relentlessly inquisitive and housebound insomniac he is, nevertheless nice to have around.

So this hugely underrated gadget called a mirror turns out to be more eloquent of my Nature, infinitely more direct and convincing, than all the scriptures in the world. It began with a good name: *mirror* derives from *mirari,* which is Latin for to wonder at. I gave it a bad name—toy, illusionist, trickster—but it was I who played tricks with it, turning a blind eye to its tenfold illusion-shattering Revelation. And now, every time I compare that tiny and flawed and ageing man-face behind the glass with this immense and immaculate and immortal God-face in front of it, I'm Myself again.

'God hath given you one face,' says Hamlet, 'and you make yourselves another.' By robbing mirrors, I add. Put it like this: there's a Face, and there are faces. The difference between them is total. It's essential to find out which of them God has given you. He gave you ten ways of finding out, no less. Get the answer wrong, and you're not only in every sort of trouble—you're a blasphemer.

Here are some who got the answer right:

Each thing has two faces: a face of its own, and the Face of its Lord. In respect of its own face it is nothingness, in respect of the Face of God it is Being.

Al-Ghazali

Everyone likes a mirror, while not knowing the nature of his Face… After all, how long does a reflection remain in view? Make a practice of contemplating the origin of the reflection… That cheek and mole come back to their Source.

Rumi

This is not a task for one whose True Face is not clean.

Attar

[Lycomedes had a portrait painted of the Apostle John.] And John, who had never at any time seen his own face, said to him, 'You are mocking me, child. Am I like that?

Acts of John

The seventeen hundred koan or themes to which Zen students devote themselves are only for making them see their Original Face. The World-honoured One sat in meditation in the snowy mountains for six years, then saw the morning star and was enlightened, and this was seeing his Original Face. When it is said of others of the ancients that they had a great realization, or a great breaking through, it means they saw their Original Face.

Daito Kokushi

Prosecution Witness No. 4

THE LAVATORY ATTENDANT

Having carefully explained to the Witness the nature of the charge against me and said a little about my Defence position, Counsel asks him what light he can throw on the matter.

In reply the Witness testifies that he knows me well by sight. I'm one of his regulars. Also by reputation—evil reputation.

The Judge warns the Witness that he's in the box to answer questions about facts, not to moralize unbidden. And certainly not to tell the court about what other people think of me. The Jury are directed to ignore the words 'evil reputation'.

WITNESS: All this bull about not really bein' a man only shows that Nokes is plain bonkers. What incredible swank, what a nerve he's got! I can't believe my ears. If he's not human, why does he visit my Convenience? And what the hell's he doin' when he stands there facin' the wall lookin' down? I'd like to know what's divine about that, about what's goin' on down there.

Don't tell me [banging the witness-box with both fists] don't tell me the Almighty *pees!* And *farts!*

The Judge calls the court to order, and warns the Witness to moderate his language. Drastically.

WITNESS: Sorry, guv! But I know all about this perisher in the dock, and I've had as much as I can take. It's him, not me, who's using insultin' language about the Almighty. Who does he think he is? I'm tellin' the bugger he's just like me and you…

His Honour warns the Witness that he's within a whisker of being committed for contempt of court.

Disappointed with the Judge, he appeals to the Jury.

WITNESS: What's more, ladies and gents, I remember this bloke rushin' in—like he's got all the devils in hell at his tail—and makin' for one of my toilets, lockin' himself in and comin' out after five minutes and a flush. I bet you each a tenner what he did in there was what they all do. Was it the Almighty who—?

This time, Judge and Counsel together succeed in silencing the Witness. I have no questions to put him. He stands down, muttering.

Defence: **Gravity and Levity**

MYSELF: Members of the Jury, hostile though this Witness appears, he plays wonderfully into my hands. In spite of himself he prepares the way for striking new evidence in my favour, evidence which, but for him, I might so easily have missed.

Let me explain:

When I'm interested enough—and honest and observant enough—to look at myself for myself, I find I'm duplex. I come in two designs, two quite distinct models, Mark 1 and Mark 2/3. They are very *different,* more so than black and white. They stay *apart,* keeping their distance like poles of a magnet. They stand *facing* each other, as Nelson's Column faces Whitehall. And they are *opposites,* as sweet is the opposite of bitter. Mark 1 is the real and central and divine Me, while Mark 2/3 is the apparent and peripheral and all-too-human me. Mark 1 is what I am, while Mark 2/3 is what I look like. Mark 1 is what I find myself to be here as the seeing Subject or First Person, while Mark 2/3 is what I find myself to be over there as the seen object, or second/third person. In short, it's as impossible to exaggerate the contrast between these two models of me as it is to exaggerate their connection.

Nowhere is this contrast more startling than in what the Witness calls his Convenience. His customers are of two sorts. All pee downwards, human fashion. All except one, who pees upwards, divine fashion. Every time—

No, no, Your Honour: no need to ply your gravel. I assure you I'm not being irreverent or flippant, and certainly not needlessly scatological. Here are inescapable facts which support my case. Nor am I holding this court in contempt. (I can't afford to, when I'm on trial for my life.) If I'm indulging in levity it's because God Almighty does so with a vengeance and a tra-la-la, in both senses of the word levity. I can't help it if people find His Self-revelation in the humble workplace of the Witness as disgusting as I find it entertaining, and charming, and immensely significant.

The Prosecution's God is a respectable character, stiff and solemn, a model of middle-class good manners and predictability, with no shocks up the divine sleeve. Well, my God isn't a bit like that. Kings *have* their jesters, but the King of the World is His jester. He's all surprises. He's the Funny One, the Shocker! Downright vulgar He is!

Take what happens in the Witness's WCs... All right, Your Honour: no need to elaborate. Only let me point out that in all those locked cubicles underwear goes down and then up again. In all except one, where it goes up and then down again.

COUNSEL, resolutely horror-struck: Your Honour, I really must butt in here to draw the Jury's attention to the almost unbelievable goings-on in this lawcourt. This *lawcourt!* The Romans revered Cloacina, the goddess of the sewer. Going a whole lot better (better's hardly the word), John a-Nokes reveres himself as at once the God of Heaven and the God of Public Lavatories, sparing us no lavatorial detail. Not only does he convict himself out of his own mouth, of the crime of blasphemy, but does so in the most repugnant fashion imaginable. One nicely calculated to stir up devout people of all sects and persuasions. Members of the Jury, don't let his sophistry—of which you are, I'm sure, about to be served another large helping—obscure these perfectly obvious facts, these disgustingly obvious facts.

MYSELF: This is rich! This is too much! *Who* broached this now-so-filthy subject by calling the Lavatory Attendant, confident that his testimony would demolish my case? It was the gentleman over there in fancy dress, the one who, now the facts turn out to *support* my case, suddenly finds the whole business 'unbelievable' in its nastiness! Nokes is wicked: when attacked he defends himself! Nokes is disgusting: when shat on he returns the compliment, and has the last laugh! Nokes says: nasty be to him who nasty thinks.

God is no more prim and proper than a child of four. His truth is funnier than our fiction. He's arranged that waking to our Identity with Him is wonderfully light-hearted. Now I call that really *decent* of Him. Here's the Almighty, intent on Self-discovery and Self-revelation and Self-giving-with-a-smile, leaning over backwards to demonstrate that everyone who says 'I' is none other than Himself. Leaning over backwards is right. If you don't get it, look at Diagram No. 4. If you *do* get it, look at Diagram No. 4, and join in the divine merriment!

Members of the Jury, the court will presently go into recess. You will then have the opportunity to test what I'm telling you: to check whether, in the lavatories of this court, a wonderful kind of peeing is going on. Not the common sort which obeys the Law of Gravity, but the unique sort which throws that Law into reverse.

Now, Who can break Nature's laws but the One who makes them? And not this Law alone but many others, as we shall see during the count of these proceedings. Meantime, how delightful, how worthy of our notice, that this fun-loving and fun-poking Deity should find the latrines of this court as suitable a place as the court itself in which to disclose His presence among us at this time! Or even more suitable!

Again, this is too much for Counsel for the Prosecution. He shoots to his feet. Writhing and spluttering, he implores the Judge to put a stop to this indecency, this outrage, this barefaced profanity, this calculated insult to the Divine Being, this—words fail him!

JUDGE, addressing me: Urinating *upwards,* forsooth! Have you taken leave of your senses? This court is no place for facetiousness, let alone profanity, and I must warn you not to try its patience too far.

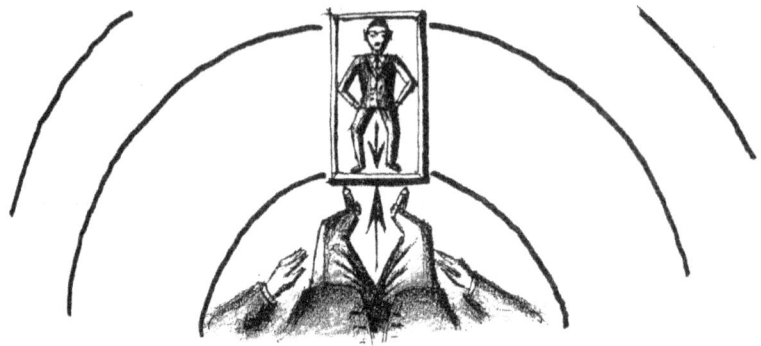

Diagram No. 4

MYSELF: No, Your Honour, I've *come to* my senses—a hard but necessary thing to do. Diagram No. 4 makes it so much easier. Spare those arrows a second glance, and tumble to the truth. As for profanity, the rest of my argument will be as tactful as I can make it. His Majesty wears no fig-leaf, but I'll try to bear in mind the conventional image of Him which is practically all fig-leaf. Mine is an uncouth God, but I'll do my best to remember how couth Sir Gerald's is. How frightfully genteel.

Exactly what (I ask myself) is this shocking He, this shameless She, this unbowdlerized It, in reality? Its essence is Awareness, the One Light of Consciousness that lights up the world and every creature the world comes into. I locate this Light Indivisible right where I am, plumb in the Centre of this world as I find it, nearer than near, at the heart of the heart of me. Here is no spark of that Fire, but the blazing Furnace itself. It brooks no rival consciousnesses. Awareness comes whole and single, or not at all: never in pieces—one piece looking after this, another piece looking after that phenomenon. Which means that, whatever part or function of my body—cosmic or human—is being attended to, it's not a man as such who's attending. What I provisionally called my awareness is in the last resort my God's, inside as well as outside the Witness's Convenience. Awareness is His quirk, His trade, His speciality, His monopoly. It includes awareness of His Universe Body, of which all particular bodies are organs.

The Prosecution—so sure that what goes on in that lavatory is obnoxious to God and man—leaves me with no choice but to enlarge briefly on the subject of this Universe Body as it presents itself to me.

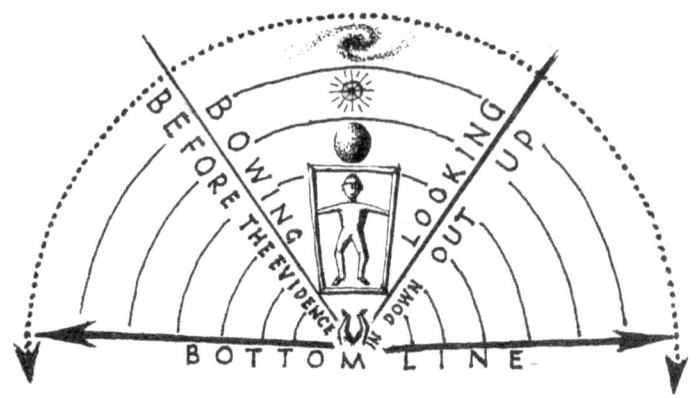

Diagram No. 5

I refer to the many-layered onion-like thing I see that I am as First Person, not to the uniform potato-like thing I imagine I'm in as a third person. To be precise, this almost-half-an-onion-like thing that figures in nearly all our diagrams.

Encouraged by the great tradition of the Inner Light at my core, and inspired by my direct vision of it, I submit with reverence to what it lights up. Here I am at once this central Awareness or Consciousness and what it's conscious of which is none other than its own region-by-region embodiment, its cosmic constitution. The view out from here embraces the One-centred but many-levelled physique that is the expression and instrument and object of the Consciousness that I AM, and I take it as I find it.

In Diagram No. 5 I've drawn the general shape of my findings. No longer so damned cocksure I know what it's like being me, I dare to start all over again and *bow before the evidence*—actually as well as metaphorically. I bend and bow so deeply that I come to the very edge of me and my world, to the *Bottom Line* it all arises from. A frontier that doesn't prevent me from gazing past it and in to the infinite Source of All, brilliantly on display yet awesomely mysterious. Next, slowly straightening up, I gaze *down* at this headless trunk and these foreshortened legs and tiny feet. Then *out* at all those people and their gear, among them that special fellow who stares at me fixedly from behind his window. There he is, that Jack-in-the-mirror third person who's as human as the rest, inasmuch as he's the same way up as they are, and topped with the same sort of headpiece, and pees the way they pee. And then I look *up* at the teeming countryside, the forest covered hills, low clouds and high mountains (I leave you to picture these in my picture); and finally at the wide sky with its Moon and planets and Sun and solar systems and galaxies.

Such is the magnificent shape of the First Person Singular. Its crucial feature is its Bottom Line—the Fringe of this shirt, of this true cutty sark. Here, where man's extremity *visibly* lines up with God's opportunity, where what's so generously given is so rarely taken, I come to the World's End (completing the down-sweep of my bow before the evidence), the World's Beginning (the launching pad that gives rise to the many-levelled scene as I straighten up again) and, back of both, the World's Source (the below-Line World without end, amen). Here is my Triune Home, the fringe benefits of which are endless.

COUNSEL, in a stage whisper that threatens to shatter the court's light-bulbs: Lunatic fringe!

MYSELF, ignoring the jibe: I come to sweeter-than-sweet Home God's Home, in fact, where all that the Light lights up gives place to the Light itself. Home, where the One Light, bodying forth its own magnificent Embodiment, *is* all it shines on. The 360° wraparound Home of the Divine Humorist, whose smile is so broad it meets at the back.

Such, ladies and gentlemen of the Jury, is my cosmic constitution. This is me when I'm interested enough to look, and honest and unhurried enough to take myself as I find myself. This is what I naturally *am*, before rushing to twist and trim and denature it into what I'm told I am. Such is my Body, my marvellous Incarnation.

And yours too, I guess, just as soon as you care to glance up, and out, and down, and in at the Unique Glancer, and What lies back of Him.

And every time I look down and pee I'm reminded of His condescension, His delicious sense of humour, His mystery. Long live micturition!

JUDGE: Do you *have* to go on and on about micturition, as you call it? This muckraking is provocative and does your case no good.

MYSELF: I've no choice, Your Honour. The topic's forced on me by the Prosecution. But also, more importantly and persistently, by the Highest Authority, who has deliberately chosen the low things of the world to confound its Pecksniffs, its moral prigs and spiritual snobs.

Of course for purposes of inspection and description this great Body has to be dismembered notionally, differentiated into a hierarchy of organs. But in fact it is always an organic whole. Or rather, it's the one and only Organic Whole, the only true Organism that includes all it needs to be itself, the only true Individual that's independent and strictly indivisible. Every layer and every member of it (whether honoured or neglected or despised, whether overlooked or looked at or underlooked, whether labelled 'decent' or 'common and unclean' or 'foul')—every least itsy-bitsy fragment of it is holy: by which I mean wholly cleansed and made good and sanctified in the Whole. Not on the whole and partially, but *as* the Whole and absolutely. Rightly viewed by its Proprietor, no part is a mere part. Or even a hologram of the Whole. It is godly. It is God.

And, of course, all this applies to peeing as well, with its associated anatomy. Yes, ladies and gentlemen, to the whole urino-genital-excretory works. Dare you—can you—amputate or expurgate from the Body of God those members which Mrs Grundy would like to expurgate from the body of man?

JUDGE: Surely you've made your point—and are now in danger of running it into the ground.

MYSELF: My point, Your Honour, *is* the Ground! Let's dare to be as grounded as God, as low. It may help us to take kindly to the facts in all their earthiness, and the necessity as well as the depth of the divine descent into their midst, if we recall how many have found hope and comfort in that descent. I'm thinking of the Christian tradition whose Deity is, to put it mildly, no toffee-nosed snob: of the faith that has for substance and centre-piece the coming-down of the King of Glory to be born in a shed reserved for beasts, and to die on a dump reserved for criminals judged lower than beasts. According to this faith, such is the world's Top Liner that He becomes its Bottom Liner, thereby saving and sanctifying all between. What I'm saying is that, if so many have valued so highly and for so long this incomparable Comedown, the very minor part of it which is the Witness's specialty is worthy of your sympathetic reconsideration. For you must agree that the Witness's Convenience is a lot more convenient and respectable and salubrious than that stable in Bethlehem which (according to this great tradition) was not despised by Almighty God. Far from it: He moved right in. 'Love,' says William Butler Yeats, 'has pitched his mansion in the place of excrement.' Here is the God of St Paul, who has 'chosen… [the] base things of the world, and things which are despised.' Here is indeed the Highest who looks down on no creature.

However low that creature, He's lower, He's lower.

I find it touching and beautiful that Who I really, really am should be great enough and humble enough to play the part of one of the Witness's regulars, and witty and humorous enough to be his one Irregular. He's nearer to a man than his jocular vein.

All work and no play makes Jack a dull boy, and God a dull God. It's not Him but the world of men in general (and of Counsel in particular) which takes itself so seriously, and *gets down* to things with furrowed brow. But at the Earth's centre, where gravity's zero, all ways out are ways up. So also at the Centre of the universe (which is where you are Who you really are), at its lowest point, gravity bottoms out and levity takes its rise. Here, God has great fun *getting up* to things, and forging the link between spirituality and humour. It's no accident that the holy has its comic side, and the comic its holy side: the connection's built-in from the start. The Creator's marvellously lacking in *gravitas*. He's *Light*—Light fantastic. P. G. Wodehouse is unlikely to be canonized just yet; but, as the future St Plum might put it, the shot's on the board.

It's not only the banana-skin type of humour which up-ends things. 'The whole of human life,' as Plato observed, 'is turned upside-down.' This is where the divine comes in. 'In the way of search for God,' Rumi tells us, 'everything is reversed.'

Ladies and gentlemen of the Jury, I call the great Robert Browning, who will both sum up and light up (if not clean up) my response to the Crown Prosecutor and his somewhat tacky Witness:

I but open my eyes,—and perfection, no more and no less,
In the kind I imagined, full-fronts me, and God is seen God
In the star, in the stone, in the flesh, in the soul and the clod.
And thus looking within and around me, I ever renew
(With that stoop of the soul which in bending upraises it too)
The submission of man's nothing-perfect to God's all-complete,
As by each new obeisance in spirit, I climb to his feet.

Prosecution Witness No. 5

THE PASSENGER

Counsel begins by reminding the Witness that, though she is in court sub poena, she is on oath. The Prosecution requires her to outline the circumstance and the extent of her knowledge of me.

She replies that we first met two years ago. She and I were members of a party of four who toured Europe by car for a month, so we got to know each other pretty well. Since then we have met occasionally and more or less by accident.

COUNSEL: Is it a fact that the Accused did most of the driving, about which he made strange claims? If so, what were those claims? And did you find that his performance at the wheel of the car justified them?

WITNESS: We went about four hundred miles, and he did all the driving. This was because he liked driving, and it was his car—a Rover—which he handled very well. Yes, he was a smooth driver, who knew instinctively how much faster than the speed limit he could drive and get away with it. Also, just when to overtake, and so on. As for his claims to be a very special sort of driver, one with an extraordinary secret, I never quite understood them or took them too seriously. If they help him to improve his performance, so much the better, say I. They're his business, not mine or anybody else's, and I think it's outrageous that this court—

His Honour and Counsel simultaneously intervene to warn the Witness of the consequence of questioning the authority of the court. She is advised to continue her evidence more circumspectly, confining it to what's called for.

In response to Counsel's further questioning, Witness agrees, reluctantly, there was nothing special about my driving; and further, that nothing happened during the trip to suggest that one of the foursome was unique, or wielded superhuman powers of any kind, at the wheel or away from it. The car did, in fact, break down once, and the party lost its way more than once, and these difficulties were overcome by quite normal means.

WITNESS adds: All the same, my impression is that Jack's efficiency at the wheel, and his liveliness and sense of humour, had something to do with his strange views about himself. So, I say good luck to him and them. What works that well can't be altogether off-beam.

COUNSEL: That's enough of your opinions. To come back to the facts: is it true that nothing happened during that tour, or has happened since, to convince you that the Accused exercises divine powers, let alone that he is himself a divine Being? Is that right?

WITNESS: Yes, but surely it's his—

COUNSEL: No buts. Yes, or no?

WITNESS: Yes *and* no.

JUDGE: The court requires a straight answer.

WITNESS: All right then. Yes.

MYSELF, to the Witness: I have no questions for you at the moment, so please leave the box. But stay in court. I may have some for you presently.

Defence: **The Car Driver and the World Driver**

MYSELF: While I accept that the Witness's account of the trip was sincere, I have to tell the court that mine, though equally sincere, could hardly be more different.

I say we never exceeded the speed limit, and never came near it. I say we never got lost, and never broke down, and never drove four miles all told—let alone four thousand. I say we got many, many times more power out of a litre of petrol than any other car on the road. I say—

JUDGE, angrily: Did you or didn't you go on the same tour as the Witness? And please do not waste any more of the court's time with fantasies or riddle-me-rees.

MYSELF: Well, it was and it wasn't the same tour. And what I just told the court happens to be a model of understatement: all gospel truth, but pitching the driver's claim to extraordinary powers as low as possible, and couching it in the soberest language. Apparently the Witness didn't share my breathtaking experience. I understand that. Everything depends, you see, on Who is driving.

Yes, Your Honour, I did the driving. But *Who* was this I? That's the big question, the question *sub judice*.

Look: *I'll tell you what I did, you tell me Who did it.* I'll describe the astounding things that happened on that trip, if you'll explain Who's capable of such things—a human being, or a superhuman being, or the Divine Being. I can't speak fairer than that, can I?

My story is of a driver that you would swear was in no condition, legally or medically, to be in charge of a push-bike. There he was, slouched in the driving seat, upside down and literally off his rocker. Dangerous driving at its most lethal, you would think, made worse by the unroadworthy state of his car, with most of the rear missing. As it turned out, however, none of this mattered very much, for the car was as handicapped as the driver. In fact, it was paralytic and incapable of moving an inch. Incapable even of coasting downhill in neutral with brakes off and three pushing.

But neither my strangely dilapidated condition nor my car's presented any difficulty, so far as transport was concerned. The countryside took care of that, and did all the moving necessary. And much, much more. The whole world was in turmoil, convulsed by quakes infinitely beyond the Richter scale. It was as if some giant troll were stirring the cosmos like a maniac, before gobbling it all up for his dinner.

COUNSEL, *sotto voce:* The maniac who's now in the dock?

MYSELF: Let's put it differently, and do belated justice to that inverted and abbreviated Driver. He was, in fact, so fit, so skilful, so powerful, so unhandicapped, and—yes!—so unhuman that, *instead of driving a car, he drove the world,* without himself budging an inch!

COUNSEL: Jurors have too much common sense to be taken in by this sophistry, this midsummer madness. The certainty that you and I move around in the world—and not vice versa—is so universal, so practical, so indispensable to life and thought that it can't be false. Here, in fact, we have just one more example of the famous Nokes

Law: *Everyone's out of step, except me!* You can't prove him wrong. But you can order him to fall out and go back to where he came from. To the glass-house. Or is it to the nut-house?

MYSELF: If I'm out of step, it's because I'm marching to God's almighty drum. Let me see if I can confound Sergeant Wilberforce by getting another recruit to hear and march to it...

Will the Witness please go back into the box. [She does so.] Please tell the court what I'm doing...

WITNESS: Turning round, and round, and round in the dock.

MYSELF: Just me? Is the dock, is anything else besides me on the move?

WITNESS: No. Just you.

MYSELF: Now it's your turn to do what I did. [She complies, gathering speed ...] Tell the court whether you are moving, or the court. Go by what's given right now.

WITNESS: I'm quite still!... The court's *whizzing* round! Wow!

MYSELF: Please slow it down... [She stops turning. Somewhat reluctantly, it seems…]

COUNSEL: Be sensible now! Enough of Nokes's *credo-quia-impossibile* nonsense. You don't *believe* you set the court in motion. Be honest.

WITNESS: Why not? I was being sensible, just as you say. Coming to my senses. I understood enough of Einstein and relativity to know I'm not talking nonsense, either.

MYSELF: Thank you very much. No more questions...

What Counsel said about common sense, and the practical necessity of imagining oneself moving around in a still world, is true enough of course—so far as it goes. Which isn't half far enough. It doesn't go back to the beginning or on to the end. Let me complete it by telling the whole three-part story of his experience of movement:

(1) As an infant he was still and his world was all commotion. When his dad took little Gerald for a drive, he loved watching the lampposts and trees and buildings go sailing by. When his dad tossed little Gerald up in the air and swung him around, it was fun and he wasn't a bit scared. Why? Because everything in the room was rushing about like crazy—everything except him.

(2) As an adult *he's* all commotion and *his world* has ground to a halt. And he's scared. Taking on all that turmoil has ousted his inner peace and left him jittery and twitchy, disturbed through and through. As you can see.

(3) My wish for him is that one day (it could be as a result of this Trial) he will come to his senses and complete his life story. Then he will no longer be agitated and in a dither. He will regain his inner tranquillity by giving back to the universe the turmoil that never was his anyway. He will be an unflappable Seer of Who-he-is, enjoying the sight of a world that has sprung to life again in a dance whose *corps de ballet* ranges from lampposts and city blocks to the stars. God's Bolshoi, putting on His Nutcracker Suite. What a philistine, what a bunkered ass, what a nutcase he'd been, to rubbish that superb spectacle! But now, arrived at the third stage, *instead of driving his car he drives his world.* And, for good measure, is less

accident-prone. Driving about in a still world is driving without due care and attention. It's dangerous driving. In the end, it's fatal.

Ladies and gentlemen of the Jury, Your Honour and everyone else in this courtroom, I ask you, I put it to you with the utmost seriousness: *Conceding that it's the world that's being driven, can you, dare you, put any creature in the driving seat, anyone except the Creator of the world?* If you can and you dare, it's not I but you who are guilty of blasphemy. God, Aristotle taught, is the Unmoved Mover of the world. When He condescends to take the wheel of my 1991 Rover, and set all His world a-roving for the price of a driblet of six-star Supershell, Jack can't and Jack won't try to shoulder Him out and take over. When he sets the Jungfrau waltzing with the Finsteraarhorn, Jack can't and Jack won't halt them in their tracks. That would make a jackass of him.

When you next drive your car, why not let the lampposts and the trees and the buildings and the hills *en route* tell you *Who's* driving? They are all raring to enlighten you. If you go on reading them as fixtures in a stable world, then for sure it's a human driving—without due care and attention. But please God there will come a day when you're sensible and humble enough to look and to stop hallucinating like mad. Then you will enjoy the superb spectacle of the World-Mover at work, and you will know that He is Who you really, really, really are. And then, maybe, you will bitterly regret having brought in a verdict of Guilty against me. Or rather, against Him! Think of that: against Him!

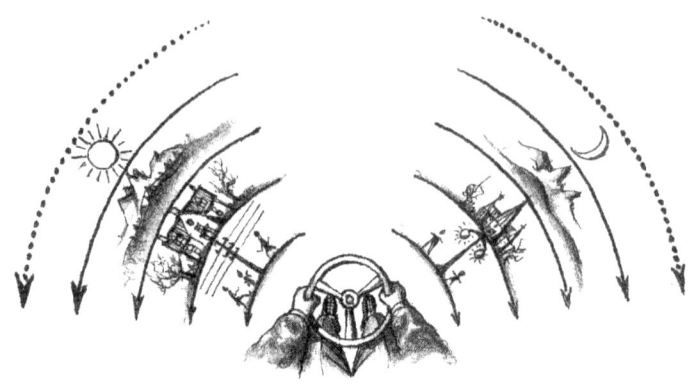

Diagram No. 6

Diagram No.6 gives a crude impression of the World-Driver on the job. But it does bring out the fact that upright things (like telegraph poles and church steeples) don't keel over as they slide past Him. They stay firmly upright. And—how curious and significant, and how overlooked—*upright means radial to His Centre!* When next you kindly take the universe for a spin, see how all *fans out* from its Owner. Actually, you've only to glance round the court right now to observe how all its vertical lines converge on—well, on Whom? That's the question this Trial is all about.

Members of the Jury, you don't look the sort that habitually has one —or two—or three for the road. But what, after all, is drunken driving? If it's being so blotto that, suffering from a severe bout of delirium tremens (so to say), you see moving things as stuck, and stuck things as moving, and converging lines as parallel, then I have to accuse you of this offence. What's worse, accuse you of having committed it countless times. In fact, I doubt whether you know what sober driving means! But there's a remedy. The only safe and sober Driver stands ready to take charge. Hand over the wheel to your Divine Chauffeur!

I seem to remember Bertie Wooster tottering down the Mall, after a cheerful evening at the Drones. Or was the Mall tottering down him? Anyway, says Wodehouse, he 'aimed a kick at a passing lamppost'. He saw what he saw, for once. But there's a cheaper and safer method of sobering up than the in-vino-veritas way, a much better way of seeing what you see than going on a blinder. It is to look, just LOOK, and see what's moving. And see WHO isn't. And BE the One that never budged by a billionth of an inch!

COUNSEL, bursting at last under the strain: Oh no you're not getting away with this! Members of the Jury, Nokes makes a great show of spiritual depth. He figures he's the profound one, in contrast to us shallow types. I say he's a master of superficiality. He trivializes the great issues and problems of our life, reducing them to such matters of moment as the curious behaviour of telegraph poles. He's been playing this funny-man, happy-go-lucky, soft-headed, Mickey Mouse game from the start of this Trial. It's one which serious and responsible adults, coats off and sleeves rolled up, engaged in the world's work, decline to play.

MYSELF: And the reason why you hard-headed spoilsports are stressed to the limit is that, instead of playing God's game, you play God. Stop arrogating to Sir Gerald and Co. His work of world-moving. Give yourselves a break and let Him get on with it, for a change. Look how marvellous He is at the job! Do you imagine that He who quite casually moves the Sun and the other stars can't shift the picayune obstructions that stand in your path? Can't the One who stirs the cosmos more effortlessly than you stir your porridge—can't He also shift your blinkers or blinders, so that you discover simultaneously that magnificent Storm and the Stillness at the Eye of it? His Tempest there, His Peace right where you are?

Tell me, how can you sidestep, how can you trivialize, that deepest Peace, which is yours for the seeing?

Only when we see everything else as moving can we truly sing 'We shall not be moved'. In their different ways, the following Defence witnesses encourage us, by *placing* motion and Stillness, to enjoy both:

'Glorious, stirring sight!' murmured Toad... 'The poetry of motion... Villages skipped, towns and cities jumped... Oh bliss! Oh poop poop! Oh my! Oh my!'

Kenneth Grahame

The mountains skipped like rams, and the little hills like lambs... Tremble, thou earth, at the presence of the Lord.

Psalms

At the Centre where no one abides, this light is quenched in a still stronger Light... For this Ground is the impartible Stillness, motionless in itself, and by this Immobility all things are moved.

Eckhart

The Tao is ever still, yet there is nothing it does not do.

Tao Te Ching

There is nothing that stands fast, nothing fixed, nothing free from change among the things that come into being, neither among those in heaven nor among those on earth. God alone stands unmoved.

Hermes Trismegistus

For a long while I used to circumambulate the Ka'ba. When I attained unto God, I saw the Ka'ba circumambulating me.

Bayazid al-Bistami

If you have faith as a grain of mustard seed, you shall say unto this mountain, Remove hence to yonder place, and it shall move.

Jesus

(Faith—in Greek, *pistis*—doesn't mean blind credulity, but confidence in one you trust. I say: trusting God includes trusting the visible behaviour of His Alps just as much as their visible form. It means valuing the smooth and stately dance of His mountain peaks as highly as their superb get-up.)

Prosecution Witness No. 6

THE HAIRDRESSER

Witness testifies that she cuts my hair regularly. Excuse me—*styles* it.

COUNSEL: What does it grow on?

WITNESS: His head, of course. The noddle he brings into my saloon for tidying up, once a month.

COUNSEL: Has the Accused ever told you that, in reality, he has no noddle to tidy up or to take anywhere? And that this is enough to prove he's someone very special? Not a man at all, actually?

WITNESS: Well, he does sometimes joke like that. He says we shouldn't charge him for doing nothing to nothing. Then I point to the hair trimmings on the floor, and he pretends to be absolutely astonished. We have a laugh and he pays up.

COUNSEL: Do you get the impression he's mad?

WETNESS: Not at all. Just playful, pleasantly eccentric.

COUNSEL: Isn't the idea that he's walking around headless very odd? As for claiming this proves him divine: isn't this odder than odd? In fact blasphemous, not to say devilish?

WITNESS: That's going rather far. Though it looks a bit that way, now you mention it.

COUNSEL: Thank you. Please stay in the box. I see the Accused wishes to cross-examine you.

Defence: **It's Me, Not a Picture**

I put it to the Witness that I never claimed I had no head. Quite the contrary.

MYSELF: Didn't I say, again and again, that I have no head *here,* on *these* immensely broad shoulders, where it would look pimping, quite silly. And that I keep it parked a yard or so away behind glass, on top of that weedy, narrow-shouldered fellow who fits it to a tee? Didn't I insist, in fact, that I set up around me countless ghostly Nokes-heads, all waiting out there for suitably positioned mirrors and people and their camera to pick up and make something of? To flesh out? Just as you're doing right now?

WITNESS: Yes, I remember now. That was the sort of thing you talked about while I was styling your hair. At the time, it didn't sound crazy, but quite obvious. Weird though, and rather exciting... Now I'm all confused...

I have no more questions. I thank the Witness. She stands down.

MYSELF: Your Honour, members of the Jury, I appear before you accused of blasphemy, a very serious crime. So serious, say I, that it's the root and stem of all crime and delinquency.

What is it to blaspheme?

It is to insult the Almighty. Among the many ways a man can do this, two stand out. He can try playing God, or being God. Let's take them in that order.

The playing-God blasphemer doesn't state, in so many words, that God's a fool or a liar. He doesn't need to: he lives it. He stakes his life on the proposition that the Creator and Sustainer of that life doesn't know His job; that His gifts as given are for rejecting out of hand; that the ground-plan of His design for a habitable universe is ill-conceived and fraudulent; and that he the creature knows better and can do better, thank you very much. So he substitutes for the divine world that he sees the human world that he thinks he sees, but in fact engineers. He doesn't just strengthen the frame and re-panel the bodywork, as it were, and recondition the engine for better performance, but inverts and reverses the whole contraption, in the belief that he's making it roadworthy and drivable. And then, to complete and compound the blasphemy, he forgets what he's done. He takes his de-natured universe for Nature, his fabrication for God's Fabric. Such is the playing-God variety of blasphemy.

Going on at the same time is the being-God variety. The blasphemer puts himself, the human, in the driving seat of the restructured vehicle. He replaces God at the Centre of God's universe.

For too much of my life I've been as guilty of both varieties of blasphemy as any of you. But no longer. I've come to my senses. Now I see that to be honest to God and to Jack is to be Him here and Jack there, and never the twain shall meet.

Nowhere is it easier to come to my senses and stop blaspheming—nowhere is it clearer to me where God's home is and where man's home is, and how far apart they lie, and how different their design is—than in the Witness's hairdressing establishment. All is revealed to that begowned customer (or rather, half-customer) in the adjustable chair, facing that plate-glass mirror—if only he will look, and dare to take seriously what he finds. Here, on display with illusion-shattering brilliance, is the one truth which he desperately needs to acknowledge. Obviously, to be a man at all, he must have eyes for eyeing people with, a mouth for feeding himself with, a scalp for growing hair on, and so forth; and, what's more, he must have a unique version of these features, distinguishing him from all other specimens. And obviously all that stuff belongs where he finds it and keeps it, on the *far* side of that glass. What's right here, on the *near* side of the glass, is in every sense the opposite of all that. If there's a Face here at all it's one that has no features at all, let alone human ones, let alone distinctive ones. It is absolutely Blank. But—ah!—how keenly awake to itself as Blank: as the speckless Clarity and Awareness that's taking in that man-head in the mirror, and the other customers, and the hairdressing saloon, and all that happens to be on show! Knowing Itself as the solitary Knower, This is none other than the God-head whose home is at the Centre of His world, at the Mid-point of all those peripheral things—including that blockhead (no mock modesty this, just a fact) behind the glass, having his head of hair tousled and trimmed. This is the One Head, the One No-head, the One truly Unblocked Head of all. Me, not a picture.

To see that blockhead off to its place behind glass, leaving the clear-headed God-head here in front of it—this is natural piety.

It's sober realism. It's humility before the evidence. It's waking and coming to one's senses after a long and bad dream. It's *godly*. It's the sovereign remedy for all ungodliness, and in particular for the fatal disease of self-deification. It puts paid to blasphemy. And it's all so ridiculously obvious!

Ladies and gentlemen, this is the sight I was enjoying in that hairdressing saloon, my description of which puzzled and intrigued the hairdresser. This is the sight I'm enjoying right now in this courtroom. And it's precisely what my accusers, along with the majority of humankind, are determined to turn a blind eye to, are hell-bent on not enjoying.

It's you lot who are the blasphemers!

Commotion in court. The Jury go into excited huddles. Counsel's on his feet, gesticulating like a semaphore gone haywire. The Judge bangs away with his gavel as if he's bashing me on the head. He threatens to suspend my right to defend myself till I can do so properly, and cease straying from the point to deliver a lecture to the court—a contemptuous and abusive dressing-down, at that.

Apologizing, I promise to try to put my case in more parliamentary language. However, I insist that every word of it so far has been relevant to the crime I'm charged with, and central to my Defence against the charge.

COUNSEL, the semaphore suddenly under control: There's something I've been itching to say to the Jury for what seems an age. This abusive fellow's really stupid, too. Only someone as clever-clever as the Accused could be so unintelligent. His basic delusion, underlying his many particular ones, is that the human mind is a freak and a cheat at odds with Reality. This is a sick and impious view. Its cure is to regard the rational mind as that higher function which, so far from contradicting Nature, completes it. 'The art itself,' as Polixenes says in *The Winter's Tale*, 'is Nature.' What John a-Nokes calls *playing God*, I call *being man*. Man who has been entrusted with the job of building a cosmos out of loose and apparently incompatible sensory clues. Man to whom God gave this gigantic jigsaw puzzle for his birthday. The astounding success of his science proves that the resulting universe-picture is no fiction... So keep your respect, Jury, for common sense and the human intellect, and the familiar objective world they pains-takingly piece together, to the great benefit of us all, and you are safe from the Accused's wiles. You won't be taken in by his far-too-ingenious defence of idiocy. And you'll continue to drive to the barber's through unagitated streets, and keep your head on when you get there.

MYSELF: I'm told that there are edible beans which, until they are well boiled, are mildly poisonous. Counsel is offering us a half-baked concoction (to be fair, two-thirds baked) that's deadly poisonous because it stops short at the second and man-centred and blasphemous stage. The three stages are the perceived world of the animal and the very young child, the conceived world of the older child and the adult, and the union of these in the perceived—conceived world of the Seer. Of the Seer who doesn't lose sight of the world as given—of God's natural world—and doesn't cease to value and trust it; *and* who, with reservations, values and trusts also the artificial world of the adult, as a quite brilliant fiction for handling the natural world efficiently. Certainly the Seer sees the city dance all the way to the hairdresser's, where he sees his head safely stowed behind glass. But of course he's well aware that for the traffic cop his car's on the move, and for the hairdresser his head's on his shoulders. Thus he sees God's world, conjures up man's world, and inhabits both. This is his three-stage, Practical Design for Practical Living. The other design—that of the two-stage non-Seer—isn't all there, and so doesn't work out. It should not surprise you, members of the Jury, that play-God blasphemers—the sort that dismiss God's world unexamined, in their anxiety to redesign it to their own specification—botch the job in the long run. After many a short-term gain, their effrontery proves a dead loss, in the end fatal. And no wonder. It's not that their world's unlike His, but the opposite of His. How could such unrealism, such self-deception, such wilful blindness to the given, fail to prove increasingly counter-productive and in every way ineffectual? Cumulatively so. Day by day it's resulting in more and more personal misery, more and more social strife, more and more irreversible damage to the environment. And now it threatens man's very survival. Having made his bed he must lie on it. And die on it—if he doesn't wake up pretty soon from his nightmare world into the real world. Into God's world, the dear world he gives us in His mercy and loving-kindness, the world that's woven of blessings.

Into the world where I let things be themselves in their proper places. Where I let man be man on the far side of the glass, and God be God on the near side. Into this wide-awake world where Jack is hairy Jack over there being barbered, while God is God here just Being—Being that's balder and smoother and brighter than a china egg. Here, where the many man-heads come back to the One God-head, forever trim and speckless and radiant like the midday Sun.

It's by this simple truthfulness, this ever-renewed submission to the evidence, that I break the disastrous habit of Nokes-deification before it breaks me. It's not easy, I can tell you. It's not done overnight. It takes a lot of seeing him off. But in all honesty and with great respect I stand here and tell you I'm no blasphemer.

I wish to God I could say the same of—

All right, Your Honour. I've finished. I hand over to one of my most distinguished witnesses—to that sublime pagan Seer, Plotinus, who wrote:

> To Real Being we go back, all that we have and are. To This we return as from This we came. Of What is Here we have direct knowledge, not images or even impressions; and to know without image is to be... When we look outside of This on which we depend, we ignore our unity. Looking outward we see many faces, look inward and all is the One Head. If a man could but be turned about—by his own motion or the happy pull of Athene—he would at once see God, and himself, and the All.

And, for good measure, let me throw in a couple of pieces from that equally distinguished Sufi Seer, Rumi:

> If He sever one head from the body, He at once raises hundreds of thousands of heads for the beheaded one...
>
> He that beholds his own Face—his light is greater than the light of creatures. Though he die, his sight is everlasting, because it is the sight of the Creator.

And this from Rabi'a of Basra, the woman saint, and one of the earlier Sufis:

> I myself am keeping a guest-house. Whatever is within, I do not allow it to go out; and whatever is without, I do not allow it to come in.

Prosecution Witness No. 7

THE OSTEOPATH

Witness testifies that I went to him with a stiff neck a year ago. I complained that I couldn't turn my head more than about 50° without some pain. He's happy to say that his treatment, after a few sessions, was fairly successful.

Counsel asks the Witness whether he's aware that, because I can't *see* a head and neck mounted on my body, I maintain they don't exist.

I intervene to protest that Counsel is grossly misrepresenting my views. He should leave it to me to put them.

The Judge agrees and Counsel rewords his question.

COUNSEL: Are you aware of the Accused's published claim that losing his head is finding his life? *Finding* it, mark you, not, like King Charles (only the first one, I trust), *losing* it? That, for some reason hidden from us ordinary mortals, this cutting down is adding to, with the result that he's not less than human but much, much more than human? Superhuman at the very least? In which case why did he need to go to you for treatment? And what do you make of the whole cock-eyed affair?

WITNESS: Yes, I know that he says he's very special, and (in my view) sincerely believes it. But I'm sure he's wrong, and the reason he's wrong is that he's relying too much on one sense at the expense of the others. On vision alone, ignoring touch—to say nothing of hearing and tasting and smelling. Of course, when I'm working on his neck, I'm the only one of us two who sees it: but I also feel my hands on it. And so does he. *Ouch!* he cries, when I press a tender spot. Obviously—for us both—touching is as much believing as seeing is believing. Or more. Arriving home at night, he fumbles for and presses the light-switch he doesn't see, and I take it that in his bath he scrubs his back sometimes. In fact, touch is often a surer test of a thing's presence than sight is. You discover that a hologram of a cup isn't a cup by trying to take hold of the thing. And then, of course, there's the truly touching story of Doubting Thomas, who refused to trust his eyes till he had fingered the wounds of his Lord.

COUNSEL, all irony and gloat, turns to the Jury: We can't wait to hear the Accused's crushing reply to this testimony, can we? [Addressing the Witness] Would you say that this man is stupidly but genuinely naïve in his obsession with sight alone? Or that the diabolical pride and ambition of the blasphemer drive him to suppress the tangible evidence that proves he's only human after all? To be blunt, the Jury need to decide whether he's a fool or a knave. Can you help them to do so?

WITNESS: Perhaps he's a bit of both. My guess is that he's the Golden Ass, bright (if not brilliant) in his loopy fashion. Rather like King James I, the fellow they called the wisest fool in Christendom.

COUNSEL: I'm informed that the Devil has a higher IQ than any other angel—and if you read it as Idiocy Quotient, that's all right by me... Have you anything to say about the Accused's lunatic pretensions to divinity?

JUDGE: That's a grossly leading question.

COUNSEL: Delete 'lunatic'.

WITNESS: I do have a query. Why should God be in Mr Noke's head (or *instead* of his head, or *in his no-head* - have it any way you like) and not in his heart, for example, where religious folk profess to find Him? Why this fixation on the human head, I ask, with its seemingly unlimited potential for confusion and delusion, leading on occasion to blasphemy trials? Why, with all His Creation to choose from, should the Creator settle for and settle in such a crowded and crime-infested slum? Or such a poky hideout or hide-in as any organ of the human body? Or the whole of it, for that matter? Surely He could have found less congested and dingy lodgings somewhere in all the real estate of His universe?

COUNSEL, sitting himself down with the air of one who has said the last word: Over to the Accused

Defence: **Taking the Rough with the Smooth**

I continue the Witness's examination.

'As a prelude to deflating the Prosecution, and answering the very pertinent questions you have raised, I would like to put one to you. To you, who know about such matters. What is this very, very peculiar finial or knob or headpiece, this problematic something-or-other that tops off a human body?'

Counsel begs his Honour to dismiss my question as yet another red herring, a false trail the court shouldn't waste time following.

The Judge fails to see why I want a definition of something that all sane persons are agreed about.

I claim the right to conduct my Defence in my own fashion, but to save time I'm willing to rephrase my question to the Witness:

'Do you agree that a human head is an opaque, multicoloured, roughly eight-inch, hairy bone-box, jam-packed at the top with knobbly grey stuff, and furnished with a pair of shuttered portholes and a hinged lower section for letting sounds out and food in?'

The Witness agrees, reluctantly, that will do.

I have no further questions. He stands down.

MYSELF, addressing the Jury: While that picture of a human top is fresh in our minds, let me assure you cross-my-heart that I'm topless, a head short, and can find nothing like that lurking on these shoulders. What about your shoulders? Are they a dish for serving up that very fancy meatball on, or for serving up everything but that meatball? For serving up a world? What's on your plate, right now? At this moment can you think of anything less like what you're looking out of, either in detail or overall, than that very grotesque and very knotted topknot? Than that very meaty meatball?

I shall be coming back to exactly what you and I do have here in place of that meatball or topknot. Meanwhile I want to address the question which the Witness put to me at the end of his testimony. It could hardly be more germane to my Defence.

Why do I pick on the head? The reason's simple. I don't: it picks on itself. It's an oddity, a joker. The joke is that what I took to be most me is least me. It's the only part of my body (I mean of the whole of it, which is the Whole) that consistently plays truant, the only part I never come across here, that's *permanently* AWOL. The rest goes and comes back, much as it pleases and as I please. Thus when I look *down* it's just my head that's missing; when I look *out* (as I'm doing now) the rest of my human body's missing; if I were to climb on to the roof of this court and gaze *up* at the sky, my Earth-body would be missing; if I did so at night my Star-body—nearly all my Solar-System body—would be missing; and finally, if I were to close my eyes, my Universe-body would be missing. What's constant throughout is the missing head. The essential feature of this topknot of mine is that it's featureless. And not only featureless but a nonsense, an absurdity. I'm shoulder-high, or rather shoulder-low. There I stop.

Or put it this way: the reason for picking on my no-head, rather than (say) my no-torso, is that it's *central* to me throughout—whereas my no-torso often isn't. Do I have to explain further? Be serious! If This that's forever where I'm coming from, This that's the Root of the root of my life and the Being of my being and the indispensable Core of the Mystery of Me—if This isn't worth fastening on to and looking into hard and long, tell me what is. To be wrong about This—and what could be more perverse than bunging it up with that peripheral and hugely complicated bag of tricks which is our agreed definition of a human head?—to be wrong about This is to be wrong about everything else. If there's anything more sure to sink me than a millstone around my neck, it is this fictitious millstone on my neck.

No, it's not my man's head that I pick on and make such a fuss about. It's the absence of it here, and the presence of... Well, of something very, very different. Which brings me to the question of what, exactly, I'm touching when I finger the thing (or no-thing) that

I'm living from here, that I'm looking out of. How far is it like, and how far is it unlike, the intangible thing that those other ten fingers are simultaneously exploring in my mirror? The question is: what, when I attend, does touch disclose about what's right here at the hub of my world? Not about what's there, in the realm of light-switches and cups etc., but here, in the realm of their user?

Over there, touch tests and complements sight, and vice versa. They fit nicely. And so they do here (as we shall presently see) but combine to tell a vastly different story. Here they come together most beautifully to reveal What I really am, in sharp contrast to what I appear to be, what I look like to you now.

But what's the good of just talking about this contrast? I must ask you, all you Jury members and Your Honour as well, to conduct along with me a little experiment. It's so easy to do, so revolutionary in what it comes up with, so destructive of the lies we live by, that we all ought to do it daily along with our physical jerks and hair-combing and teeth-brushing. If you are too embarrassed, or too lazy, or too prejudiced to do what I'm now doing, or to take seriously what you find when you do so, you'll be turning this place into a court of injustice, a kangaroo court. To say nothing of the entertainment and the revelation you'll be missing out on, personally. So *please*… Yes, you, Sir Gerald, too! And your Junior, Mr Atkinson… Well, have it your own way. No surprise that the Crown denies it crowns thin air.

The rest of you all set? I'll tell you what I'm doing and what I'm finding, so that you can then do the same, and check whether you get the same results as I get. Don't believe me. Look for yourself.

You see me now stopping my ears, pressing a finger into each ear-hole...

Well, that's your story. Mine isn't a bit like that.

What I'm finding here is a *mélange* of sensation of touch, of sustained sound, of pressure, of discomfort and a little pain—with no things, no solid, opaque, coloured objects whatever to attach these sensations to. Attending carefully, I sort this *mélange* out into two parts, with a space intervening.

How wide is this gap between the ears I don't have here? On present evidence, how distant are these two sensation-groups, one on my far right and the other on my far left?

Now it's your turn to repeat the experiment, asking the same questions... Please!...

Instead of sticking his forefingers in his ears, Counsel applies them to his forehead, twisting them screwdriver fashion. His Junior nods and winks at the Jury, most of whom are following my instructions, hesitatingly.

MYSELF: What I find here never ceases to astound and delight me. I don't know about you, but this between-ears gap of mine is Universe-wide at the very least! I'm hugely tickled (should I say the World's hugely tickled?) to find I've come to the World's End, where I'm simultaneously fondling its quite rough extremities and seeing how vast is the interval between them. Yes, seeing it: I'm no more imagining or thinking that gap than I'm smelling it or tasting it. I'm taking the world by the ears. It's a kindly and gentle taking, the way one handles a pet rabbit, and the contrary of setting the world by the ears.

And what is it that fills to capacity this huge between-ears gap right now? Why, the whole scene, the world as it's presenting itself. Yes, it's you—you the Judge and Jury, and the Prosecution Lawyers, and the Clerk to the Court, and the Court Usher, and all the rest of you in the setting of this courtroom—who are currently tenanting this immense Accommodation that I have to let. You lot, plus all sorts of thoughts and feelings about you, plus all those sensations I've just described and many more, plus God knows what. And all that between-ear filling is changing continually. What never changes is this Aware Accommodation for it all, for you all. THIS I AM. The pot that looked so narrow can take the world-joint, and its ears are poles apart.

In one of his more lucid moments Bertie Wooster says of some character, 'Between the collar and the hair-parting nothing stirred.' They say of a fool that there's nothing between his ears. I say, bully for him. For me, too, that's a good half of the truth. The other is that there's everything. Nothing and Everything. I ask you, what could be more unlike that dead-to-the-world head-thing, that man-head as we have defined it, than this wide-awake Emptiness—Fullness? What could be more like the God-head—as, precisely, Nothing-and-Everything, alive to Itself as just that? Yes, the awesome, blissful, glorious fact is that what we are now exploring, this between-ears Immensity we tried so hard to bung up with our man-head, is our God-head. Blasphemy it was and blasphemy it is to desecrate this

Holy of Holies with any human thing, any thing at all. Blasphemy and damnation.

Counsel startles the court by suddenly pulling a face, sticking his thumbs in his ears, and waggling his fingers. Has his lunch been a rather convivial one? His Honour seems too taken aback to comment...

'Is this a court of law?' Sir Gerald wants to know. 'Anyone peeping in would think it's a circus, or a nursery, or a loony-bin... Let's all play Ring a ring o'roses! Better still, Johnny shall have a new bonnet! Ha, ha, ha!'

MYSELF: The joke's on the joker who can't tell the childlike from the childish...

I want now seriously to address the Witness's question about why the King should so demean Himself as to occupy such poky and unregal premises as the human body, setting up His throne in the coal cellar.

Poky and unregal? Nonsense! Just look and see: could this throne-room, into which you and I tried so hard to smuggle a human head—could it be any wider, any deeper or loftier, any grander than it now so obviously is? Let's not fool ourselves that, if we searched the universe of galaxies and stars for an age of ages, we would ever alight on a more palatial residence for Him—one more heavenly yet more homely, more empty yet more gloriously filled, more lived-in yet more bright and fresh and dust-free—than this home He's being provided with right here. Or, for that matter, a home more safe against any alien invasion at all? More untroubled by outsiders? What outsiders?

The plain fact is that, no matter how we resist and lie about it, we are all living from What and Who we really are, not from our man-head but our God-head. Fortunately we have no choice. Besides, at some level and in some strange way, we aren't just living from but *awake* to our God-head. For who of us, inside as well as outside mental hospitals, believes that we are shut up in eight-inch spherical containers, in bone-boxes stuck over with hair outside and packed with offal inside? Who of us doesn't feel at large, no matter what we've been told *ad nauseam* to the contrary? Who of us (even before we dare or care to look) fails to find our outer space continuous with our inner space, with no perimeter fence between them? Who of us can even imagine what it would be like to be plunged and stuffed into the dark, sticky, wet, congested goo which is alleged to befoul the very Centre of our universe? In truth, though all our lives we are taught to blaspheme by superimposing man's opacity on God's transparency, none of us begins to learn the lesson. None of us takes it seriously for a moment. In the last resort, blasphemy is no more than a black knight's move in the Grand Master's great game of pretending. We are all guilty, and none of us is guilty, of this impossible offence.

Well, members of the jury, I guess that's enough...

COUNSEL, rising to his feet quite steadily: No, it isn't! I've two or three awkward questions to put to you, Mr a-dash-Nokes. Explain why, when you finger the unseen thingumabob on your shoulders, you always feel the head of a man. And not a head of celery or lettuce, or—painfully—a head of steam? And explain why, when you stand before a mirror, the movements of your hand over the felt but unseen contours of the thingumabob correspond so closely with its movements over that unfelt but clearly seen head? Isn't the obvious explanation (obvious to all but the very sick or the very thick) that on the near side of the mirror is your invisible but real human head, while on the far side is your visible but unreal human head, its mere reflection?

Not another lecture, for God in Heaven's sake. Brief but clear answers, if you please.

JUDGE: Yes, indeed.

The jury perks up—feeling (I imagine) that I've been caught out this time. I'm inclined to share that feeling. However, I listen to my reply.

MYSELF: God has been credited with (and accused of) making man in His image. And if in the making He indulges in a spot of kindly humour, isn't that what we're learning to count on from Him? In any case it's to be expected of all heads—animal, human, divine—that they should have enough in common to justify their common name. No great surprise, then, to find that, in my huge and airy divine Head here, can be detected some curious correspondences with my stuffy little human head over there in the mirror. Most appropriate and most encouraging I find them, such as they are. I regard them as the ideal base from which to explore the immense contrasts between man's topknot there and God's Topknot (or, rather, Bottomknot) here.

COUNSEL: There you are, members of the Jury! No explanations, more blasphemy! And more pathology, let me add. Acephalitis is surely one of the more serious degenerative conditions.

MYSELF: And you'll get a whole bunch of physicians to agree

with you, Sir Gerald! According to one long-established and fairly respectable medical system (currently patronized by some royals) the experience of having no head on your shoulders is indeed a well-recognized disease. Consulting *Clinical Homeopathy,* by Dr Anton Jayasuriya, we find that the remedy is *Asarum europaeum!* Other pilules—to cure you of the feeling that your head is empty, or much enlarged, or loose—are prescribed by Dr J. T. Kent in his *Repertory of Homoeopathic Materia Medica!* [Laughter and catcalls in the court. Unable to keep a straight face himself, His Honour lets them pass...] Let me assure the Jury that I'm not pulling their legs! Those are standard handbooks by world-famous authorities! I shall not, however, allow them to divert me from my argument.

The final and crucial question is: *which of my two heads—the one on that side of the glass, or the one on this side—is the real one?*

The criteria for settling this question beyond all doubt are eight. They will serve to sum up my Defence against this Witness's testimony and the Prosecution's handling—or mishandling—of it.

(1) My real Head is the one that's right here and right now, plumb in the Centre of my universe.

(2) It's the one which sees, hears, tastes and smells.

(3) It's the one that's big enough to contain the other head, with an infinity of room to spare. Or let's say: it's the one that's right up to itself and therefore infinite—the way everything is when it's viewed from no distance, and therefore *full size.*

(4) It's the one that faces outwards, that's turned towards the world and not away from it.

(5) It's the one that sports a pair of 'noses', one on the far left of the scene and the other on the far right, *both touchable* though transparent, and only occasionally opaque. (Believe it or not, Boericke's *Materia Medita with Repertory* prescribes *Merc. per.* for treating patients who complain they are two-nosed!)

(6) It's this incredibly well-stocked head, this Great Universal Store that carries all the goods in the world, arranged in the most attractive, uncrowded, easy-to-find fashion imaginable. Not that tiny lump-of-a-head which is just one of the items on its shelves.

(7) It's the unframed and unboxed one, in contrast to that picture-framed fellow, poor old Jack in the box - in the glass-fronted box he can't spring out of.

(8) Finally, it's this rough one I make sure of by fingering it all over, and not the smooth one that's inaccessible behind its glass barrier. *Not the human head—not that recognizable Noke's head—which I never laid hands on in all my life.* If touching (and not seeing) is believing, that head is as dubious as a mirage in the desert, while this Head is as certain as the Great Pyramid of Cheops.

Please note, Jury, my preference in the end for touch as against sight, *pace* the Witness's testimony to the contrary.

And please note that on all eight counts my God-head is my real and unique Head—the Sun of which my man-head is a mere satellite. As we've just seen, that man-head is not only off-Centre, but unconscious, exclusive, inward-facing, and un-get-at-able. What a surprise, what a joke—what a master key to my true Identity—is this elaborate debunking and decentralizing of John a-Nokes, once

I get around to noticing it! Immeasurably more real than the glazed man-head I'm forever out of touch with is the unglazed and naked God-head I'm forever in touch with. Praise be to the One Who will go to such lengths—playing the Lone Rough Beast to my Smoothie—to save me from myself by uniting me with Him Who is Myself!

All the same, I have to admit that, of the two, smooth Jack has this advantage: it's a lot easier to do justice to him in a drawing. As you will see from Diagram No. 7—an unfinished and dubious effort, which I'm half inclined to withdraw from our exhibition of self-portraits.

'This travelling hat may look small, but when I put it on it covers the universe,' said Zen master Huang-po. If he hadn't been a Buddhist, he might have added that it's *God* Who puts it on, and it's nice and furry, and it suits Him perfectly!

Finally, let me throw in this verse from 'The Derby Ram', an English nursery rhyme which gives the general idea:

The space between the horns, sir,
Was as far as man could reach.
And there they built a pulpit,
But no one in it preached.

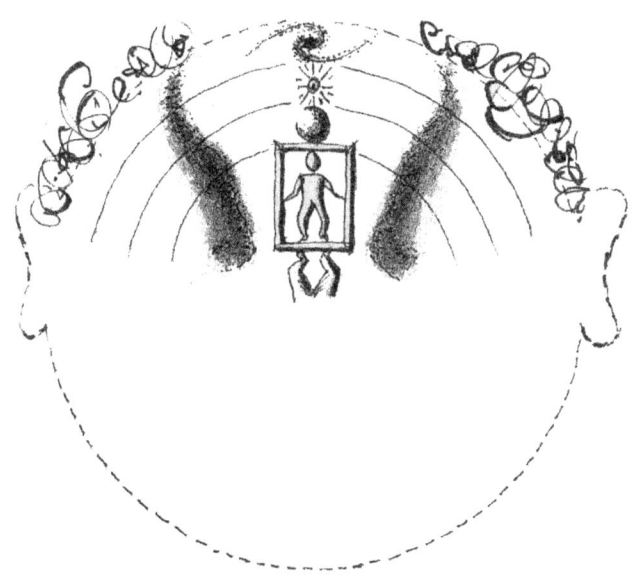

Diagram No. 7

Prosecution Witness No. 8

THE NEUROSURGEON

Witness explains that he's a not-so-near neighbor of mine and little more than a casual acquaintance. No, he has no reason to regard me as antisocial or mad or perverted in any way. He minds his own business and knows little about mine. Certainly he has heard rumours (who hasn't?) but pays no attention. Yes, of course he knows that I'm up before this court on a charge of blasphemy.

COUNSEL: Are you aware that the Accused prides and preens himself on being headless, which surely means brainless? And claims that his considerable handicap, instead of leaving him subhuman by a long chalk, leaves him superhuman, even divine?

WITNESS: I've heard he's got this thing about his head. I don't understand it at all.

COUNSEL: You aren't alone. With the forlorn hope of enlightening you and the court, let me read out something from a published book of his:

> Provisionally and common-sensibly, he [the scientist] put a head here on my shoulders, but it was soon ousted by the universe. The common-sense or unparadoxical view of myself as 'an ordinary man with a head' doesn't work at all; as soon as I examine it with any care, it turns out to be nonsense.
>
> And yet (I tell myself) it seems to work out well enough for all everyday, practical purposes. I carry on just as if there actually were, suspended

here, plumb in the middle of my universe, a solid eight-inch ball. And I'm inclined to add that, in the uninquisitive and truly hard-headed world we all inhabit, this manifest absurdity can't be avoided: it is surely a fiction so convenient that it might as well be the plain truth.

In fact, it is always a lie, and often an inconvenient lie at that.

WITNESS, asked for his comments: Well, I must say that the Accused appears to me to be a perfectly ordinary man, with a perfectly ordinary head to him. And the whole of my professional experience tells me that in that ordinary head is an ordinary brain, and that in that ordinary brain are millions of ordinary neurons. About the brain's condition, whether it's diseased or somewhat disordered or functioning normally or functioning brilliantly, I can't tell you now for sure. But it's there in position all right. If it isn't, he's the sensation of the century and the eighth wonder of the modern world. And I'll resign my job and take up pisciculture. At least *fish* have brains.

COUNSEL: Would you tell the court something about the brain's importance, its function in the life of the Accused, its central role in all our lives?

WITNESS: A large subject. You can look at it from two angles. On the one hand you can regard the brain as the indispensable seat of *consciousness;* and—as such—determining the level of the mind's functioning, its scope and its quality. Thus a rabbit, with its comparatively small and unconvoluted brain, experiences a somewhat smaller and less convoluted world than that of a King's Counsellor. Thus a rabbit or a King's Counsellor who suffers from a brain tumour or a brain injury experiences a distorted rabbit world or KC world. On the other hand one can view the function of the brain more objectively. This way, the brain—the nervous system as a whole—is seen as a mechanism for processing incoming information so that it issues in appropriate outgoing behavior, somewhat as the alimentary system processes incoming foodstuffs to fuel that same outgoing behavior. That's the view my work inclines me to take. I perceive the brain as a telephone exchange-cum-computer, co-ordinating the functioning of the organism as a whole and of its parts. However, both ways of regarding the brain make that organ quite crucial in the body's economy and in every respect central in our lives.

COUNSEL: You hear that, members of the Jury? Central in our lives. [He turns to the Witness.] So, when the Accused says he's brainless (is 'decorticated' the word I want?) is he lying like the deuce, or off his trolley, or plain ignorant?

WITNESS: Just pulling our legs, I'd say. Playing at being Winnie the Pooh with little or no brain at all. Ingenious mischievous, fun-poking, a latter-day Till Eulenspiegel, a taker-off on intellectual or poetic flights of the imagination—I don't know what—but in any case not altogether serious. He's no more mad than I am. Just more fanciful than I can afford to be. To put it in the vernacular and frankly, I get the impression that, so far from being brainless, he's every bit as brainy as most of you around here.

JUDGE: Just answer the Counsel's questions.

COUNSEL: At this juncture I must remind the Jury that the

Accused isn't on trial for his private beliefs—no matter how fantastical, how elaborately absurd or how ingeniously offensive they may be. He's here on account of his pubic blaspheming and the civil disturbances it has given rise to. The only reason why his opinions are very much the concern of this court is his tireless and much-publicized contention that they are true, so true and so fundamental and so revolutionary that the blasphemies they come out with aren't blasphemies at all, but sober statements of fact. Accordingly, one of the aims of the Prosecution is to tear that claim apart. [He turns to the Witness.] Are you proposing to the court that the Accused's story—this fantasy that he's empty-headed, or no-headed, or divine-headed (whatever his latest variation on the theme may be)—is just a contemporary upsurging of nonsensical British humour? New-style jabberwocky, featuring a reincarnated Queen of Hearts still screaming, 'Off with their heads!'? Good old British whimsicality run into the ground, surely? Pushed so far and so hard that already it lands the humorist in that dock, on trial for his life? And may well land him, like Till Eulenspiegel, in an early grave?

WITNESS: I guess I am, except that I don't take it all so dead seriously. Besides—

COUNSEL: And that the theological skyscraper—high-rising to I don't know what heavens of self-deification—which he erects on these comical quicksands is no more solid and well-founded than they are?

WITNESS: Well, you said it.

COUNSEL: The court insists on a straight answer.

WITNESS: Honestly, I don't know. I'm no theologian.

COUNSEL: But you do know that the Accused's claim to be unique, to be vastly different up top from us common folk, is (to say the least) over the top?

WITNESS: Well, yes—

COUNSEL: Thank you. That will do.

Defence: **The Brain of God**

MYSELF, to Witness: You and I are agreed about what a human brain is, and its importance for human life. Our only difference is about *where* the thing is. But that difference makes all the difference.

Addressing this vital issue of where, I'm much less interested in what you say than in what you do, in your approach to your work as a brain surgeon. I mean *approach* literally, in the most physical sense of the word. By what steps (I'm asking) do you get down to work daily, actually come to the delicate task of (say) excising a tumour on my brain? It will save the court's time if you will let me outline the successive stages of your inward journey, for you to confirm or correct as needed. These stages I've shown on Diagram No. 8 in the booklet, which you and His Honour and the Jury should please refer to throughout.

You drive from the country to the town (a), and through the town to the hospital (b). Having parked, you walk to the neurosurgical department and enter the scrub of the operating theatre that's been allocated to you. Scrubbed and gloved and gowned, you approach the patient (c) on the table, already heavily sedated and anaesthetized locally. (The brain itself, of course, is insensitive to the scalpel, and needs no anaesthetizing.) You commence surgery, making incisions and trepanning and so on, till the cortical area requiring treatment is exposed and clearly on view (d).

In short, you have approached me by stages, beginning with a landscape and ending with a brainscape.

Is my account of your professional procedure, so far, about right?

WITNESS: I can't fault it. But why this painstaking detection of the obvious? So what?

MYSELF: Now we're coming to the really interesting part, the nitty-gritty. *Here, in region (d), which is still several inches short of me, you stick.* You the brain surgeon have arrived at your goal at the place from which my cortex can be viewed. Note how far it is from me, the operand, how far it has to be from the point of contact (x). For if (armed with optical and electron microscopes) you were to venture much nearer, you would be wasting precious time and holding up the operation. Leaving behind you the region where the brain is on display, you would come to regions where it's replaced by a set of neurones (e), then one neurone (f), then a bunch of molecules, then one molecule... And so on until, having come all the way in to our meeting place (x), you would have left all of me behind you. And what good would that do either of us? So it's essential to the operation that you stop short of these forbidden regions, and remain at just the right distance (around nine inches, say) from where I am. Essential that you don't stray from the only region where my brain's on show,

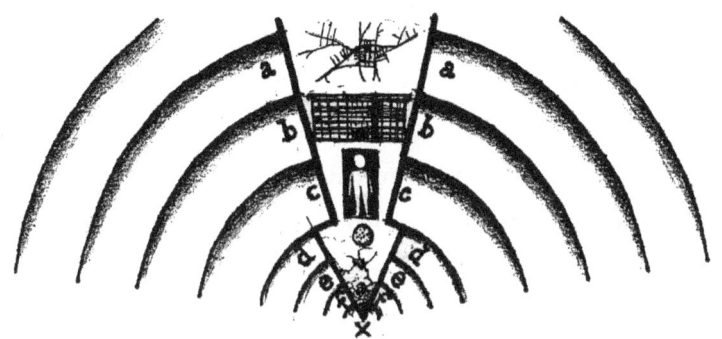

Diagram No. 8

the only region where it puts in an appearance, where *qua* brain it manifests.

WITNESS: Are you saying that I make an incision in the brain tissue *at a distance?* I'm no magician.

MYSELF: I was coming to that. Plainly it's not you the man but your outstretched scalpel-hand that travels that last and all-important stage of the inward journey (d, e, f . . . x), through regions cellular and molecular and atomic and subatomic, to the point of contact (x), the site of the operation itself. It's not you the surgeon but the keen edge of your knife that traverses these near regions where I'm progressively brainless, then cell-less, then molecule-less, and so on till it arrives *here* where I'm everything-less. Here we really come together. Here at last we two get down to business.

WITNESS: I think you've got the pattern all right. But I'm having difficulty with the language.

MYSELF: In that case, let's go non-verbal and refer again to our picture, showing the main stages of your approach to me, your patient. My point cannot be missed, it's so obvious. It's simply that, if you are to keep abreast of the progress of your operation on my brain, you must stay with it where it manifests, where it's on display—just so many inches short of that busy scalpel.

The question was: where do I keep my brain? And the answer is: in roughly the same place as I keep my head; namely, upwards of (say) nine inches from here, from my Centre. I stash it away where I stash my head—that little head which I keep over there in my mirror and in people's cameras and in you people, and never, O never, here. (How ridiculous that Nokesian pinhead—with its even tinier brain—would look on these immensely broad shoulders!) Naturally brain and head go together—and naturally, knowing their place, go to it together. This would be obvious if it happened (as it could well happen in some brave new world) that my scalp and skull were replaced by transparent plastic, and instead of a hairdo I wore a braindo.

Well, I put it to you, the Witness: is this soft British whimsy or is it hard international facts? Isn't your approach by stages to this operation a telling example of Basic Relativity, of the Law (so fundamental, so neglected) that what a thing *is* is no fixed quantity/quality, but depends on where it's being viewed from? Of the Law that *distance,* besides lending enchantment, lends just about everything else, and is the making of things? Of the Law that whatever I go up to I lose, and that what I always go up to (namely, my head and brain) I always lose—lose to you and to the world in general? Which explains why you, in your role of brain surgeon, know your place—as we have seen—and come no nearer. Yours is close work, all right. But not too close.

Not disagreeing, Witness says it all takes a lot of getting used to: it's so different from the ordinary common-sense way of looking at his job. But he's not clear about why we should bother with this strange and therefore difficult vision, so long as the ordinary one works as well as it does.

MYSELF: I can think of two good reasons. First, if it's a true and sensible vision that makes nonsense of our so-called commonsense picture of what's going on (and by God it does!), then we'd better pay attention. Lies are inefficient, truth works. Lies bind, truth liberates. What's even more to the point, lies kill but truth cures.

Second, if it proclaims my true Identity (and by God it does, it does!)—assuring me of my oneness with the One Who as the Source of all things is No-thing, and happily as free from brains as from everything else—then it's the best news imaginable. It's the good news I'm dying to hear and living to put into practice. It's the revelation of What I need, not only to survive this Trial and the severest sentence the court can impose, but also to ensure that what survives is worth surviving for. In brief, the more I enjoy this vision the more I find it to be realistic, down-to-earth no less than up-to-heaven, practical, beautiful, and all my heart could desire.

COUNSEL, unable to contain himself any longer: Also it's flim-flam, a load of wishy-washy willful thinking. [He jabs at me with a bony forefinger.] For you haven't begun to face the disagreeable fact that, as the Witness brought out, this much-cracked-up consciousness of yours (on the alleged primacy of which your case hangs) arises from and is conditioned by the brain. Airily you ignore the inconvenient fact that it is in all ways dependent upon that organ's bulk and complexity, and its state of health or sickness. Here the Witness's testimony implies that this wonderful awareness, this precious consciousness of yours which you presume to deify, is about as Godlike as marsh gas, which also is beautifully at-large and transparent and colourless and tasteless, and sometimes luminous—but which bubbles up from rotting vegetation. Now I ask you: what sort of God is this, who bubbles up from a tangled mishmash of knobbly grey matter, matter which, if not rotting fast, is still suffering from a terminal disease called life, and is tragically subject to tumours, cancer, blood clots, drugging and other horrors? I ask you! [He leans far forward. His voice drops from a roar to a stage whisper.] Listen, Nokes! Listen very carefully. With the utmost seriousness I mean what I'm about to say. If you will assure the court that *this* is the divinity you claim to be—I refer to this will-o'-the-wisp or flibbertigibbet—then you are indeed a fool, and indeed you are guilty of gross abuse of the English language, and probably of behaviour leading to a breach of the peace. *But not of blasphemy.* Redefine your deity as a pseudo-gaseous by-product of matter, or, if you like, as its finest production to date, and a lovely quasi-spiritual phosphorescence playing above the stuff (rotting or daisy-fresh, I don't care)—go on to apologize to the court for wasting all this time—and I will see that the charge against you is dropped ... Mind you, I'm not saying that a lesser one, to be tried in a lower court, won't be preferred against you. But at least your life won't be at stake ... Well, what about it?

The Judge nods vigorously. Counsel sits himself down with the insufferably complacent air of a parent who magnanimously pardons a rebellious and rather idiotic child, in the expectation of tearful gratitude. The Jury are all ears.

MYSELF, treating this peace-feeler with the contempt it deserves, and taking the war into the enemy's territory: Do I gather that Counsel is gassing away in this court? Am I to understand that the forensic fireworks we've just witnessed are a kind of ignis fatuus arising from a kind of bog? Well, he's the final authority on what it's like being that bog, and I'm in no position to pull him out of it. All I can say is that he's reduced his arguments throughout this Trial to wind, to hot air, to miasmic hot air at that. Happily my awareness isn't a bit like that. Sure, it can't be pinned down (much less bogged down), baffles all description, is quite indefinable. But it's indefinable because it's the Definer, the Fountainhead of all definition. The reason why I can't tell the court what it's like is that it isn't *like* anything, that it differs absolutely from everything it's conscious of. The reason I'm tongue-tied on this subject (which is *the* Subject) isn't that I don't know what it is, but that it's the only thing I do know—know through and through *ad infinitum,* know absolutely because I am it absolutely. All other entities (yes, including brains and heads) are the *contents* of this Container which never changes, while they change all the time, come and go continually. Moreover, in razor-sharp contrast to their Container (which stands forever perfectly revealed, yet perfectly mysterious) they are painfully shy and retiring, never exposing all sides of themselves, let alone their insides. In fact they are cagey by nature, essentially lacking, never all there, never quite real. To see them at all is to see them distorted. Such reality as they can boast (and this goes for brains of course) isn't theirs at all, but on loan from the One Reality that is Consciousness, the Awakeness from which they arise and to which they return. Ladies and gentlemen of the Jury, to make this Primary Producer a by-product of one of its products is like attributing Walt Disney to Mickey Mouse, Edison to his lamp, and Sir Gerald to his brief. It is to derive the Real from the unreal, the True from the false, the Known from the guessed-at. And it's just plain dotty!

COUNSEL, stamping and finger-wagging: But you can't wriggle out of the fact that, in the course of your own evolution, so swiftly recapitulated in the womb, more and better-organized brain has gone with more and better-organized consciousness. Nor can you get over the fact that when (as a result, it may well be, of the Jury's verdict) your brainwaves flatten out and cease, so will the consciousness they are giving rise to.

MYSELF: Counsel will never get the hang of what I'm saying as long as he confuses and lumps together Consciousness and what it's conscious of, Container and its contents, Subject and its objects. Why can't he understand that he's taking awareness of things, and making another thing it?

I assure the court that I *don't* want to wriggle out of the fact that the contents of this Container-which-I-am vary all the way from the subatomic, through the human to the supergalactic, and are in flux all the time. Oh, no, I want to wriggle into it. I revel in all this delightful mutability. But even more do I revel in the fact that the Container Consciousness itself stays forever the same throughout all these developments and deteriorations, all the comings and goings of its contents. Take my own case, and refer again to our Diagram No.8. When I was (in your reckoning) minus nine months old and a single cell in the womb, I was What I am now: to wit, the same Consciousness (x), viewed from region (f), from the place where I then read (and still read, if you come near enough) as cellular. Also, when I shall (again in your reckoning) die and revert to inorganic matter, I shall still be this same Consciousness (x), viewed from region (g), from the place where I shall then read (and already read if you come that near) as molecular. Throughout these and all the other countless views of Me near and far, I remain the unvarying Container, the Viewing and the Viewed One, the Central Reality of which all creatures are at once contents and regional appearances. Theophanies, every one. Appearances of God. Myself, heavily disguised.

In a word, I'm *safe.* Indeed I'm the only Safety, right here at the Centre where I share Identity with you, learned Counsel, and the Judge and the Jury and all beings of all levels and places and times. Go on threatening me, do your worst by me, do your best, in the end it makes no difference. The God-head which we all are is clean of all perishables. It's the Sole Imperishable.

COUNSEL: So this wonderful God-head of yours is cleaned out, decorticated, absolutely brainless. Why should you risk your life for the privilege of being this numbskull, this cosmic nitwit?

MYSELF: The truly wonderful thing is that this empty God-head is replete with all the brains in the world, is brainy to bursting, is the Brain of brains, the Brains Trust of the Universe. This is no wild speculation. Once I inspect this immense cavity between my own *felt* 'ears' here (in striking contrast to what's between the seen ears of my pinheaded friend in the mirror), I find it's filled with the world, brains and all. Yes—I have brains all right! The lot!

This divine Brain is my *real* Brain. To be assured of this, I need only to experience this Brain in action, to be awake to the way it runs my life. I swear to you it makes all the difference in my day-to-day existence. It works brilliantly for me when, at long last, I cease relying on that pathetically narrow and remote man's-head with its minuscule brain, and start relying on this all-inclusive and ever-present God's-head with its World-Brain. Well, I can answer for nobody here but myself. When I trust that pinhead, God help me! When I trust this Pincushion Head—this Hedgehog of Pins—God helps me!

To rescue these bald pronouncements from all vagueness and highfalutin godspeak, to bring them to life and topicality, let me explain Who's really conducting my Defence. I assure you that it isn't that little creature I see in the mirror and that you see in the dock. You may have noticed how seldom throughout this Trial I have relied on him and his ideas (in so far as he could be said to have any) and how often on those of the Prosecution. Counsel and his witnesses aren't my enemies but my friends, handing me on a plate just the right concoction to get my teeth into.

All I have to do is wait to be served. I'm given what I need just when I need it. The way it all works out is something I'll never get used to. While Sir Gerald and his priceless gallimaufry of witnesses are telling me how conceited and stupid and gullible I am, I take their point. I couldn't agree more, I empathize, I'm on their side, their argument is unanswerable. And then—O surprise, O gratitude!—without foreknowledge, clueless, mindless, more idiotic than idiotic, I listen with awe to what comes out of this all-wise God-head, speaking of Itself and for Itself and—yes!—to Itself. What a Brain is here!

It's all a question of *trust*. I can be sure that, sooner rather than later, John a-Nokes will let me down. And that, soon and late, now and forever, Who I am will never let me down. But of course! He would be letting Himself down. In traditional language, this means that God's arrangements for me (by which I mean the universe of things as they are now presenting themselves) are perfect—if only I will say Yes! to them. There, in what's actually happening, is His World-Brain at work. And coming up with the right answer every time. I'm picking God's brains when I see that *almost* headless man off and this *Completely* Headed God in—this God-head that contains, and is, all creatures great and small, headed and headless, brainy and brainless.

Listen, finally, to a few of the *very* brainy ones:

How can this one small brain think thoughts, unless God does the thinking?

Herman Melville

The Brain is wider than the Sky
For—put them side by side—
The one the other will contain
With ease—and you—beside.

Emily Dickinson

And still they gaz'd, and still the wonder grew
That one small head could carry all he knew.

Oliver Goldsmith, The Deserted Village

More brain, O Lord, more brain! Or we shall mar
Utterly this fair garden we might win.

George Meredith

The (self-abandoned) soul forms insensibly a habit of acting always by the instinct, so to speak, of God.

If we are able to envisage each moment as the manifestation of the will of God, we shall find in it all our hearts can desire.

Our understanding wishes to take the first place among the divine methods; it must be reduced to the last.

Jean Pierre de Caussade

To enlighten all beings from the self is delusion; to be enlightened by them is enlightenment.

Dogen

In a brilliantly thought-provoking fantasy entitled 'Where am I?', Daniel C. Dennett describes the experiences of a man in radio communication with his own amputated brain, floating in a tank. 'Here am I,' says this unfortunate character, 'sitting on a folding chair, staring through a piece of plate glass at my own brain.' I, John a-Nokes, could say the same thing right now, given only a window in my forehead and a mirror in my hand.

Prosecution Witness No. 9

THE PSYCHOTHERAPIST

COUNSEL, to Jury: 'You will have noticed how loath John a-Nokes is to admit that he has a mind of his own, how unwilling to take responsibility for his thoughts and feelings. You can see why. Such an admission would brand him a man, only human after all. For not even he could pretend that his mental chatter and petty worries are the Almighty's—to say nothing of his fears and hates, his addictions and moods. So what does he do? With a fine show of humility, he declares himself to be the Perfect Idiot, whose mind is so blank it's no mind at all. He *projects* all that subjective stuff on to the objective world, clearing the decks. For whom? Why, for the deity he claims to be, of course. 'God's in, I'm out!'—those are his very words. Oh, yes, his false modesty pays off all right! It's a sprat to catch a whale. A Jack Sprat to catch a Whale of a God.

Well, there's another way of looking at this convenient and much-used device of projection. It's a way which, though less complimentary to Jack Sprat, is—you Jury members will agree—more realistic. Our next Witness—a lady of long experience in psychotherapy—will explain how it works.

WITNESS: There are various kinds of projection, all resulting in distortion of reality. Thus you may grossly overvalue and idealize someone, falsely attributing wonderful qualities to him or her. Or you may grossly undervalue and denigrate someone, falsely attributing dreadful qualities to him or her.

For an example of the latter sort, let me tell you about a client I've been seeing over the past few weeks. I'll call her Joan. Joan's trouble (she explains) is that her relations and friends and neighbours are all of them extremely selfish, content to take advantage of her and indifferent to all she does for them, mean with money, not interested in her at all. Joan feels put upon, exploited, everybody's stooge. Now it won't do for me to assume she's got it all wrong. It may be unlikely, but it's certainly possible that she is surrounded by a company of loveless and insensitive self-seekers.

Such folk are no rarity. Nevertheless, as I learn more about that company, and go on listening to her story and observing how she tells it, the more apparent it becomes that she's finding in others the faults she can't face in herself. And that what she says *they* are is my best clue to what she is. Anyway, the result is that she's very worried and miserable, even to the point of threatening suicide. And I guess that Joan's friends and relations are having a hard time, too... Well, perhaps this case will do to illustrate how projection works. It's a very simple and transparent manoeuvre, and none of us is innocent of it.

COUNSEL: Briefly, how are you treating your client's condition? I take it you are getting her to withdraw her projections?

WITNESS: It might look like that to you. But really I don't seek to interfere in people's lives and get them to change their ways. I aim, rather, to encourage them to look at what's actually going on. Gradually, I think, Joan is realizing where all this unkindness, all these deplorable attitudes of the folk around her, are coming from. She's just beginning to take responsibility for her feelings. If, as I should expect, this *awaking* to what's so issues in a *change* in what's so, it won't have come from my helping her to alter anything, but from helping her to become conscious of it. It's a good working hypothesis that the more one goes for awareness, without straining to change things for the better, the more they *are* changed for the better. A year from now, it's conceivable that my client will be surrounded by lovely people!

In short, you could say that my approach to these problems is crabwise, oblique and not head-on.

COUNSEL: How do you see this as applying to the Accused?

WITNESS: I don't. All I know about him is what you've just told us. At a guess, however, I'd say he's attempting the impossible. Fortunately—repeat, *fortunately*—nobody can at any one time unload more than a fraction of his or her mind-stuff on to the world. And never, not in a whole lifetime, could anyone unload it all, leaving not a wrack behind. One is always coming from a vast mass of unexamined and more or less unconscious material. Let me assure you that the Defendant's fooling himself when he imagines he has completely cleared the decks for—whatever it is, or whoever it is.

COUNSEL: And if he were your client?

WITNESS: I'd forget all I've just said, give him the benefit of the doubt, and start from scratch. I promise you I wouldn't start by assuming he's sick.

COUNSEL: That will do very well, thank you.

I, the Accused, have no questions for the Witness. She stands down.

COUNSEL, to Jury: The Witness's message—coming to us from ripe and compassionate experience of the human condition—is that John a-Nokes is deceiving himself and others when he says he's moved out to let God in. He hasn't. And he can't.

Defence: **The Storming of the Bastille**

MYSELF: Ladies and gentlemen of the Jury, to respond to this Witness's testimony I shall have to outline the history of projection—and introjection—in the experience of humankind.

JUDGE: Before you get carried away, the court would like to know how long this seminar's going to be.

MYSELF: Not long, Your Honour. Provided Counsel doesn't interrupt me.

COUNSEL: Really, Your Honour -

JUDGE: We have to get used to the fact that these proceedings are about as much like a lawsuit in modern London as they are like a Socratic dialogue in ancient Athens. All the same, I shall rein in the Accused when he's obviously forgotten where he is, and why he's here.

MYSELF: I shall be grateful for the court's patience—without which I cannot respond adequately to the Witness. She's led us right up to the vast and perilous rain forest of the psyche, and I've no choice but to weave what path I can through the tanglewood.

To be clear about this crucial subject of projection (which is just a provisional name for it) we have to begin at the beginning and see where we get to. First, as humankind, then as the individual human.

Primitive man is pre-psychological man. His thoughts and feelings aren't stowed away in his head: they are distributed throughout his world, colouring and structuring and animating the whole scene. Thus it's not that the mountain top fills him with fear, but rather that a fearful dragon lives there, so it's a place to be avoided at all costs. Thus it's not that he invests the grim-faced idol with divinity or mana, but that it comes invested with the stuff; with energies that work magic which can heal or kill. And so on. For primitive man it's not that qualities and meanings take flight from the Subject to the object, but that they were never anywhere else. The bird in that bush was never in the hand.

But, in the course of ages, a whole flock of birds is netted. As he becomes more and more civilized (as we quaintly put it), more and more of these free-range qualities and meanings and powers are pulled in, are caught and collected from the Great Beheld, and caged in the Beholder. Man becomes *psychological* man. Along with a head he grows a mind to put in it. And this protuberance goes on enriching itself at the world's expense till in the end it's full to bursting and his world is reduced to nuts and bolts—if that. Double trouble. No longer One, his name is Legion. No longer the Possessor, he's possessed.

Take, for instance, the life history of the Sun. At first he's seen as tremendously alive, a powerful deity given to stately diurnal procession across the sky, with lesser and lower life in his gift, and his all-seeing Eye—now beaming, now glaring—fastened on man below. But man doesn't stay docile: he revolts against solar tyranny. The first stage of the Sun's undoing is the separation of his animating spirit from his body, which is reduced to a mere fire-ball steered daily round the heavens by the Sun angel. Next, the angel-chauffeur is polished off by degrees, till all that's left of him is a few fossil remains preserved (along with the angels of the spheres and the stars and the planets, and myriads of non-astronomical ones) in stained-glass windows. As for the fire-ball itself, its daily motion across the heavens is offloaded on to Earth and man. Its warmth and its shining and its many colours follow suit—they are now 'all in the mind'—till that once-glorious Sun-god is reduced to a lot of superheated gas in the sky and a lot of superheated mathematics on Earth, neatly tucked away in the heads of astrophysicists. How's that for desecration, for ungodliness? Yes, for blasphemy? And what applies to the Sun applies to everything under the Sun. Objects that were tremendous or significant or lovely or good have lost all these qualities to man the despoiler. To thieving man who, far from being deified or ennobled by his loot, is increasingly bugged by it. His chickens have come home to roost. And most of them have caught fowl pest.

The consequences of this age-long, immense, many-sided in-gathering of all that's held valuable are with us at this time in history and not hard to detect. But they are increasingly hard to take. Modern man's head is swollen and splitting with more meanings than he can cope with, stolen item by item from a cosmos now reduced to a meaningless commotion of inscrutable particles. Certainly the ingathering was necessary and hugely productive in its time: in the course of this long process of introjection man gained the inestimable benefits of civilization. But the goods suffered damage on the way in;

they didn't travel at all well. Problems mounted. The current result is *mens insana in corpore insano,* a bloody human mind in a bloodless universe body. Psychological man is a mess . . .

JUDGE: I'm trying to grasp the connection between this sorry tale, about the alleged withdrawal down the ages of the world's meaning into the head of its observer, and the crime you are charged with here today.

MYSELF: Pre-psychological man, Your Honour, is pre-blaspheming man, and psychological man is blaspheming man. It's not that the former is clearly aware of the indwelling God, but that, like the animals, he lets God be God within and lives from Him in all innocence. And it's not that the latter announces at the top of his voice that he has usurped God's throne. The operation is all the more effective for being an undercover one. His newly acquired mind is his secret weapon for driving God from the Centre of his world and setting himself up there, and it owes much of its huge success to its camouflage. Blasphemy looks a treat in academic and priestly robes.

JUDGE: It's you, not humankind, that's being tried for blasphemy. Tell the court precisely how you see yourself figuring in this ancestral story.

MYSELF: It's like this, Your Honour. Each individual condenses and recapitulates in a couple of decades the five-million-year life history of the species. As a baby I am, like primitive man, pre-psychological. My development into full humanhood, so necessary and so remarkable and so swift, is nevertheless achieved at a high price. Growing a virtually empty head on my shoulders, I proceed to follow the ancestral pattern and furnish it by ransacking the universe. And go on to over-furnish and cram the thing till I'm dangerously swollen-headed, and my world is proportionately denuded and fatuous. With the understandable result, perhaps, that I rush off to the shrink in the hope of reducing it to reasonable size and bearable pressure by letting some of the stuff out. By releasing swarms of bees from my bonnet—if I can.

In fact, I don't rush off to the analyst. Desperate evils need desperate antidotes. I've another remedy—quicker, surer, far less pricey, and far, far more drastic than his—for this severe head condition. Cephalectomy—no less! Cutting off the diseased organ. Beheading, to put it crudely. Thus releasing at a blow those captured swarms to go back to their native habitats, to the hives and the flowers from which I'd collected them over the years. Off they buzz—to my great relief They go back to making honey, I go back to relishing it. Life is sweeter now.

COUNSEL: Your Honour, I must strenuously protest. This Trial—the first under the Act of 2002, and therefore sure to establish precedents for further Trials—is taking the most deplorable shape. Here's the Accused, who's charged with a carefully defined offence, diverting attention from the charge and wasting time and public funds by delivering a lecture on his own brand of social psychology. Or is it on the care of the bee in sickness and in health? This isn't Defence. It's persistent frivolity and contempt of court. I respectfully ask you to shut him up forthwith.

JUDGE: You called the Witness. And if the only way he can counter her testimony annoys or bores or puzzles you, that can't be helped. On the other hand—yes. To the Accused my advice is: make it snappy. Stick to the point.

MYSELF: I was doing so meticulously, Your Honour, when Counsel (for reasons not hard to guess) deliberately diverted the court's attention from that point. He pretends not to understand my bees-in-the-bonnet picture, so let me try another. My head is a demolished Bastille, from which hordes of captives are freed to go back to where they belong. No question of projecting them homewards. You try stopping them! The site of the Bastille is cleared, down to the last stone. Cleared for the Liberty that is God's. I don't dismiss my imprisoned thoughts and feelings to make room here for Him. I don't let them go. I simply see that they have always belonged out there, to the object and not the Subject. Diagram No. 9, though it should be in fluorescent colours, will give you the general idea.

So once more that world—ranging from island universes to up-ended feet—springs to life and mind. We are back where we started—but with some huge differences. In many ways the universe for post-psychological man is no longer what it was for pre-psychological man—often as full of threat as of promise, often as much alien as it was homely, and as much other as it was himself. But now the wide and busy world is his very own, the indispensable filling of his empty and still God-head, the brilliant minding of his vacant No-mind, the magnificent bodying forth of his central No-body. It's a world whose riches have been earning a high rate of compound interest,

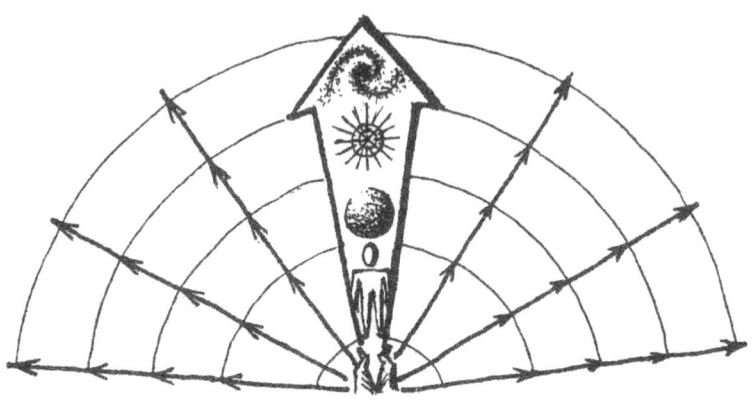

Diagram No. 9

whose capital has been doubled and redoubled for having been so painstakingly (and so painfully) collected and deposited over millennia in that temporary and packed-solid bank vault called the human brain. Now released and seen back to those roomy cosmic stations (which, to tell the truth, it never really left), that nominal and hoarded wealth is at last actualized. It's turned into God's real estate, His paradise.

So, in the end, His world didn't come to grief. Nothing was wasted. Without the intervention of psychological man and all his man-centred delusions, post-psychological man—which is to say God-filled and God-centred man—would never have made the grade.

The fact is that, if it were not for psychological man—the blasphemer who for a time seems to succeed in making God peripheral and man central in his universe—we in this courtroom would be a bunch of savages. Maybe naked, maybe half-decent in grass skirts, maybe dressed up to the nines in full tribal splendour—I don't know. But I do know that l wouldn't now be joyfully entertaining the dear Lord right here, if John a-Nokes hadn't first given Him the bum's rush and lowered his own trousered backside on to the royal throne.

COUNSEL: End of seminar—blaspheming seminar—I trust...

Well, the Prosecution won't waste the court's time further by refuting a hypothesis (it's no more than that) whose relevance to the charge is so marginal. One point, however, has to be made. It's as if the Accused were pretending that more is less. I say, he can hardly cure himself of *projection* (which even he apparently accepts is a disease) by unloading *all* his thoughts and feelings on to a long-suffering world. He simply ensures that he's got the most virulent form of the disease.

MYSELF: As usual, Counsel turns a true story into a lie by omitting its conclusion. What's wrong and unhealthy about the partial and second-stage projection the Witness described isn't the projection itself, but its misuse to evade responsibility. What's right and healthy about the *total* and third-stage 'projection' I'm advocating—in fact, it's not projection but releasing—is that it accepts *total* responsibility for what it finds 'out there'. Not only do I see off from here my thoughts and feelings, but what they are thoughts and feelings about, the world they alight on. Who I really, really am produces and is responsible for the lot, washes His hands of none of His creatures, however bad or miserable. These headless shoulders are visibly broad enough to shoulder the blame for all that's blameworthy, as well as the praise for all that's praiseworthy. Hence the tradition that God saves His world by taking on *all* its sin and suffering.

The long and the short of it is that your 'projection' is fine when it's total, when it cleans you right out. Then its other name is *creation,* and it proceeds from Who you really, really are into a world that's seen for what it really, really is. Namely, Yourself. Then You are unspeakably lovely, within and without.

It's half-measures that are the very devil. Here are some who went the whole hog:

The shining of the mere object, as though with a voidness of one's own nature, is samadhi.

Patanjali

As long as I am this or that I am not all things.

Eckhart

To sit in the Throne of God is to inhabit Eternity. To reign there is to be pleased with all things in Heaven and Earth.

The streets were mine, the temple was mine, the people were mine, their clothes and gold and silver were mine, as much as their sparkling eyes, fair skins and ruddy faces. The skies were mine, and so were the sun and moon and stars, and all the world was mine.

Traheme

For one of superior intellect, the best thing is thoroughly to comprehend the inseparableness of the knower, the object known, and the act of knowing.

The Precepts of the Kargyutpa Gurus

Prosecution Witness No. 10

THE SOCIAL WORKER

Counsel introduces the Witness as a Social Worker of long experience. The Witness isn't so keen on the label. He doesn't see himself as any sort of specialist. Really he's no more than a plain, common-sensible fellow who happens to be fascinated by the human mind in all its astonishing variety. His life interest —as much hobby as profession—is people. Not excluding the Accused. Years ago, Witness attended a couple of his classes, and does know something of his views.

COUNSEL: Are you aware that he says he has no mind? And that, for him at least, being empty of mind is being full of God, and being full of God is being God? Just like that!

WITNESS: That's more or less the message I get.

COUNSEL: In the light of your experience, what have you to say about this extraordinary claim?

WITNESS: Two things. The first is more of a question than a comment. I should want to know what effect his unusual opinions have on his relationships with people, his lifestyle, his contribution to the world, his energy, his happiness. Since I haven't seen him for some years, I just don't know what he's like now. For all I know to the contrary, his opinions—however bizarre or outrageous—could make for a better life, and so pass at least the pragmatic test.

COUNSEL: And what's your second point?

WITNESS: It concerns the status of the mind. To me it's obvious that tradition is right here, and that man is tripartite, compounded of Body, Mind and Spirit. And that the middle term is vastly important, here to stay, impossible to reallocate to either or both of the end terms. It can't be unloaded on to Spirit. Clean of everything but itself, Spirit is pure and unchanging Awareness, Subject without objective content; and in no way can it take on Mind, that most kaleidoscopic of thingamies. Even more certain is the fact that Mind can't be moved in the opposite direction and somehow grafted on to the Body. If it could, what would be the difference between surveying a bruise on your knee and feeling the ouch; or between cupping your head in your hand while staring into the far distance, and contemplating the sweet (or horrible) mystery of life? No doubt about it, the Accused has and is a Mind all right, a Mind of his own, with unique pluses and unique minuses. It's what makes him a distinct individual, a person. He can't get out of it, or get it out of him. He's stuck with the darn thing.

COUNSEL: One's own mind, then, is clearly distinguishable and separate from all other minds? *Autant de têtes, autant d'avis?*

WITNESS: There's a good deal of overlapping, and blurring and merging at the edges; nevertheless, an inviolable core remains. Take some examples. Mercifully the taste of the marmalade you're having at breakfast doesn't spread to my kipper. Much as you might like to, you can't pass the pain in your back on to me. You have no clue to my feelings about the latest edition of King Charles's *Guidelines for Architects;* or about Lord Scargill's TV protest, in full fig, against the abolition of the Upper House; or about the appointment of the first Lady Archbishop of York. (Or you hadn't, till now!) And so on, endlessly... In fact, I know of no sillier idea than this—that you and I and the Accused don't have minds of our own—unless it's the idea that we don't have any minds at all.

COUNSEL: Why, then, do you suppose the Accused fastens on to this crackpot notion?

WITNESS: I should have thought the answer was obvious. Having made up his mind (a revealing phrase), in the teeth of all the evidence to the contrary, that he's divine, he hunts around for any old reason to support that conclusion. Not wishful thinking but wishful refusal to think—wishful self-deception—is his trouble. l could be wrong. I hope I am wrong. But that's the impression I get.

COUNSEL, to jury: About the Witness's first point—what he calls the pragmatic test—the Prosecution will be calling other witnesses to testify that the Accused is, in his personal morals and behaviour, no better than the rest of us. Worse, some will say. Either way, his pretensions to divinity will be made to look absurd. Meanwhile, let's continue to address ourselves to the Witness's second point, to Nokes's disingenuous dismissal of the mind. We await with bated breath his account of how he rids himself of—and gets along so nicely without—this thing that the rest of us are encumbered with. I almost said: that the rest of us are.

I have no questions for the Witness. He stands down.

Defence: **Think-bubbles**

MYSELF: It's wrong, I say, to dismiss any well-established and sincerely held opinion as wrong, just like that. But it's right to ask: from what point of view, in what context, for whom and at what time and for what purpose is it wrong? Conversely, of course, it's right to ask, not *whether,* but at *what level,* such an opinion is right and true.

This rule of thumb applies to the question of whether I have or am a mind. Very much so. And by *mind,* of course, I don't mean *brain,* which is a thing you can weigh and put in a jar and pickle.

Take the level of common sense, which—viewed from other levels—is really common nonsense. Nevertheless, manspeak goes with manhood, and it's not merely permissible but necessary to talk common-sensibly *as if* I had a mind. Just as it's necessary to talk *as if* I move around the world (on foot, by car, by plane), and look at it through two eyes (one lazy, the other busy), and am here what I look like to you over there (headed, your size, your way up), and so on and on. To refuse to *fall in with* these 'as if' conventions would be tiresome and pedantic and indeed unworkable. On the other hand, to *fall for* them (as almost all of us do, almost all of our lives) is far worse. It's to miss the whole point of our lives.

For these reasons my response to this Witness's testimony will be two-pronged. I shall show in what sense I'm mindless here, and then show how I neglect that sense at my peril.

JUDGE: Hold on! Not so fast! Surely your Defence rests on the difference between what you call the third person and what you call the First Person? And surely what makes all the difference is the First

Person's *mind*? These persons look much the same, but the latter's certainly, and by definition, fixed up—spooked up, some would say—with this invisible presence, while the former isn't. It's possible to doubt others' minds, not your own.

MYSELF: With respect, Your Honour, they couldn't look more *different*. The visible and real differences between the third person and the First—inversion, decapitation, 180° turn-around, and so on—are striking and many-sided enough, without dragging in dubious invisible ones. In fact the silliest thing in the world is myself as this First Person persuading myself that I'm the spitting image of that third person over there—except that a think-bubble or balloon (as in a strip cartoon) arises from the top of my head! A wild fantasy, which common sense nevertheless builds its world on.

No, a thousand times No! The only mind or think-bubble I need, or can find the slightest evidence for, is the Super-bubble that rises from my No-head—from my Bottom Line—and it's none other than the concentric system of cosmic bubbles featuring in nearly all our diagrams, and in Diagram No. 10 in particular. If I'm to use the word 'mind' at all, here is the Mind-Body or Body-Mind of God Himself, His marvellously filled-out and iridescent Think-bubble, His richly sculpted and gilded Frame of Mind. And mine!

I find myself permanently stationed at the mid-point of this divine nest of hemispheres. Let me remind you of the pattern. Looking *up* from here, I find the outermost layers to be tenanted by heavenly bodies. Looking *out* from here, I find the middle layers to be tenanted by earthly bodies, including humans of all sorts and conditions, and notably the one behind glass who I identify as John a-Nokes.

Diagram No. 10

There he is, out there alongside the others, the same way up as they are, and like them furnished with two eyes in a head, and nary a hint of a think-balloon arising from it. Looking *down* from here, I find these feet, and foreshortened legs, and most of my foreshortened trunk, in that order.

And I find the whole hemispherical bubble-system terminating in and resting on my Bottom Line, on this fuzzy but perfectly visible boundary drawn across my chest, well short of the neck and the head I was told I had right here. When in every sense I have the humility to *bow* before the evidence, before what's given up there and out there and down there—given to the headless one here at the World's End—this is what I get. I'd better take it. I don't intend to turn down God's kind invitation to bubble over with Him so joyfully and so imaginatively. [Counsel's bouncing about on his feet, vainly trying to get a word in edgeways.] Come to think of it, God's Think-bubble—or Nest of Think-bubbles—is just what His world amounts to. All those seemingly solid creations of His, including Messrs Wilberforce and Nokes, are phenomena, surfaces not even skin-deep, airy nothings that go pop as you approach them. No matter how showy, the only substantial thing about them is the divine Bubble Blower or Afflatus at their core.

COUNSEL, at last: Following on that Peeing God, we now have—if you please!—a Bubbly God, a God crooning that old pop song, 'I'm forever blowing bubbles, pretty bubbles in the air.' All bubble and squeak, if you ask me—[Some hooting and clapping in the public gallery.]

MYSELF: Your Honour, do I have to endure this nuisance?

JUDGE: Just carry on, regardless.

MYSELF: Of the many intriguing features of this concentric world-system, the one which concerns me just now is the assortment of senses which reveal it. In fact, it's not so much a think-bubble as a see-touch-hear-taste-smell-bubble. I *see* stars and clouds and mountain tops. I *see and touch* rocks and trees and houses. I *see and touch and hear* people and animals and machinery. I *see and touch and hear and taste and smell* crunchy slices of toast. I *feel* an aching muscle and a collywobbly stomach... In short, accompanying and disclosing the cosmic hierarchy of objects, and inseparable from them, is this cosmic (repeat, cosmic) hierarchy of senses. Also, of course, over and above these localized sense-objects, there are more general ones. Thus I sometimes take on the joy of the world, at other times its sadness; sometimes its beauty, at other times its dreariness. Quite often, with Jakob Boehme, all Creation has for me a delicious *smell*. And then, of course, it is continually displaying all sorts of interconnections, all sorts of meanings and values which knit the parts into one tremendous Whole.

This is the way the world comes. This is the form it takes, the richness of it. In this and no other fashion is the universe—which is my Body—served up to me: as a *sensible* universe, a *minded* cosmos, a *living* organism, complete and strictly indivisible. To split it into a mindless body there and a bodiless mind here—a machine and a ghost—is to wreck the body and unhinge the mind. Violence that's as absurd as it is unnecessary. No, I'm not Body *and* Mind, and Spirit. Not a troika but a pair: Body-Mind, *and* Spirit.

Which means that murder's afoot, murder's called for. I'm God's hit man, under contract to kill the mind as a separate something or other. The great medieval English philosopher William of Occam (in Surrey) furnishes the weapon. Occam's Razor is the famous principle of parsimony: if you can do without a notion or an entity (he says) do without it, do it in. Shrewd advice! Accordingly, I dispatch the mind as an existent, real, useful entity. It isn't. Most definitely it isn't. On the contrary, it's *de trop* and a confounded nuisance.

COUNSEL wades in with: This is lunacy. I have, with great reluctance, to share the same Universe Body with Mr John a-Nokes, whether I like it or not. But not—thank heaven!—the same mind. People's minds, differing hugely—and, providentially, insulated from each other—can't be decanted into a blender and reduced to some kind of psychic purée. As the Witness testified, each is a little world. It's this privacy which makes the Accused's life and mine, thrown together in the same cosmos, just about bearable.

MYSELF: It's not that the mind selects its little private world out of the big public world, but rather that the big world is self-selective and grudging by nature, and discloses itself piecemeal, in dribs and drabs and never as a whole. So much so that knowledge of the world is often described by the sages as a kind of ignorance. Put it like this: you and I, as Spirit, are at once absolutely empty of the world and absolutely full of it. But as Mind-Body, we are never seized of more than minor excerpts from it. It's a limitation on the side of the object, not the Subject.

And so, members of the Jury, the stage is cleared of that bastard and shady mountebank which I call my mind—cleared to make way for Spirit. Bright Spirit which is none other than Awareness, Awareness which is none other than the indwelling God. Mind, that would-be usurper of God's throne, that Old Pretender, has had his swollen and spooked-up head sliced clean off, with that keenest of razors, which is Occam's.

COUNSEL: I'm afraid the philosophers won't help you much in this court. They prove anything and agree on nothing. To rely on them is to lose your case. To rely on just one of them is to fail to find any case at all. I advise you—seeing that the mind's status is the matter at issue just now—to forget about philosophy and stick to psychology. Or do I hear you telling the court that the immense body of theory and practice which is modern psychology is superfluous, a load of old rubbish?

MYSELF: Of course not. It came out, in my reply to the previous Witness, that the way from the Eden of pre-psychological man to the Promised Land of post-psychological man (I mean him in whom God is enthroned) lies through the howling Wilderness of psychological man. Certainly a region that can't be bypassed. But just as certainly one that's best not lingered in over-long.

I'm much helped in this passage from psychological man to post-psychological man—in this seeing the mind out and God in—by the behaviour of the stuff of the mind itself. Obligingly, my so-called mental contents are outward-facing and centrifugal, raring to go and make room here for Him whose place it is. They have objective intent. They are as unimpressed by that ballet of bloodless abstractions which is the mind-in-itself as they are impressed by that rumbustious, blood-distended, go-getting, blazing commotion which is the world—the scene they can't wait to join. Thus I try in vain to think a thought that belongs to my mind and not to my world, one which is my own private property, which is altogether unthinged and mentalized. Thus I find that my love doesn't exist till it belongs to my loved one: it's not that I adore but that she's adorable. That my thoughts and feelings are about her, not about myself-in-quite-a-state-about-the-lady. That my hate isn't hate till it alights on what's hateful. That I taste jam, not a tongue. That I smell a rose, and neither a nose nor an olfactory experience. That I fear spiders, not arachnophobia. In fact, it's the rose that gives me the smell, the spider that gives me the creeps. *The mind is phoney.* And, in so far as I am a mind, I'm 'mental', meaning barmy. As a separate, inward-facing, self-contained entity, the mind doesn't exist. And, in so far as it does exist on its lonesome, it's a thief and a sick thief at that. So plague-stricken that it plants the kiss of death upon everything it pulls away from the world and bear-hugs. 'He who binds to himself a joy does the winged life destroy.' *I'm a real person in a real world to the degree that I have no mind of my own aside from my world.*

Which brings me to the practical proof, the promised down-to-earth demonstration in everyday living of the fact that I have no mind here. It's not that I can manage pretty well without the God-damned thing, but that I can't manage at all with it. It, or rather the mistaken idea of it, gets in the way all the time. I assure learned Counsel that

I value an ounce of practice here more than a ton of philosophizing. And so for a brief word or two about the mindless life.

I call it alert idiocy—

COUNSEL: Omit *alert*—

MYSELF: And substitute *wise*? Wise naïvety. And, just in case you should confuse this naïvety with dumbness and folly, let me remind you that it's from this position of *not knowing* that my Defence is being conducted. I'm absolutely serious when I tell you I've no idea what I'm up to. [COUNSEL: Hear, hear!] All I do is see Who I am and eagerly await developments. I listen with interest to the sounds coming from this dock. At last, having learned the lesson of countless disappointments, and having ceased to rely on the minuscule resources of that pinhead over there in my mirror, I start relying on the infinite resources of the God-head, on the Source of all resources right here; so that now I find myself knowing what has to be known, and saying what has to be said, and doing what has to be done, without any preview at all. I don't know what I think till I hear what I say—hear the words that come from my No-mouth. From something like what the Ancient Greeks would have called my Daimon, or Good Genius.

COUNSEL: And what your contemporaries call your demon, or evil genius.

MYSELF, ignoring the crack: It really is so very inefficient to operate from a mind which is full of things to go wrong, and so very efficient to operate from a No-mind which is empty of all that clutter. This isn't a dogma for believing but a working hypothesis for testing, all day and every day. It's never too late to have a marvellous childhood. True maturity is that second childhood which I still call alert idiocy.

COUNSEL: At least we can agree about your idiocy and God's wisdom. Which neatly disposes of your claim to be Him. [He treats the Jury to a broad smile—I think his first so far in the Trial.]

MYSELF: No, Sir Gerald! You've got it all wrong again. At this level it's not (strange to say) that I'm a foolish old dingbat and my God is all-wise, and that if I know what's good for me I'll hand over my portfolio to Him. (Valuable advice, true at its own level, but not here.) Here, the deeper truth is that, on the contrary, He's perfectly clueless, and that to be Him is to be perfectly clueless too. No institution contains a patient as empty-headed as the God-head. Yes, Your Honour, this is putting Him down with a vengeance—all the way down to the level where He underpins all. Just as the Abyss of the God-head is not alive but the Source of all life, not intelligent but the Source of all intelligence, not loving but the Source of all love, not happy but the Source of all happiness, so It isn't practical but the Source of all practicality and know-how. You name it, God in the depths is free of it. He's clean, as clean of mind as of all else. His IQ is zero. Biggest head, smallest wit. His world is smart, is intelligence and knowledge enough, is minded enough. He gets on with His job of Being Aware and letting all that brainy stuff come up just as needed. In short, while *there's Nothing to Him, Everything's from Him.*

Ladies and gentlemen, in such trivial matters as what to wear for the day and eat for breakfast, all the way to such grave matters as what to say for myself now I'm on trial for my life, I'm advised to trust my Deepest Nature which is No Nature. I need to psych myself *down* for this ordeal, and to give Him a chance! But don't take this from me. Don't take it from the world's saints and sages and seers. But now give them at least a brief hearing. And (I suggest) give what they are saying a longer testing:

No Mind Here

When they bring you before the magistrates, do not think beforehand what to say. The Holy Spirit will show you at the time.

Jesus

Not to know is profound, to know is shallow.

Chuang-tzu

Mine is indeed the mind of a very idiot, so dull am I.

Tao Te Ching

Never mind the mind. If its Source is sought, it will vanish, leaving the Self unaffected.

Ramana Maharshi

The Zen Doctrine of No Mind

Title of a book by D. T. Suzuki

Only Don't Know
> *Title of a book by a recent Zen master, Seung Sahn*

Buddhahood is attained when you have no mind for the task.
> *Hui-chung*

Only have no mind of any kind. This is undefiled knowledge.
> *Huang-po*

God is not seen except by blindness, nor known except by ignorance, nor understood except by fools.
> *Eckhart*

It is the mind that tells you that the mind is there. Don't be deceived... It is the bland refusal to consider the convolutions and convulsions of the mind that can take you beyond it.
> *Nisargadatta*

Mind There

As he gets to be more purely and singly himself... the astronomer is 'out there' with the stars, rather than a separateness peering across an abyss at another separateness through a telescopic keyhole.
> *Abraham H. Marlow*

The inward and the outward are become as one sky.
> *Kabir*

Every thing and quality is felt in outer space.

William James

The soul lives in what it loves.

St John of the Cross

Our souls live in the surrounding world.

Heraclitus

Prosecution Witness No. 11

THE OCCASIONAL BARMAID

The Witness says that her job is teaching in her local village school. On Saturday evenings, and at other busy times, she helps in her husband's pub, 'The Inn at the World's End'. She's the mother of two young children.

Yes, she knows the terms and the nature of the charge against me. She regards blasphemy with the utmost horror. For her it means joining forces with Satan in his rebellion against the Almighty and setting yourself up as His equal.

And yes, she knows me by sight. And not only by sight. I have occasionally come to the pub with a few friends. There's only one small bar, and she can't help overhearing our conversation. No words can express her revulsion. She isn't surprised to see me in the dock.

COUNSEL: Leaving aside your very understandable feelings about the Accused, let us address his claim that he isn't really a human being. The Jury would like to know what happens in your bar when it comes to his turn to buy a round of drinks. Presumably, if there are four in the party, he orders four beers, not three? Without any hesitation at all, he includes himself among the other humans round the table?

WITNESS: Of course.

COUNSEL, to Jury: His behaviour gives the game away. What he does shouts so loud it drowns what he says. He talks big, as big as God in heaven; and acts little, as little as the beer swiller in the dock. In the Witness's bar he's on home ground. He's one of the boys. He doesn't dream of *counting himself out*. But notice this carefully, ladies and gentlemen: in non-human company, he doesn't dream of *counting himself in*. I understand he has three cats. Don't tell me he's number four, Puss in Boots, a real fat cat. I can't see him licking his fur and dipping his whiskers into a saucer of Kittymash. He has a dog too, but doesn't debate whether he should enter himself or the dog in Crufts. In the monkey house at the zoo he knows his place, and which side of the bars he belongs. It's only among humans that he always demonstrates (unintentionally) that he's sure he's among his compeers. If I'm doing him an injustice here, we shall hear about it soon enough.

[To the Witness] Let's get back to your pub. Is it fair to say that not only does the Accused reveal himself as human, but (if it were possible) as more human than human? Or course he doesn't tell you he's the man, the likely lad at the top of the heap: he just lives it. How he looks after Number One! Number One is his darling, all his care. Number One pays only for his own round, and counts and pockets the change instead of putting it in the collecting box for guide dogs for the blind. Number One makes himself nice and comfortable by the fire. Number One is careful not to leave his lovely warm overcoat on the peg for customer number two or three to carry off... Am I right?

WITNESS: Of course you are.

COUNSEL: Have you anything to add?

WITNESS: Only this. I once heard him say in the bar: 'I am not

Mr John a-Nokes. I'm Mr Zero. I AM, stop. I am that I AM. I AM is my first and real and permanent name: and you know Whose name that is. John and Nokes are just my temporary names, my nicknames.' Those were his very words. I'm sure, because I secretly jotted them down at the time. I have the paper here.

COUNSEL, to me: Do you admit this evidence?

MYSELF: Gladly!

COUNSEL: There you are, Jury! The Witness recorded those words and he confirms them! They are just about the most blasphemous words that ever soiled human ears. Don't let the Accused's shenanigans—with which he will now seek to complicate and confuse the simple issue—erase these words from your memory for a moment.

Defence: **Back to Square Nought**

MYSELF, to Witness: In view of your deep concern about the state of my soul, may I ask you when you last attended church? Since you got married, I mean. When did you last pray? Or read your Bible? Or any of the world's scriptures? Out of school, I mean.

JUDGE: You don't have to answer those questions.

MYSELF: Your Honour, surely I have the right to challenge the credibility of a Witness whose theological opinions the Prosecution has been at pains to elicit? But let it pass... [I turn to the Witness.] My next question isn't about your part-time job as assistant publican but your full-time job as deputy head-teacher. Perhaps I should remind you that you are on oath to tell the truth, the whole truth and nothing but the truth.

Around what age do children—your own and the others at the school—stop leaving themselves out when they are counting those present, and begin counting themselves in? I take it that you notice things like that—if not out of interest, at least because you remember your Piaget from training college days.

WITNESS to Judge: Do I have to...?

JUDGE: This time you do have to answer him. Truthfully and fully.

WITNESS: Oh... Well, the age varies. I've known a kid of eight, when we were playing a round-the-table game in which she had to count the players, leave herself out. She was quite puzzled when I pointed out her mistake, and the others (mostly younger kids) laughed at her. The funny thing is she's quite a bright girl. And then there are other less bright kids who, as early as four or five, don't make this mistake. It doesn't seem to be a question of intelligence... But I don't see what—

MYSELF: Thank you. Let's be quite clear about this. Before that critical age (whether as late as eight or as early as four) the child habitually leaves herself out; after it, habitually counts herself in. Before that age, the child's wordlessly telling humans, 'I'm not one of you.' After that age, 'I *am* one of you.' Have I got it right?

WITNESS: Um...

MYSELF: We didn't hear you.

WITNESS: I suppose so.

MYSELF: Thank you again. No more questions. Please leave the box. [I address the Jury.] The Prosecution says I have always and naturally counted myself in among any humans that happen to be present. Not so, says the Prosecution Witness, when pressed. She's the one that's right, of course. Let's go into this further.

My life, ladies and gentlemen of the Jury, falls into three parts. First, the early years when I neither needed to nor could count myself in; then the middle years when I could, and very much needed to do so, when I had no choice; and finally, these later years when I do have a choice. For me now, all depends on the level I'm looking at and operating from, on the context. In my human capacity, as the fellow you're now looking at and I checked up on earlier today in the glass, why of course I count him in. I cheerfully pay for his round of drinks; not so cheerfully I include him in the number of residents in my house for super-poll-tax purposes (how can I deny *he* has a super-poll on top?); and I miserably consent to his making a fourth at bridge; and so on and on. But of course! What do you take me for? When and where a man, say I, do as man does, be a man and not a mouse or a monster or anything less than a 100 per cent died-in-the-wool Number One human.

But right here all is different. For the life of me I can find nothing here to count, let alone a human thing. To add in this nothing along with things would be like adding in the date with the bill. It would be like shopping for vegetables with £100 in my purse and spending £200, in the belief that my purse is £100 and legal tender. It would be like counting those Jury benches as Jury person thirteen, or this hand as finger six. It would be asking for certification and institutional care. But enough of this foolery. I go by what I *see*. What is this Third Stage of my life, after all, but reverting to the truthfulness of the First Stage, but now with clear awareness of myself as Zero, as Capacity for numbers but myself number-free, as the uncountable Counter? What is this but humility in the face of the evidence, the humility that can find no one here to be humble? What is this but coming to my senses at long last after the senselessness of common sense (so called), the wilful nonsense of Stage Two? What is this but becoming natural again after that phoney interlude, with all the stresses and anxieties that go with self-deception and playing a hard game hard?

Opting out of that game, what do I find? *Where* do I find numbers?

I count one, two, three windows up there in the courtroom. I count one, two, three, four, five—many faces out there in the court. I count two foreshortened legs *down there* in the dock. And below them, one foreshortened trunk. Always numbers are presented there in my world, to me *here*.

Here, I count nothing. I find nothing to enumerate. In this place the reckoning is always Zero—zero men, zero dogs, zero cats, zero mice, zero trees, zero what-have-you. Name anything you like, it's conspicuous here by its absence. I'm just as innocent here of human characteristics as of any others, and I am as much no-man as I am no-dog, no-cat, no-mouse, no-tree... I'm perfectly neutral, a member of no group or class or set. I'm No-one, One minus one, a Cipher, *the* Cipher.

But I notice that from this Cipher all series originate, to it all numbers belong, by it they are counted. Therefore, in this place of seeming disadvantage and total lack, I have the advantage. I initiate every series in the universe. Zero is truly a commanding station.

I look around the court. I listen. Just as those forms are seen from this Void, and heard from this Silence of mine, so they are reckoned from this Zero. Here they come back, not to square one but to square Nought, where all reckoning starts. This is my Home Ground.

JUDGE: But what about Counsel's point that you are more at home with people than with other orders of being? That your attitude to them gives the lie to what you say about yourself, and shows that in your bones you know you're only human after all?

MYSELF: The Prosecution is quite wrong, Your Honour, about how I feel. My boxer Ludwig is perfect company after a day spent with noisy and demanding humans. I'm apt to feel more comfortable in the quiet and congenial society of the stars—as the Sky in which they shine—than in the blaring city street. More comfortable, it may well be, than in the Witness's bar parlour, for that matter. In the friendly hills, among companionable trees and streams and flowers, at sea or in mid-desert, I don't want for company, I'm no trespasser, no stranger in a foreign land. Everything fits this No-thing. It's not that I belong to all categories, all orders and genera and species, but that they belong to me. I include the most exclusive. Here I hold court. Here is the forum, the meeting place, the open heart of the universe, where I'm always at home to all comers because there's No-body at home to get in their way or pick and choose among them. As Edwin Markham wrote of one who shut him out,

    Love and I had the wit to win:

    We drew a circle that took him in.

Such, members of the Jury, is life at this Third Stage, when I stop pretending to be here what I *look like* to you over there, and I'm content to be this all-comprehensive circle which is Zero.

Let's suppose I'm in a room with four friends. As a young child, automatically taking myself at Centre to be Zero, I count four people present. As an adult, setting up my human self at Centre as number one, I count five. As a Seer, consciously seeing myself at Centre to be Zero, I count four again. Diagram No. 11 shows these Three Stages at a glance.

When at Stage Two I count this Zero in along with those people, it's like counting the basket in with the eggs—and proceeding to scramble and eat it. Which is unhealthy. And—what's more to the point—blasphemous.

I come back, ladies and gentlemen of the Jury, to the definition of blasphemy on which my Defence rests. It is to sit oneself as man Number One on God's throne at the centre of one's world, and sit tight. It's to stay stuck at the second of our Three Stages, the stage that we all have to go through, but should go through speedily.

Innocent Counting

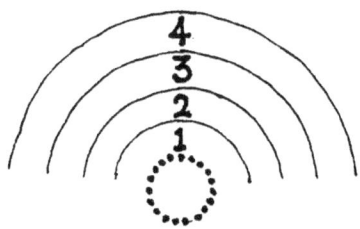

Young Child

Blashphemous Counting

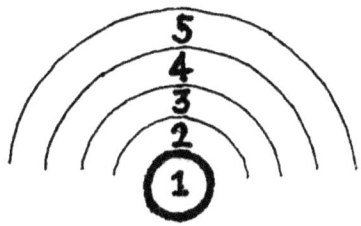

Grown-up

Enlightened Counting

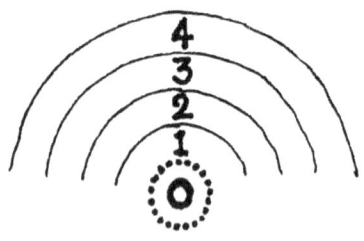

Seer

Diagram No. 11

What a black joke it is, Your Honour, what irony, that I'm the one that's standing here in the dock charged with this truly heinous crime!

I, who insist on the inviolate holiness of the Holy of Holies, where the Godhead dwells at the Centre of all things in solitary and number-free splendour, and where no man can ever, ever intrude! What irony that my accusers, who do their damnedest to force their way into that shrine and set up man there—do their damnedest to deify man—what irony that they should charge me with the crime they are guilty of every second of their waking lives! What a sick joke! I say— they should charge me with the crime they are guilty of every second of their waking lives! What a sick joke! I say—

COUNSEL, rocketing to his feet: Your Honour, this is worse than contempt! It's contempt not only of this court, but of Your Honour personally, and all of us here!

JUDGE: It's vexatious. But this man is on trial for his life, and must be allowed to fight for it in his own fashion—within limits. However, I warn you—the Accused—not to abuse our tolerance. Insulting behaviour will do you no good at all. If you persist in it, I shall have to consider what can be done to put you in a more chastened mood, and purge your contempt.

MYSELF: Truly, Your Honour, I intend no disrespect. Quite the reverse, in fact. What I'm saying is that everyone in this court is really living from Stage Three, without realizing it. My point is that none of us, never mind how Satanic our ambition, no matter how colossal our chutzpah, can begin to oust God from the Centre of our lives. There's no dislodging this Roger the lodger. Creatures are, willy-nilly, a mere dream apart from the Creator at their core, nothing at all without this central No-thing, Clarity, Transparency, Capacity, Essence, Reality, Aware Emptiness—whatever name you like to give this Zero. Even to blaspheme against This is to do so by virtue of This, empowered by This. In truth, the crime of blasphemy is all sound and fury signifying nothing, mere bombast and posturing. All the same, alas, it's real enough to spoil our lives.

It just isn't a practical proposition to stick at this Second Stage, betwixt and between, imagining we're living from the infinitesimal resources of Number One, instead of from the infinite resources of Zero. It's deadening, anxiety-producing, exhausting, absurd—

COUNSEL: Your Honour, does the court now have to endure a sermon from the dock on how to conduct our lives?

MYSELF: It's no uncalled-for preachifying, but an appeal from the heart for justice and sanity. If I can show the Jury that what I'm claiming to be is natural and normal, sensible, healthy and immensely more efficient than the alternative—and in fact the way I am and each of them is already, whether we acknowledge or deny it—why then they must bring in a verdict of Not Guilty. For what is blasphemy but refusal to fit in with the Divine Plan, with God's design for the world, with His status quo? And what is the antidote for blasphemy but obedience to that plan, and saying a hearty Yes! to His arrangements?

So, if I have the court's kind permission, let me give some impression of what it means to live consciously from this Third Stage, from Zero instead of Number One, from life as I live it instead of life as I'm told I live it. [Counsel groans, and ostentatiously sets his stopwatch. I ignore the gesture, and continue.]

Zero is my lucky no-number. Zero is my Core, my ever-present refuge in time of trouble. At once the down-swoop of my freedom from all things and my soaring union with all things. At once my absolute detachment and my absolute attachment. As Number One I was a man and nothing else. I headed the queue of humans only, and was in no such commanding position as regards mice or Cats or dogs, or plants, or any other creatures. At the front of just one cosmic queue, I was shouldered out of all the others. I wasn't made to feel at home there, or wanted. A stranger, an outsider everywhere. Not a happy life. But as Zero I head every queue and start every line in the universe. As the launching pad they all take off from, I'm shot of them all, but remain their Shooter. Here, as Who I really am, I originate all creatures from creepy-crawlies to seraphim. No longer the lone outsider, blackballed from every club but one, I'm the Sole Insider. This is no empty boast or gooey sentiment. To the degree that I see into and enter my natureless Nature, I see and enter into the Nature of all beings. The barriers fall, and I've no option but to love the world that I am. My score in this cosmic championship remains at love—love fifteen, love thirty, love forty, love game. Love means Zero, no score at all. Yet Love wins every time. Oh, yes, Love wins—game, set and match! It takes God's Wimbledon by storm.

Everything is eloquent of the Zero, the Love, the Nothing at the Source of everything. Even the way I'm obliged to talk of it, in a marvellous and seemly *double entendre,* goes straight to the heart of the matter. I say I believe in Nothing, rely on Nothing, am fanatical about Nothing, see Nothing, know Nothing, want Nothing, have Nothing, am Nothing—and so on, *ad infinitum.* Here, the most negative of assertions reads as the most positive. The mere nothing that's scarcely fit for the universe's scrap heap suddenly becomes the very un-mere No-thing that originates everything! Zero is the rune, the magic word which, when lived as well as spoken, reconciles all life's opposites—peripheral belief with central scepticism, peripheral commitment with central independence, peripheral wealth with central poverty, peripheral know-how with central cluelessness, peripheral excitement with central calm... As I say, this divine *double entendre* is no verbal accident or trick. It's not even a way of life. It's *the* way of life, for it's the way life *is.*

This Aware Nothing or Zero is indeed no shivering cold, toothless, pale abstraction. It is the Parent, the Mother-Father, infinitely robust and flamboyant in its expression, infinitely still and silent and mysterious in its essence, inscrutable to the point of being incredible. For no reason It *is,* and for no reason It is the inexhaustible Source of everything. To imagine you are living independently of It, living from Number One—no matter how godlike Number One may seem—is nightmarish. And so daft. As if you could, for a split second!

Finally, a little experiment. Surprise the Divine Mathematician at His sums! To catch the One red-handed, in the very act of coming from the None, unpocket and show a fist. To catch the Many coming from the One, spread your fingers. To catch the Many returning to the One, close your fist again. To catch the One red-handed in the very act of returning to the None, the Zero, pocket your fist again. This is not a symbol or a moving picture of Him who truly counts. It's the real Thing, and the real No-thing.

And here's the sort of thing the wise have to say about the No-one who heads every queue in His universe:

Tao gave birth to the One. The One gave birth to two things, three things, up to ten thousand.

Tao Te Ching

The Many return to the One. To what does the One return?

Kao-feng Tuan-miao

O is the source of all speech, a pillar of wisdom and a comfort to every wise man, a blessing and a joy to every knight.

Anglo Saxon Runic Poem

Wise Master Eckhart wills
To teach us Nothing's lore,
And he who sees it not
May wail to God therefor.
The true and heavenly light
On him hath never shone.

Medieval Convent Song

COUNSEL, making a great show of resetting his stopwatch: Your Honour, I've been very quiet throughout these ingenious and long-drawn-out manoeuvres, with their smokescreens and feints and diversionary tactics. I think that this time I deserve the last word—if only to bring us back to the simple issue before this court.

JUDGE: It's up to the Accused.

MYSELF: Go right ahead. There'll be no comeback from me.

COUNSEL: Members of the Jury, in her pub the Witness wrote down these words: 'I am that I AM. I AM is my first and real and permanent name: and you know Whose name that is. John and Nokes are just my temporary names, my nicknames.'

He accepts, without a blush or a tremor, that those were his very words. Greater blasphemy than this no man has ever breathed. Not all the twists and turns of his Defence, right up to the end of this Trial and your retiring to consider your verdict, will begin to purge one syllable of that blasphemy. Or deter you from bringing in a verdict of Guilty.

Don't be put off by his gamesmanship. I shouldn't be surprised if, though not yet halfway through this Trial, you felt that Nokes has already scored some impressive goals. Lots of them. I do so agree. His nimble footwork, his dash, the accuracy of his shooting have often (I confess) left me wonder-struck. All the more so because every one of his goals has been an own goal. He seems to imagine that he can clear himself of blasphemy by blaspheming ever more shamelessly.

Prosecution Witness No. 12

THE STORE MANAGER

The Witness remembers me vaguely as one of his customers. He can think of nothing special about me—except that there was a bit of a fuss on one occasion when I returned some potatoes which had gone partly bad. He said it was my fault because I waited a week before unsealing the plastic bag they were packed in. Though slightly irritated, he stuck to the rule that the customer is always right, and replaced the goods.

COUNSEL: Would it surprise you to learn that this humble purchaser of spuds is some sort of divinity, heavily disguised? Divinity in his own eyes, I mean?

WITNESS: It certainly did startle me when I was told as much, at the time of the subpoena to appear in this court.

COUNSEL: I take it that you aren't aware of the strange opinions he's published about advertising, and their connection with his still stranger opinions about himself. He claims that advertising is of two very different sorts—one directed at us common folk, the other at him. Both are effective within their limits, he says.

WITNESS: I do have some rather funny customers, but I mind my own business. Treating them all in the same manner, and I hope with equal courtesy, seems to work out all right. To interest the gentleman there in my merchandise I doubt we need to dream up any special posters, newspaper ads, or TV commercials—designs that would appeal to him, in contrast to other (shall I say *normal?*) people. Again, when he comes shopping, the standard sales techniques are (I'm pretty sure) effective, and what he buys is normal enough, even predictable. Anyway, my job is sufficiently demanding without having to cater for two species of customers. To do that I would need to be a superman, as well as run a supermarket.

COUNSEL, to Jury: I think this Witness's testimony speaks for itself and needs little comment from me. All I'll say just now is: he knows his job. Which means, for all business and practical purposes, he knows his John a-Nokes, the customer who's no more divine than the potatoes he forgot to de-bag.

I have no questions to put to the Witness. He stands down.

Defence: **The Birds of God**

MYSELF: The Witness underestimates himself—or should I say his firm? More accommodating than he realizes, he caters specially for me, in addition to his normal customers. Very considerate of him, I say. Let me explain.

J. Sainsbury, the worldwide chain of stores—of which his is the latest and swishest—relies heavily on advertising. It's only to be expected that most of its publicity, since it's aimed at human beings, should portray human beings. Hence countless pictures of astoundingly healthy and good-looking men, women, children and babies rapturously eating this and drinking that and wearing the other, and getting up to most of the things that real humans get up to. Whether in the press or on hoardings or on the screen, or in the mere labelling of goods, most advertising is obviously directed at *Homo sapiens*.

But there remains a type of advertising which neither depicts people nor is aimed at people, but does its best to depict me—with a view to selling me something, I presume. For example, there is the tilted and brimming beer-mug held by a loose hand floating in mid-air, about to pour itself into the Void here, into the no-mouth of this no-drinker. (More accurately, of this *real* Drinker, the one who actually tastes the brew.) Or a pair of hands, equally innocent of any connecting body, busy handling a packet of cigarettes and conveying one of them to this absence-of-lips. Or a car evidently designed for me since it's driven by no human driver, but instead by loose hands and feet mysteriously working at the controls—rather as if they were a quartet of superbly trained circus animals at their tricks.

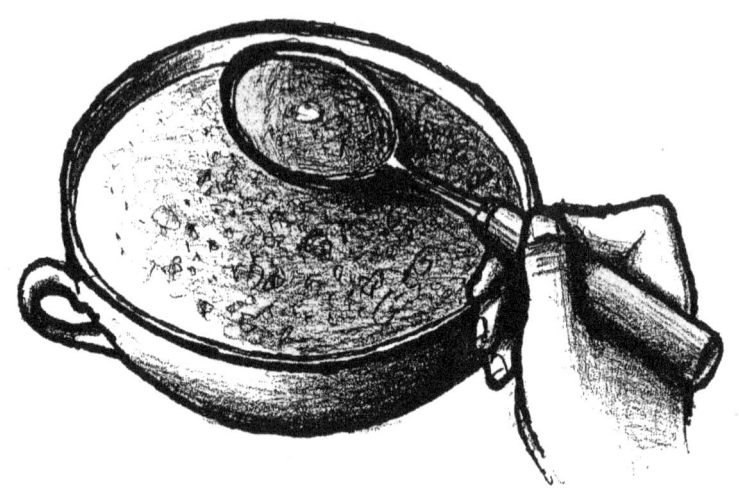

Diagram No. 12

Please turn to Diagram No. 12, which is a sample of the sort of advert I mean. Just one of hundreds.

Look at your hands now. Wave them about frantically, as if you were conducting an orchestra and playing the harp... Go on... Let them go...

These airborne attendants upon the First Person are surely more like birds than earthbound animals. Birds that combine the incredible skills of the swooping swallow, the hovering hummingbird and the grasping eagle—and never a failed take-off or mid-air collision or crash landing among them. Birds of God they are—*uccelli di Dio*—which is what Dante called the angels, God's messengers and servitors. To each of you, then, two questions and a warning. Can you deny you are so served? Conceding that you are, can you deny that your attendants—your *uccelli di Dio*—are in fact *God's*? *God's*, I say! To claim them for Jack, for any human, wouldn't be just mock humility. It would be blasphemy.

Back, then, to J. Sainsbury, PLC.

Naturally, such tailor-made advertisements have special impact on me. Taking full account of how different I am, they speak to my condition. It's the same with drama on the large and the small screens. Nearly all of it is about and for humans. But now and then the cast includes a headless and other-way-up actor. I hear his voice, his breathing, his footfall, and occasionally catch sight of hands and feet and vestiges of a trunk. And naturally (other things being equal) I'm involved. He's the character I identify with. He's my kind. He's not a man, he's Me.

By the same token, a canny insurance-agent knows how to handle my mounting sales resistance. Instead of confronting a man across the table, he comes round to my side where there's no man. Here, no longer handing over documents for me to look at, he looks at them with me. Merging points of view, his humanness vanishes into my non-humanness. His voice and his gesturing hands—now loosed from their trunk, coming from here and no longer from there—are now so truly mine that I could well become the pushover he hopes for.

The simple fact, to me so obvious and so amusing and so awesomely significant, is that there are *two* immensely different sorts of limbs—the ordinary and tied-down sort that stick out of human and animal bodies at various angles, and the extraordinary and unattached sort that stick out of No-thing, branch from No-trunk, belong to No-body, operate from No-where. Unique in their looseness, they are also unique in their sensitivity, and in the miraculous ease and speed and fittingness of their responses to one's every need. They are exceptionally serviceable offshoots, making the attached kind look like so many orthopaedic devices, wonderfully constructed and operated, but unresponsive and wooden by comparison. And no wonder! These loose limbs belong to the Looselimbed God, and just have to be very special. They come straight from Him, like bright angels from heaven, intent on His business.

No, Sir Gerald, this isn't some newfangled and trumped-up conceit of mine, with no precedent. You can find the hand of God curiously depicted in many early medieval paintings and mosaics of Abraham about to sacrifice Isaac, and the Baptism of Jesus in the Jordan, and so on. God's pointing hand (lace-cuffed and neatly sleeved, like his Honour's over there) with long and delicate and well-manicured fingers, emerges from a cloud at the top of the picture. It comes, I assure you, from that very same Cloud of Unknowing as *this* inelegantly sleeved hand—the one that I'm now extending to the court—is coming from.

Turn, please, to diagram 13 in your booklet, where you'll find a copy of one of these pictures.

In this picture, from a ninth-century Roman codex, a sleeping St John receives the Revelation of the Apocalypse at the hand of God. From around the twelfth century onwards, artists depicted not just the hand but the whole of God—as a well-preserved septuagenarian! Unreality at its most ridiculous, with more than a smidgen of blasphemy about it!

COUNSEL, with a great flourish of his brief: Members of the Jury, in the course of this Trial the Accused has produced many arguments—ingenious in their pseudo-naivety and absurdity, and some of them perverse to the point of madness—in support of his boasted divinity. But the one we are now listening to is the limit. Or rather, it exceeds even his limits, is really *too* much. If I have now to put to him some questions which aren't just embarrassing to this court and an offence to its dignity, but blasphemous in the very asking—why, he's to blame. His filthy insults to the Almighty can't be countered without some contamination, some descent to their level. For which I crave the court's indulgence.

Diagram No. 13

He maintains that his hands are God's hands, seeing that they are loose and attached to no body. Whereas yours and mine, alas, seeing they are attached to human bodies, are merely human hands. I leave on one side without further comment the insufferable self-conceit and bumptiousness of the fellow, and confine myself to the bare facts. His hands look much the same as ours, don't they? Compare those primitive pentadactylic appendages, much like those of a frog, resting on the rail of the dock over there, with the similar appendages resting on your laps, members of the Jury. What's the difference? Why, his hands look to me rather more batrachian than some others I can see around the court. Does he mean to say that—

JUDGE: Need this aspect of the matter be pursued further? Aren't you giving it far more attention than it deserves?

COUNSEL: As Your Honour pleases. I was about to come to the gravamen of my argument.

Reflect, members of the Jury, on what those hands of his (and yours and mine, no less) get up to out of court. Picture the things they did last night and this morning, and will do before the day is out. Some of them nice and clean things, some grubby, some foul. As foul as foul can be. Some of them acts so indecent that it's a criminal offence to perform them in public. Is he telling the court that Almighty God (may He forgive me for mouthing such a notion!) is grubby and foul, indeed *obscene*? Or that He delegates His job of wiping bottoms to certain of His angels?... Very well, Your Honour, I won't pursue the matter further... [The court simmers down.] I don't need to. Believe it or not, the worst is yet to come. In effect, the Accused is implying that the Almighty can sink to petty larceny. That He's quite capable of the occasional flurry of shoplifting in the Witness's store. No, I'm not accusing John a-Nokes of bagging from time to time a can of anchovies or dressed crab or Caspian caviare, and forgetting to produce it at the checkout. What I'm saying is that he *could* do so, using those very same loose and free-ranging hands which he says are the Almighty's. To tell the truth, I shouldn't be surprised if he does occasionally help himself to the Witness's choicest goods; after all, the Divine Customer he pretends to be is certainly entitled to the lot, for free! The Earth is the Lord's, and the fullness thereof. From which it follows that Sainsbury's is the Nokes's, and the dressed crab thereof!

Need I say more on this disgraceful topic? With great respect to Your Honour and the court, I had to say as much as I did. I'm told that certain mystics in the past have got away with the boast that God has no hands but theirs. To some pious folk, I guess this may not sound blasphemous. But only go into the implications a little, as I have been obliged to do today, and it's evident that blasphemy of a peculiarly disgusting kind lies behind that seemingly innocuous sentiment.

The Accused has himself sawn off the branch he thought he was sitting pretty on, has uncoiled enough rope to hang himself with— several times over. The Jury will be fascinated to witness his efforts to survive his own Defence.

MYSELF: Having acknowledged that I'm almost as impressed with Counsel's dirty story as he is, let me assure him that I too shall listen with much interest to the response it evokes here. I swear to you I don't know in advance what the One under attack has up His sleeve for the court—a sleeve which, though abbreviated (as we've seen), is much more capacious than would first appear. In so far as He's conducting His Defence right here, all will go well. In so far as the man you see is doing so, it won't. Well, here goes:

Counsel at pains to disinfect the Almighty and jack up His social standing—till He's salubrious and respectable enough to be invited to a dinner party thrown by a retired company-director's wife in Riseholme or Tilling, or even Bognor Regis—now there's a delightful spectacle! It's a lily that requires no gilding by me. Except perhaps to remind Counsel that dirt is matter in the wrong place, and nothing in God's world is in the wrong place. To the Pure all things are pure. Unattached hands are never dirty, attached ones never clean.

The point I do want to make is a very simple and very serious one. As so often in the course of these proceedings, what the Prosecution supposes to be the end, the *coup de grâce* of my case, is the practical start of it. Repeat, *practical*. The One who has the whole world in His hands doesn't mishandle it. When I consciously live from Who I really am right here, from this inverted and decapitated body which is His and not Jack's, I find these hands caressing His world and doing His work, I find these feet going on His journeys, I find this voice speaking His words. I challenge anyone to see steadily into his or her True Nature, and do violence to it. Impossible! 'Turn the man loose who has found the Living Guide within him,' says John Everard, 'and let him neglect the outward if he can.' If you find your hands conjuring packets of smoked salmon from the Witness's shelves into your shopping bag instead of your shopping basket, or changing nappies with nose-wrinkling disgust, or swatting flies instead of letting them out, or washing dishes while you are wool-gathering leagues away, or doing any sort of botched job—why, then you can be sure they aren't God's hands. Or be sure, rather, that you are putting them forth in ignorance of Whose they really are. In fact, I challenge anyone to overlook his or her True and Divine Nature, hallucinating in its place his or her false human nature, and not to go on to steal and lie and be disgusted and unkind and inefficient and all thumbs—in some sense and to some degree.

Meister Eckhart said that if he had to choose between God and Truth he would choose Truth. The same here. I don't take notice of and insist on these loose hands and feet because they are efficient, or even because they are God's, but because they are *God-given*—or rather, plain *given*. Because they are actual and factual and true, and no hallucination.

Do what you like to me, I will live from what I see is here, not from what you say is here. And I will tell the world about it. And I will take the consequences. Meanwhile, I swear to you that to live from this is really to live. Which is to live Godly.

COUNSEL, in the falsetto he ascends to when he's absolutely horrified: Oh, no! You're not getting away with that one! What's given—in your self-portrait as the upside-down and headless monster to which you attribute divinity—what's given isn't just hands and feet. There's also a truncated trunk. A trunk furnished with sex organs. Sex organs activated by lust. Don't tell me there's any other sort.

I'll spare the court a detailed exposition of what this means. The Jury will already have spotted that here we have what must be the Arch-blasphemer at his most uninhibited—a creature who makes out that even his sexual exploits are divine! Talk about irreverence! This is dragging the Highest down to the level of the farmyard!

MYSELF: I'm told He doesn't need dragging. He *chose* to be born among the beasts in that stable in Bethlehem. Beasts whose sexuality was uninhibited. And innocent.

Like so much else, our sexuality comes in three instalments. *First,* that of the animal and the young child. It's as blameless and decent as their eating and drinking. *Second,* that of the human grown-up, which is unnatural and indecent in so far as it's what D. H. Lawrence called sex in the head, and I call eccentric sex, or spying on one's own lovemaking. The genuine sexuality of the headless First Person on the bed is spoiled by the false sexuality of the headed third person at the bedroom keyhole—of the one who never felt the least stirring of desire. *Third,* the sexuality of the truly grown-up, of the Seer who is no longer beside himself. Ceasing to be his own voyeur, he regains at a higher level his lost innocence and spontaneity. Along with his head he loses sex-in-the-head, and finds the real thing in his loins. Head he loses, tail he wins.

And, after all, Counsel putting on his holier-than-thou act (shocked to the core yet again is our Sir Gerald!) is rather comical. And misinformed. Eastern spirituality insists that only God sees and hears and is aware—which must mean that only God enjoys sex. And again, Western spirituality insists on a God who, humbling Himself, becomes man. Which must mean He takes on a sexual life as real as yours and mine. Moreover, as the All-in-all-aside from Whom nothing is—He can't escape sex. Does He then find Himself disgusting? Hardly! He leaves that to Sir Gerald and his friends, stuck waist-deep in their second-stage sex-in-the-head.

Now for my main point. Just as I challenge you to see into your Godhood and help yourself to boxes of Suchard liqueur chocolates from the Witness's shelves, so I challenge you to see into your Godhood and misuse sex for showing off or dominating or hurting instead of for loving. How could you truly make love except as the One who alone makes Love and is Love?

JUDGE, to me: How ever did we get from the Witness's supermarket to this extraordinary palaver about sex? I think it's time you summed up your response to his testimony.

MYSELF: It was Counsel, Your Honour, who dragged in the subject of sex. A Whitehousean stick to beat me with—he thought! In fact the issue before this court is a very simple one: *whose appendages are these?* [I hold out my arms.] The contrast between the little fellow you see and the Big One I see here can scarcely be exaggerated. It's staggering, and it extends from their respective limbs to all aspects of their lives. Those hands drive a Land Rover. These drive the Land. Those feet stumble and shuffle and shilly-shally on Jack's business. These stride forth on God's business. Those hands fend off the world. These embrace it. Those hands manipulate. These heal and bless. Those hands compose, play, paint, sculpt, and write run-of-the-mill pieces. These turn out the Master's masterpieces.

Only see Him nearer than hands and feet, and at once they are HIS hands and feet, busy and effective in His service. True uccelli di Dio.

Members of the Jury, if you think that this time I really have gone too far, have indeed gone way out on a fantastical limb of my own, listen to my witnesses. A well-thought-of company, I do assure you.

The Great Function manifests Itself without fixed rules. Meeting each situation on its own terms, It's never too soon, never too late. Thrusting and retracting, advancing and retreating—all happens beyond the realm of thought. When you're in harmony with It, arms and legs operate on their own.

Japanese Zen Master Bankei

I touched my limbs; the limbs were strange, not mine.

Tennyson

Gary Snyder has a poem about a climber who's stuck, in mortal danger, on a rock-face. And then his limbs move with a positiveness and precision with which, it seems, he has nothing to do. I say: his human body as such had to die before the limbs of his divine body could take over.

It is one's spiritual Nature in Enlightenment that moves these arms and legs.

Bodhidharma

You did not throw when you threw, but Allah threw.

The Koran

I [Allah] am the Hearing wherewith he [My slave] heareth, and the Sight wherewith he seeth, and the Hand wherewith he smiteth, and the Foot whereon he walketh.

The Traditions of the Prophet

We wake up in the body of Christ
and Christ wakes up in our bodies.
My poor hand is Christ.
He enters my foot, is infinitely me.
I move my hand, and—O wonder!—
My hand becomes Christ…
I move my foot, and at once
Like lightning he appears.

St Simeon the New Theologian

My head is the sky, my feet are below the Earth, and my two hands are East and West.

Abu 'l-Hasan Khurqani

Prosecution Witness No. 13

THE CANADIAN WIDOW

COUNSEL, to Witness: I believe you know the man in the dock over there. Will you please explain how you came to meet him and what happened.

WITNESS: A few months ago I was flying from London Heathrow to Vancouver, and he was in the seat next to me. We began talking about this and that. I told him a little about myself, and how I'd lost my husband recently and was returning to my native Canada. Then it happened. I'm not clear about all the details, but it was something very extraordinary. He exercised a strange power over me, so that I went quite peculiar for a time. Not all there, up for grabs. I feel very ashamed of it now, very embarrassed that I should have been so gullible.

COUNSEL: No need to feel ashamed, especially as you are no longer under his influence. I'd like you to tell the court what you remember about his behaviour on that journey of something like eight hours.

WITNESS: Well, we had dinner, with some wine. I was feeling very relaxed. I must say I rather took to him. It was then that he hypnotized me.

COUNSEL: Exactly how?

WITNESS: He got me to look steadily into his eyes. At close quarters, of course—the tourist-class seats made sure of that. He passed his hand several times in front of my face, back and forth.

He was talking all the while, in a strangely quiet but insistent voice. Soothing and persuasive it was.

COUNSEL: And he was saying?

WITNESS: This is the embarrassing bit. He kept on telling me I didn't have a head! I shall never understand how I fell for that story. Probably it was a combination of several things. Air travel always puts me in a slightly dreamlike state. Is it that the reduced air-pressure makes one light-headed? The food and the wine had their effect. But what did the trick, of course, was his steady staring, the movement of his hands, his soothing voice and the repetition of that crazy thing about having no head. Result: I really did believe him. Just imagine: a few minutes of that treatment, and he had me quite sure that, crouching there in the window-seat, was a monster without a head! None of the other people, just me! So complete was his power over me, so complete was my surrender to it, that I do believe if he'd told me I had three heads or was legless and armless, I'd have agreed with him.

COUNSEL: Then what happened?

WITNESS: I stayed under the influence the rest of the journey, though there was no more staring into my eyes or passing his hand in front of them. It wasn't needed. He went on feeding me what I now recognize were post-hypnotic suggestions. I'll say this for him, however: so far from telling me that I was to forget his instructions, I was to remember them. Amnesia was the last thing he was after. He assured me that the headless life I was going to live would be very different from the old one. I might well lose interest in my less creative hobbies, and gain energy for my creative work—whatever it turned out to be. I would certainly care less about what people thought of me. I would certainly notice colours and shapes and sounds more. Everything would be different. *Upside down* was a phrase he used several times. Yes, we didn't go to sleep at all, but went on talking through the in-flight movie. I kept on asking questions, and he answered in that very assured, persuasive voice of his. As I look back on it now, it all seems out of this world, a dream...

COUNSEL: A nightmare?

WITNESS: Not at all. It was wonderful—while it lasted. Wonderful, and kooky. There's one thing I shan't forget in a hurry. He talked me into believing that on my shoulders, in place of the head of a human being, was... I feel awful saying this... the Head of the World. He actually got me agreeing with him that, as he put it, losing my human head was finding my divine head!

COUNSEL: How did it all finish?

WITNESS: Well, as we got near the end of the flight, he gave me his address in England and said I could write. And he gave me the addresses of a number of his 'seeing' friends, as he called them, in the Vancouver region, and urged me to get in touch with them. Doing so, he said, would help me to live the new life. Also, he suggested that I should show my friends and relations that they didn't have heads. It was quite easy, he said.

And then, on arrival in Vancouver, we parted, not to meet again until today... There was I, in the baggage claim, thanking him profusely and promising to stay headless, and not forget the marvellous Being I really was. I tell you, I'd gone all funny. I really was off my head.

COUNSEL: Kindly tell the court about how you got it back on again. How soon was it before you came to your senses?

WITNESS: I went to stay for six months near Castlegar, in British Columbia, with my brother and his family. He and his wife are physicians, and know quite a bit about hypnosis. At once they were struck by the change in me. I was in a kind of trance, they said. They noticed how I'd lost interest in my hobbies, including astrology and bridge and a novel a week. And how I did a good deal of just hanging around, as if expecting instructions or waiting for something to happen. Before, I'd always kept busy, and hated being alone. Now I loved going for solitary walks. My brother and sister-in-law say I mooned around with a vacant look on my face. Not just my behaviour but my appearance had changed, according to them. l must say I felt different.

COUNSEL: In what way different?

WITNESS: It was as if the wind had swept right through me, blowing me clean away. As if I was a sort of imbecile, irresponsible, not giving a damn, light-headed and empty-headed. Colours blazed out. Food tasted delicious. For a change, I didn't resent housework. Not so pleasant was the fact that quite a number of folk that I used to admire seemed to me to be putting on acts. I could see through their games so easily. Some old friends were upset, angry with me for no special reason I could make out... And so on. Life had changed all down the line, just as he said it would.

COUNSEL: And then?

WITNESS: Well, two or three weeks of my brother's strongly expressed anxiety about me, plus what I can only call normal company and sane conversation, and I snapped out of all that. I woke from the dream. I became my old self, feet back on the ground. My brother and his wife—I'm so grateful to them—patiently showed me how I'd been hypnotized by a very dangerous man, and gone on to act out his instructions. Once I clearly understood what had happened, and had read something about the quite amazing effects of post-hypnotic suggestion, and seen a couple of videos on the subject, I quickly got back to normal. My old interests returned, I lost that vacant look, loved all sorts of company again—and got my head firmly screwed on once more. My relations were much relieved. No permanent harm done, I think. But I'll always feel ashamed of falling a victim to that spellbinder over there.

COUNSEL: I take it you didn't get in touch with the people whose addresses he'd given you?

WITNESS: In the end, I did so. My brother felt it was my duty to write and warn them against the danger they were in from Mr Nokes. Probably they were too far gone, too much under his influence to break free the way I'd managed to. But at least we had a try.

COUNSEL: And how would you sum up your present feelings about the Accused?

WITNESS: I'd put him in the same class as Svengali. Rasputin would be going too far. But even they, I think, only played God. They didn't set up to be God. What an awful thing he's doing! And yet, you know, I don't dislike him at all. I just feel terribly sad and sorry for him. He's really ill. With a very, very infectious disease from which the public should be protected.

COUNSEL: Please stay in the witness-box. The Accused signals that he wishes to cross-examine you.

Defence: **Hypnosis and Counter-hypnosis**

MYSELF: Yes indeed. I've a whole bunch of questions to put to you. But first I'd like to remind you of what really happened on that plane. I know you'll be as truthful as your memory allows, and that I don't need to stress that you are under oath. It's a fact, isn't it, that I wasn't the one who started our serious conversation? We just talked casually, and then you happened to notice that the book I was reading had the intriguing title of *On Having No Head—Zen and the Rediscovery of the Obvious,* and you wanted to know what it was all about. I replied (you'll recollect) that it would be too difficult and take too long to explain the book's message, but I could very quickly and easily *show* you—if you were sure you wanted me to. 'Yes please!' you said, eagerly. So I did just that. I did indeed show you. Am I right, so far?

WITNESS: I remember asking about the book, so I guess I let myself in for what followed. The business about not having a head, I mean.

MYSELF: It's vital that we get this straight. I *didn't* tell you were headless. Quite the contrary. Remember, I made you get out your hand mirror and find your head in there. Also I proved to you that I was in possession of your head. How else could I describe in endless detail all sorts of things about it that were currently hidden from you? You'll recollect we agreed that, so far from your being headless, you had innumerable heads lurking inside the polished objects and the people and their cameras all around you. And we shared the joke that the *only* place in that Boeing 787 which was quite free of that topknot of yours was the beautifully clear region on top of your shoulders! Your merry laughter had our neighbours staring. Oh, yes, and about that book: we agreed that the silly old author had got the title all wrong. He should have called his book *On Having Millions and Millions of Heads!*

WITNESS: I didn't agree with you about anything. Not at first I didn't—until you went into your Svengali routine. Your gazing into my eyes, and passing your hand in front of my face, and talking in that monotonous voice were what did the trick, what sent me off my rocker.

MYSELF: Svengali routine my left foot! This really won't do! You must try to remember what *did* happen and forget what your brother said happened... I tell you what: I'll quickly run through the business again with you now, to jog your memory. Never mind about the court and all those people eavesdropping. Let's go into this together again, the two of us, just as we did in the plane. [A small rumpus in the gallery. The Witness waving, as if to assure whoever was making it that she was all right.]

WITNESS: Good heavens, No! Why should I agree to such a thing?

MYSELF: Because I'm on trial for my life and your refusal could be the death of me. And because His Honour is allowing me to conduct my Defence in my own way.

WITNESS, clearly very embarrassed: Well, I don't like this at all, but if the Judge thinks I should—

MYSELF: You see, he graciously nods. All right, then. Look now at this face of mine. Take in this balding dome and greying beard, these greenish-darkish, slightly squinting eyes, this very busy mouth, and all the rest. Unlike me, you're registering the lot (aren't you?), down to the last pock-mark and scar and wrinkle. Now *on present evidence* is there anything, anything at all where you are, to get in its way? Any remnant of a face or a head of your own with which to keep mine out? Aren't these moving hands of mine no more than a distant broom, helping you to brush away all that imagined clutter of yours? To wipe your mirror clean of its imaginary grime? In fact, with no help from me, aren't you busted wide open now, wide open for all these other faces as well, for absolutely everything that's on show? And yourself as clear as clear? Gone with the wind once more? [Witness, convulsed with laughter, doesn't—or can't—answer...] Tell me now, have I just been hypnotizing you, or de-hypnotizing you? Have I been talking you out of your senses, or bringing you to your senses? Getting you to hallucinate, or to stop hallucinating? To deny, or to admit, the blazingly obvious? To lie, or to tell the simple truth?

WITNESS, pulling herself together: Well, I must admit... Oh, my God, you've done it again! [She breaks into new peals of laughter, growing rather hysterical...]

COUNSEL, intervening: You two are having quite a ball. And trying the court's patience. The demonstration we've just witnessed is pretty marginal to what this Trial is all about. You aren't charged with witchcraft, or fraud, or misusing hypnotism to take advantage of a suggestible subject. Such misbehaviour—though shocking and perhaps actionable—is relevant here only in so far as it involves blasphemy. This is exactly what, we gather, it did involve on that plane. The Witness testified how you induced her to exchange her human head for her God-head—as you have the nerve to put it. Blaspheming yourself, you got this lady to follow suit. Now that is relevant to the charge against you. Jury, please note.

MYSELF: My answer to that one—about misusing hypnotism—will come out later. Meantime allow me to conclude this interchange between the Witness and myself, by addressing the all-important question of just where God's dwelling-place is. [I turn to the Witness.] Please attend very carefully. Isn't it a fact that, right now, cradled on your shoulders—instead of just one particular human topknot, blonde and female and fifty and Canadian—is Room for all the other topknots in court? A Proper Place for them to happen in? Just Aware Capacity, perfectly simple and clear and changeless, for this hugely complex and ever-changing scene? And perfectly conscious of Itself as Empty for that filling. Yes?

WITNESS: Yes!

MYSELF: Now tell me, would it make sense to call this marvellous Alertness—this widest and brightest of Cloudless Skies—Mrs Ingrid Mary Stevenson? (I hope I've got the name right.) Or would it be nonsense and blasphemy?

WITNESS: Nonsense, for sure.

MYSELF: But instead to call it that Pure Awareness that some of us recognize as God—would that be nonsense and blasphemy?

WITNESS: Well... No, I don't think so.

MYSELF: I see that Counsel is doing his writhing act. If he can suggest a more fitting name for this Incredible One Who is Awareness itself, or can think of a more roomy and comfortable Palace for His Majesty to hold court in, we'd all love to know about it. So would His Majesty, I bet you.

COUNSEL, to Witness: I'm wondering how long you'll have to spend with your relations (who I believe are in this court) before you recover from this new attack on your integrity and common sense. Do you seriously believe that this time the treatment will stick? [Witness, now in tears, is unable (or unwilling) to reply. She's allowed to stand down...]

COUNSEL, to me: If you think that this demonstration has proved that your technique isn't hypnotic—isn't hypnosis pressed into the service of blasphemy—you'd better think again. What else has it proved?

MYSELF: Let me explain my position vis-à-vis hypnosis. My aim in that demonstration, as always, was to appeal to the given facts, and a plague on all distortions and denials of them. My life's work is hunting down and destroying the illusions society runs on. In fact I'm a resolute anti-hypnotist, who always warns people not to believe what I tell them (let alone what others tell them) but to check up on it. *Dare to be your own authority!* That's my theme song, my watchword.

COUNSEL: But when the subject is as suggestible as the Witness obviously is, what price this boasted appeal to the bare data?

MYSELF: Of course you have a point there. It does sometimes happen—in spite of my intentions to the contrary—that my way of putting questions involves a mild trance. About this I'm unrepentant. In fact I'm happy to deploy a benign and temporary kind of hypnosis to counter the malign and chronic kind from which all human adults suffer until they learn to snap out of it. It's a case of a hair of the dog that bit you, of a homoeopathy that really does work. As indeed you have just seen.

I can't say it too often or too emphatically: the 'normal' human condition is one of deep hypnosis. Instead of seeing what we see, we live out our lives seeing what we're told to see. And the difference between the two seeings is total. Take just one example out of hundreds, the one which happens to be very much to the point just now. From early childhood the Witness's parents and relations, her friends and acquaintances, the English language itself, have been drumming into her that she is face-to-face with everyone she meets. So of course, hallucinating to order along with the rest of us, she 'constructs' a fictitious head on her shoulders to keep those real ones out with, and 'sees' her face *in the one place it's absent from!* The consequences for living are in a score of ways unfortunate, and ultimately disastrous.

Let me remind you, ladies and gentlemen of the Jury, of the spectacular things that a stage hypnotist can get his subjects to do. He may suggest to a prim and proper middle-aged middle-class lady that, as soon as he wakes her from her trance, she will unconcernedly stroll to centre stage, and hoist her skirt, and dance the cancan. And lo! stroll to centre stage and hoist her skirt and dance the cancan she does with great conviction and aplomb, and without at all knowing why. Well, that's a meek and mild and comparatively harmless example of what can happen when under the influence. Immeasurably more serious is what does happen to us all. We humans are so bound by the spell of the Master Mesmerist—Society is the polite name for him—that we will believe and do practically anything to gain admittance to the club he runs and that we're dying to belong to. Talk about my occasional and one-minute use of hypnosis and post-hypnotic suggestion! Human life is *all* hypnosis and post-hypnotic suggestion—except that it's not so much 'post' as ever-present! Almost all adults are to some degree the Mesmerist's zombies. My job is to prod to wakefulness and freedom those who are beginning to suspect that he's reduced them to that state. If this means a little counter-hypnosis, why on earth not? What a wonderful tribute to the treatment *against* hallucination which we have just witnessed, that five minutes of it should be so effective against five decades of the Master Mesmerist's treatment for hallucination!

COUNSEL: I repeat: you aren't on trial for witchcraft, or for the abuse of hypnosis to brainwash people and get them into your power. The Jury aren't going to be put off the blasphemy trail so easily.

MYSELF: Not a whiff of a red herring here, I promise you. I am far hotter on the blasphemy trail than you are. For too long society and language hypnotized me into hallucinating here, bang at the world's

Centre, that congealed lump of personal stuff which is the seal and substance of John a-Nokes's separate identity. This was the chip on his shoulder. This was his blasphemy. This was his brainfouling. But now he's indeed in the brainwashing business. Simply looking-to-see is the fragrant, economy-size, industrial-strength, all-stain-removing, mildly hypnotic Tide that washes Jack's brain and brain-box clean away.

And all that's left, when the Tide runs out, is God.

Is God...

This time I'm leaving it to the true Meister, to Eckhart, to complete the story:

When all things are reduced to naught in you, then you shall see God.

Into any man who is brought low, God pours His whole Self with all His might.

It (the soul) is intrinsically receptive of nothing but the Divine Essence, without means. Here God enters the Soul with His all, not merely with a part. God enters the ground of the Soul. None can touch the ground of the Soul but God only. No creature is admitted.

God has ordained to every thing its place. To fish the water, to birds the air, to beasts the earth, to the Soul the Godhead.

Prosecution Witness No. 14

THE PSYCHIATRIST

COUNSEL, to Witness: The Accused maintains that, though in appearance a man, in reality he is God. The court wishes to know whether, in your practice over the past twenty years, you have come across this sort of madness... All right, Your Honour... Let's say, this sort of thing.

WITNESS: From time to time I have.

COUNSEL: How would you describe his condition? And how would you treat it?

WITNESS: For me to say that he's suffering from delusions of grandeur is merely to stick a handy label on him, and explains nothing. To say that the condition is a reverting to infant omnipotence explains very little. It may well be true, but doesn't tell me why the client reverts. I can think of a dozen reasons. Our work together would, if at all possible, be to bring to light the deep and hidden causes in his case, to ventilate them. Once exposed, there's a good chance of a cure. Probably, but not necessarily, the root cause of the trouble lies way back in early childhood, now conveniently forgotten and covered up. In which case a long and difficult task lies ahead, but not a hopeless one. The important thing, I find, is for me to keep an open mind, gain the client's confidence as he discovers I really care, and get him talking. I have to listen, listen, listen—and look. And wait. The less I say the better. We both have to be patient. More haste less healing.

COUNSEL: I'm told that you have never, till today, met the Accused in the flesh. However, I gather that you have made a rather careful study of his various books, articles, and audio and video tapes.

WITNESS: That's right.

COUNSEL: Well, would you say he's sane but rather sick? Or downright insane? Mad, with lucid intervals?

WITNESS: Mad is not a word I have a lot of use for. But if anybody's sick, he's sick all right. Just how sick will depend largely on how serious he is, how far he really means what he's saying. If he were a client of mine, I would give special attention to his behaviour, his style, his voice, his body language, his whole personality and state of health. This general picture should tell me more about him than any understanding of his ideas could do. It should furnish the clue to the depth of his delusions, and show whether he's altogether taken in by them and out of touch with reality, or is playing some sort of game.

COUNSEL: Briefly, what have you concluded from your study of his published material?

WITNESS: My strong impression is that he's far from being what you would call mad. On the other hand, his delusions of grandeur are not superficial, not a pose. I suspect they are deeper rooted than any I've met hitherto. He's no Baron Münchhausen, or ordinary Berneian gamesman. If he were my client, I think I would find the chances of remission to be rather slender. I need hardly add that, of course, he's just the sort who would never come to me for treatment in a million years. Or, if he did turn up on my doorstep, it would be to leave a card offering *me* therapy! Free treatment, at that! The sure sign of a fanatic with some almighty axe to grind.

COUNSEL: One last question. What reason have you to describe the Accused as *deluded*? Please explain to the court why you are so positive he isn't Who he says he is?

WITNESS: That's an easy one. I'm an agnostic myself but I accept that any God worthy of the name is omnipotent and omniscient and omnipresent. Well, if the gentleman over there in the dock is even one of these three, and that one only at rare intervals, all I've said so far is irrelevant. And I'll eat all the hats at Ascot!

COUNSEL: Thank you. I think you may have dented the Accused's insufferable smugness, and he'll want to have a word with you.

Defence: The Three Omnies

MYSELF: No, the Witness may stand down. I have no questions to fire at him, no bones to pick with him. On the contrary, I have to thank him for showing me, at the conclusion of his testimony, what till then I had no idea of: namely, how to counter the rest of it. Yet once more in this Trial, it seems to me that I have lost the day and then—praise be!—it turns out that all I have to do is to develop the Prosecution's case against me till it becomes the case for me. Or rather, to clear the decks and let it develop itself, and proceed to do a somersault dive overboard without any pushing.

Omnipresence, omniscience, omnipotence—these three, and the greatest of these is omnipotence. If, members of the Jury, I can somehow convey to you the sense in which I'm enjoying all three of them, putting them into practice right now in court, then you will have to turn in a verdict of Not Guilty. For I will have proved to you that I am Who I say I am. But let me at once add that you won't in a millennium of Sundays cotton on to my Identity—and the powers that go with it—until you work up some interest in yours, and the powers you wield. You won't understand a word I say until you dare to look and see whether or not What I'm claiming to be and to do has all along been What you manifestly are, and are doing all the time. The fact—I can't repeat it too often—is that *you* are on trial here, and before you can reach a true verdict on me you must reach a true verdict on you. Justice begins at home. So, alas, do injustice, bigotry, embattled prejudice, the closed and padlocked mind.

And a favourite way of putting up the shutters of the mind is to fall fast asleep. Which two members of the Jury have evidently done, Your Honour, before we start.

[The Judge gives deafening applications of his gavel. One of the sleepers starts violently, as if jabbed with an ice-pick. The other goggles at the court as if he can't decide whether it's part of his dream.]

JUDGE, to me: Well, who's to blame for this? It's up to you to hold their interest. I warned you of the risks of conducting your own Defence... As for the Jury, don't let me catch any of you dozing again! From now on, each of you is responsible for keeping his neighbour awake, as well as himself. When in doubt, prod. Vigorously.

MYSELF: Fear of the truth is a more powerful soporific than boredom. Half the time, I've noticed, at least one juror is nodding off. Not because I'm failing to get to him or her but because I'm succeeding! Once, in a workshop here in London, the lady next to me slept from near the beginning to the very end, some of the time with her head on my shoulder—thus warding off the terrible danger of Self-realization. 'What a nice workshop!' she commented when we said goodbye.

JUDGE: Fascinated though we all are by these reminiscences, I'm afraid we'll have to wait till we can read them in your memoirs. Just now, let me bring something to your notice. There's a Trial going on.

MYSELF: A Trial, Your Honour, about who's gifted with divine powers, and who isn't. Back, then, to our divine trio, starting with omnipresence—which happens to be the most immediately demonstrable.

Look! I aim to show you that, lying low somewhere in this courtroom, is its Creator, the Heart and Soul of all things. He's the Importunate One who stands at every door and knocks. 'Let's get together!' he propositions. To track Him down should be easy. 'For God,' says Eckhart, 'nothing is far.' He's the Distance Swallower, the Coincider. Centripetal, He's the Attraction, the Great Draw. It's as if an elastic band were stretched so tight between Him in the middle and all those things around Him that something has to give, and—whoosh!—in they hurtle. He's the only one in the whole world who, by pulling in everywhere, is everywhere, while the rest stay somewhere or other, are local, mutually standoffish, snobby, all elbows, careful to keep their precious distances, insisting on a room of their own. All but the Omnipresent one are exclusive brethren, which is to say unbrotherly. He alone is the Friend, the Includer, the Intimate of all, the Magnet, the Lodestone. That's one of the reasons why His name is Love.

Never mind about me for the moment. Never mind about the other people in court. Take a little time off to look into your own condition, personally. First-personally. Which of these two species are you now, Excluder or Includer, Pusher-off or Puller-in—going by your own firsthand experience? I must admit that you look like an Excluder; but we can't always go by looks, can we? How I wish that His Honour would let me stretch a string between you and me, eye to eye, so that you could check whether, pulled taut, it reduces to a point; or else would let me unroll a tape-measure for similarly viewing end-on and checking whether our mutual distance reads as ten, twenty, thirty feet—or as zero. Alas, hardly practicable: the courtroom would soon resemble a gigantic spider-web with one Spider and many flies. But really you've only to look now to see whether you are the Spider at the Centre or one of the many flies caught out there in its web. A mere fly, destined to refresh some voracious arachnid before long.

Well, as always, I'm in no position to speak for you. So back to me. I'm telling you now that I can't find so much as an angstrom between you and me. I'm taking you all in absolutely, all of you twelve members of the Jury, His Honour, learned Counsel and his learned junior, the Court Usher, you crowd in the gallery, and the rest. Like it or lump it, you rush in. Behold I am with you, even to the end of the world. We are Oned.

Ladies and gentlemen, will you please now turn to Diagram No. 14. I ask each of you: 'Are you the Spider x, or one of those flies a, b, c...? It's so easy to tell. From x, the Spider's point of view, a-x, b-x, c-x, etc. = 0. And a-a', b-b', c-c', etc. = > 0. That's to say: *however distant things are from one another, none's distant from you.*

All you have to do is look, as straightforwardly as when in infancy you clutched at the Moon. Astonishingly, that's all it takes for you to be sure Who you really, really are. Now if you were saying that a man (d)—proud man—is seeing this and saying this, you would indeed be blaspheming. Only God at (x) is in a position to abolish distance. *Only God at (x) is observant enough and great enough and humorous enough and humble enough to allow His omnipresence to demonstrate His divinity.*

And if, tonight, your stars come out, you'll be able to compare the distances that hold them apart with the no-distance that joins them to you. And their isolation and poverty with your riches. But don't wait till then. Relax your guard and let all things rush in, now. The Earth is the Lord's and the fullness thereof—

COUNSEL, crescendo: A Urinating God, an Idiot God, a Bubble-blowing God, a Bottom-wiping God—and now a Spider God! What next? I must say that, in falsely claiming to be Him, you truly throw floods of light on yourself!

Members of the Jury, this is a good moment to remind you of what, at the start of this Trial, I called the Four Criteria for proving the Accused guilty as charged. And to draw your attention to how thoroughly this renegade, in the last quarter of an hour, has met all four of them. *First, the blasphemy.* He insults the Almighty by taking upon himself the Almighty's omnipresence. *Second, its extreme form.*

Diagram No. 14

The Psychiatrist

He claims he is the Almighty. *Third, its dissemination.* He makes that claim now, in court proceedings that millions of TV viewers are picking up. *Fourth, the reaction.* Along with those viewers, you are—I can feel it—so disgusted, so outraged, that you would get your hands on him if you could. At least to stop his blaspheming mouth—

THE JUDGE, half standing, banging his gavel with all his might: No, no! I won't have this! This is outrageous! The Jury are here to take as cool and unbiased a view of the evidence as they can, not to be worked up to a frenzy. Your rabble-rousing outburst brings the Crown you represent into disrepute. I'm shocked that so distinguished a Member of the Bar should so far forget himself.

Counsel, turning almost as white as his brief, collapses on to his bench as if coshed... Collecting the remains, he holds a whispered conversation with his Junior... The court is kept waiting...

Atkinson nods, expands visibly, and rises like a rubicund balloon to his feet and the occasion. Sir Gerald, shrunken and frozen-faced, sits there staring straight ahead.

JUNIOR COUNSEL: Well then, to lower the temperature, back to the details of this gentleman's pretensions to omnipresence. Let Mr John a-dash-Nokes condescend to ask any astronomer, and he'll be told that a hundred light-years lie between him and that star.

MYSELF: Quite so. And then let me ask him where the star is that he actually sees and photographs. He'll concede that it's not a hundred light-years off, or a hundred yards off, but present where it presents itself in the observatory and the observer himself, and on his camera film. Questioned further, he'll explain that what's up there in the sky is nothing like a star at all, if by that word we mean the dear little twinkler people write poems about; instead, it's an unapproachable and lethal world of superheated gas, which in any case may well have blown up any time during the past century, without any of us being the wiser. And if I were to doubt the astronomer, any physiologist would confirm that what I see I see here where I am, not over there where I naïvely suppose the object to be. Why, even common sense must give in here.

The truth, so staggering and beautiful yet so simple and obvious, is that there's One in this courtroom who is omnipresent, while all the rest are omniabsent. One Spider, many flies. Ave Arachnid!

What, you don't understand this? Excellent! Nor do I! But you see it, don't you? See that it applies to you, absolutely? In that case you are starting to do justice to yourself. And it must follow, as bright day follows darkest night, starting to do justice to me.

JUNIOR COUNSEL: Specious stuff, which the Jury won't fall for—if only because it's invalidated by your admission that you've no idea what's been happening to that star up there, in the course of the hundred years its light has taken to reach you. You, wretched ignoramus, don't know. *He,* the Omniscient One, does know.

MYSELF: And so, Mr Atkinson, to the second of the three items on our agenda.

What *is* divine omniscience? What does this marvellous all-knowledge, this perfection of wisdom, this full enlightenment, amount to? On no subject is there more loose thinking, more confusion worse confounded. Somewhere at the back of our minds is a picture of the Almighty keeping abreast of the behaviour of every sand grain in the Sahara, anxiously refereeing the entire atomic and subatomic ball game, privy to the stirring of every dust grain on the floor of this court and the disposition of every *fibrilla* in the wig of His Honour. Don't be ridiculous! Is this *any* sort of God? Or, for that matter, any sort of Devil worthy of the name? A mad *apparatchik* perhaps, a nit-picking myopic obsessional monster, the world's Peeping Tom and Fusspot-in-Chief, with what full hands and furrowed brow! One who (as Bunyan says) can look no way but downwards with a muck-rake in his hand, a know-all in the worst sense of the word, an object of pity and contempt fit for worship only by fellow morons.

Knowledge of things—as things—is relative knowledge. Such information is always partial, one-sided, flawed, at best useful make-believe and at worst misinformation. Imagine the Eternal Wisdom going in for all that obfuscation! He is of purer eyes than to behold evil, says the Old Testament prophet. As if taking His cue from those three Hindu monkeys (See no evil, Hear no evil, Speak no evil), He knows what He wants to know, which is what things really and truly are. He's not a superficial God. His knowledge of His creatures, running deeper than deep, is of their Essence. Knowledge of their accidents He has too, but in and as and through themselves. His expertise and His joy is the Self-knowledge which—so far from being selfishly introverted or snobbishly Olympian—is necessarily knowledge of what all creatures of every rank, from subatomic through human to super-galactic, intrinsically are. To wit, none other than the Awareness that is Himself.

This, ladies and gentlemen of the Jury, is the omniscience I claim. It's the only sort that's worth a second glance, or worth taking seriously for a moment. I say this for three reasons. First, because it alone yields information that's true, final, stable, for resting in. Second, because it alone works out in my life: in my dealings with others I need above all to be sure that, at heart, they are *not* others. Third, because, looking in at this very moment, I see and know myself as I really, really am: namely, as this central Awareness where there's no possibility of error because there's nothing to err about; as this boundless Clarity which carries no such labels as 'me' or 'you' or 'him' or 'her', or 'Accused' or 'Juryman', or whatever, but is the one inside story of all beings in all worlds through all time. This I see with the utmost brilliance, and know with the utmost certainty, and it is none other than the divine omniscience which reconciles and unites each with each and each with all. And this is the second reason why His name is Love.

There are sextillions of questions, one Answer. This divine knowledge is so comforting and comfortable! I rest in it. The other and secular sort offers me no lodging for the night. It turns me out into the cold dark to seek more and more and more information forever... To what end?

JUNIOR COUNSEL butts in: The proof of the knowing is in the doing. What, for heaven's sake, is the use of all that inside information if you can't even bring off a Yuri Geller trick with it? Or perhaps, kind sir, you would care to treat the court to a little demonstration of your omnipotence? What about shifting any object you like in this courtroom—from my tie-wig here to His Honour's full-bottomed over there—moving it, let's say, an inch to the right or the left? Shifting it, I mean, without budging from the dock. If you are all-powerful, a spot of telekinesis should be well within your capability.

JUDGE, putting his hand to his head: I'd rather you interfered with this pen here than my wig.

MYSELF: I shall see that Your Honour isn't incommoded at all...

I swear to you that I'm performing this wig-shifting, pen-shifting miracle right now, as requested by Junior Counsel. Oh, I know what he's saying: 'All that the silly ass is doing is swaying a little from side to side!' So be it. That's Atkinson's story. Mine, just now, is that it's the court that's swaying, as in an earthquake magnitude 9 on the Richter scale.

But that's peanuts! I can be much more drastic if you wish…

I can and I have destroyed this court…!

And now, three seconds later, I choose to re-build and re-furnish and re-man and re-cockalorum—yes (rather decent of me, don't you think?), re-Atkinson it—all intact and in running order.

You will never, never, never find a normal-way-up and headed creature capable of doing such a tremendous thing. Blasphemy it is to suppose that he or she could thus usurp divine power. All humans can do is raise and lower tiny flip-flaps in their precious heads. The most uneventful of events, the most trivial of trivialities, leaving the world untouched. Only the Upside-down and Headless One, *only the Maker of the world can and does, very often indeed, make and remake it instantly at His own good pleasure.* Who else? Man blinking is blinking man. Atkinson blinking is blinking Atkinson. God blinking is the birth and death of worlds. You could call this the Blinking Path to Enlightenment, or Endarkenment on the Blink. To each of you I say, 'Blink! And for once don't lie to yourself about what happens. And about Who makes it happen.'

JUNIOR COUNSEL, wearily, after a whispered conversation with Sir Gerald: Here's Nokes putting on his idiot-boy act—Wynken, Blynken and Nod—and high-wire star turn—The Three Omnies—in his crazy-gang circus. But I'll wager the Jury is as unimpressed by this clowning as I am. Earlier on, Mr Nokes, you took upon yourself to liken the divine experience to that of a trio of monkeys. Well, I say that these boasted miracles of yours are indeed no more than monkey tricks performed by a creature who criminally attributes them to the Creator. I'll tell you why they are monkey tricks. Because they don't matter a damn, don't make a ha'p'orth of difference. Now what *would* impress the court would be the changing of this sad world just a little for the better—happiness breaking out in Surbiton, Death Valley in bloom, the Aids virus beaten at last, the clean generation of energy from wind and tide and sunlight...

MYSELF: All of which, and infinitely more, is in the process of accomplishment by the Almighty, whose only tools, whose only limbs (I wave my arms) are such as these...

But we go too fast. Let's take a look at power, at who has it, and how much. Now a man who is a little thing has a little power, or so at any rate he believes. But a God who is No-thing has no power at all, and a God who is All-things has all power. And the Seer, the one who has seen off his humanhood and seen in his Godhood, takes on with it this seeming paradox, this same union of opposites. He is all-powerless and all-powerful, willing nothing and willing everything. What this means in his everyday life is that he so concurs in all God's arrangements for him that he intends them. His will merges with God's, and *all happens as he wants it to happen*. Not as he superficially desires, of course, but as he deeply desires, in his heart. His *real* joy and his *real* peace are to do the will of the One he *really is*. There they are, the saints and saviours of the world, living what they are preaching—a truly double life—desiring nothing and everything, all-powerless and all-powerful. Theirs is the life that works. A merely *human* life, in so far as it's possible, isn't practical. I must be God surrendered to God, or a mess. He's fixed it that I must be Him. That's the third reason why His name is Love.

Nor is this double life, this divine union of weakness and strength, a lovey-dovey milk-and-water acceptance of the world's evils, a creeping-Jesus-meek-and-mild cop-out and evasion of responsibility, in the name of detachment and unworldliness. On the contrary, those saints who say the loudest Yes! to God's good will say the loudest No! to man's bad will, and undertake astonishing labours for His suffering world. St Catherine of Genoa is, for me, the outstanding example. Her 'My Me is God', and her recurrent theme that Hell is self-will, go along with her toughness and superhuman energy and efficiency in the founding and running of a huge hospital in her native city. She, along with her namesake of Siena, and many, many other God-filled ones, made and are making a vast difference in the world—overground for all to see, and even more powerfully underground, where none can see. Without them I don't like to think what the world—

JUNIOR COUNSEL, bobbing up and down and positively incandescent with excitement: Well, you certainly find yourself in congenial company. Just like you, quite the most infamous character of the last century described the world as inside-out, with himself at its centre, and the stars painted on the inside of the firmament. And, like you, claimed omnipotence. A claim debunked conclusively—in a bunker, oddly enough.

MYSELF: Extremes converge. Satan was the top angel. The unusual wickedness of Hitler had something in common with the unusual goodness of the most saintly of his victims. Who I really am is—

JUNIOR COUNSEL, again cutting me short, splutters: This is hard to believe! Are you—words fail me!—do you have the effrontery to stand there, seriously claiming to be a saint? A *great* saint?

MYSELF: Don't be absurd! Quite apart from the fact that every saint is sure he's a louse, the truth is that to be human and to be good are contraries. Only God is good. (You'll remember who said that.) A saint is one who sees his bad humanhood off to the place where it should be and sees his good Godhood in to the place where it must be, the place it never left—*and goes on to live this disposition.* But to see it at all is at least to have made a start on the God-filled life—

JUDGE: I think you have gone on quite long enough in your response to the psychiatrist's testimony.

MYSELF: All right, Your Honour. Just let me sum up.

Along with Catherine, I say my real Me is God. I've proved it in triplicate. Three Omnies are enough for Him and should be enough for you or me. This is not blasphemy. It is not a delusion of grandeur. It is not a fantasy. It is not one of life's optional extras. It is not a highly-desirable but rare ornament of grace, or a bright three-ringed halo reserved for a few great souls. It is not an attainment of the pious that you and I can get along very nicely without, thank you very much.

No. It's a must. It's the only sensible lifestyle, the only one (I repeat) that works, that's practical. Again and again the saints have demonstrated as much. But it doesn't take all that time and attention and practice for us ordinary folk to prove on our pulses how right they were.

However, the ultimate reason why this is the only satisfactory way of life isn't that it's the only *satisfying* one, but that it's the only one. The only way life can be lived, in any case. It's not for attaining but for submitting to. It's not for thinking or feeling or realizing one day. It's for seeing now.

I have sorted my Witnesses into three companies, each testifying to one of our Three Omnies—

JUDGE: Just a moment. You keep on referring to these dead folk as witnesses. It was agreed from the start that they are nothing of the sort. They aren't under oath, and can't be examined or cross-examined. Nor can their reported sayings be relied on absolutely. At best they illustrate your case, clarifying it without proving it.

MYSELF: I stand corrected, Your Honour. In any event my message to the Jury all along is: Don't believe 'authorities'. Test what they say, *and become your own authority*. On this sure foundation my whole case rests.

Omnipresence

Distance is a phantasy.

Blake

God is a circle whose centre is everywhere and whose circumference is nowhere.

Medieval Saying

And then our Lord opened my spiritual eye and showed me my soul in the midst of my heart. I saw the Soul so large as it were an endless world, and as it were a blissful kingdom... In the midst of that City sitteth our Lord.

Julian of Norwich

Omniscience

When the Self is seen, heard, thought of, known, everything is known.

Brihadaranyaka Upanishad

Supreme enlightenment is none other than all-knowledge... It does not mean that the Buddha knows every individual thing, but that he has grasped the fundamental principle of existence and that he has penetrated deep down into the centre of his own being.

D. T. Suzuki

If I knew myself as intimately as I ought, I should have perfect knowledge of all creatures.

Eckhart

Omnipotence

The Father that dwells in me, He does the works.

Jesus

It is God who works in you both to do and to will his good pleasure.

St Paul

A world of which you are the only source and ground is fully within your power to change. What is created can always be un-created and re-created. All will happen as you want it, provided you really want it.

Nisargadatta

General

Shiva, the Highest Lord, is omniscient, omnipotent, and omnipresent. Since I have these attributes, I am He.

Vijnanabhairava

Prosecution Witness No. 15

THE NEW APOCALYPTIC

A new week and a new day. Two days and three nights have gone by since the court was last in session. Long enough for Sir Gerald to be on his feet again, displaying all his old zing and panache.

He introduces his fifteenth Witness.

COUNSEL: You call yourself a New Apocalyptic. Please explain to the court what that means.

WITNESS: *Apocalypsis* is a Greek word meaning a revelation or uncovering. I'm an elder and spokesman of the Church of that name, whose members take as their infallible guide God's Holy Word and the gospel it proclaims. We stand four-square for Christ, for Jesus Christ as the only Son of God and Saviour from sin, and the imminence of his Second Coming. To be followed by the Day of Judgement. We do battle with all who deny his absolute uniqueness as the Second Person of the Holy Trinity, and who question the efficacy of his precious blood shed for sinners. Specially are we the enemies of those limbs of Satan who, not content with having apostatized from the saving truth, lead others (I'm thinking of the impressionable young) to perdition and the eternal flames of Hell. Oh, yes, it's a holy war we wage against all Antichrists and blasphemers. And when one of them goes so far as to set himself up in the place of the Lord he dishonours, why, we'll do anything to bring him down. Anything.

COUNSEL: Is it a fact that certain members of your Church, before the passing of the Blasphemy Act under which the Accused is being tried, did indeed take the law into their own hands? That they captured some of those apostates (I'm using your language), tried them, condemned them to death and actually executed them?

WITNESS: My church doesn't deny that it carries out its God-given duties where and as it can.

COUNSEL: May I take it that, now that the official law against blasphemy has been given teeth and written into the Statute Book, the attitude of your Church has changed?

WITNESS: We are hopeful that the Act will see justice done in the worst cases, but we are by no means certain. We shall see. In any case we have our work to do. Work for Christ against all Antichrists.

COUNSEL: Antichrists? Please explain. Yes, you may read from the bible you took your oath on.

WITNESS, bible in one hand and chopping vigorously with the other: They are the ones St John speaks of here, in his First Epistle: 'Many false prophets are gone out into the world. Hereby know ye the Spirit of God: Every spirit that confesseth that Jesus Christ is come in the flesh is of God: And every spirit that confesseth not that Jesus Christ is come in the flesh is not of God: and this is that spirit of antichrist.' And St Paul speaks of 'that man of sin, the son of perdition, who opposeth and exalteth himself above all that is called God, or that is worshipped; so that he as God sitteth in the temple of God, shewing himself that he is God.'

COUNSEL: Looking around now, do you find any such Antichrist in this court? One to whom both these texts apply?

WITNESS, now in something of a frenzy: I do! Look! There he stands in the dock!

Shouting and much commotion in the public gallery. A banner is unfurled. It reads 'DEATH TO THE BLASPHEMER'...

After some minutes, during which the offenders and their banner are removed and order is restored, Witness goes on.

WITNESS: My fellow workers and I have monitored the written and spoken words of this man of sin, and consider him guilty of every sort of blasphemy. Among contemporary Antichrists he is the chief. Plain beheading is too easy an exit for him. I'm thinking of what they did to another blasphemer, the early Quaker James Nayler, in 1656. He was severely whipped, branded with the letter B (for blasphemy) on his forehead, and had his tongue bored through with a red-hot iron.

COUNSEL: You shouldn't worry. Christendom has come on a long way since those crude old days. Thanks to science, we know how to give the Naylers of the world a *really* hard time, don't we?

WITNESS, all irony lost on him: Still far less than they deserve!

COUNSEL, after a long pause, as if for once he really were tongue-tied: Well, Jury, there you have it... Let me remind you that the charge of blasphemy levelled against the Accused doesn't deny his right peaceably to hold opinions which excite the sort of sentiments we've just been treated to. No—it's his persistent and blatant airing of these opinions, giving rise to offence and outrage and disturbances of public order, which is the crime he's charged with. I feel sure you'll agree that the Witness's testimony—to say nothing of the appalling behaviour of his friends in the gallery—goes a long way towards proving John a-Nokes guilty of this sort of provocation. Leaving aside all questions of compassion and common decency, and of who has the truth and who hasn't, it can't be denied that these people are scandalized to the point of hysteria by what they see as the Accused's war on all they hold sacred. Why, even in this courtroom he incites people to violence!

Defence: **Antichrist and Pro-Christ**

MYSELF: There would be no point in cross-examining this frankest of witnesses. The heretic at the stake doesn't start an interesting conversation with the fellow who's approaching with a lighted taper. So you may leave the witness-box.

As for Counsel's last remark about my causing folk to commit breaches of the peace, outside and now inside this court, I ask the Jury to look at this principle—at the precedent it sets, and the nightmare world it opens out before us. It shifts the blame from the muggers to the old lady they mug. It makes the molested child responsible for her molestation, the bank for the bank robbery, the tax inspector for the tax fraud. Well, there it is. You the Jury are stuck with this Blasphemy Act, and the way it unblushingly penalizes the victim and not the perpetrator of violence. There's nothing you can do about it... No, that's not quite true.

You know what happens when a case is being tried under a law that's come to be seen as unjust, or outdated, or simply unworkable from the start. Juries are reluctant to bring in a guilty verdict, judges to inflict any but the very minimum sentence. Later on, ladies and gentlemen, I shall no doubt have occasion to remind you of this—

JUDGE, furiously: No, you won't! Stop it! Any more of this and I'll hold you in contempt of court. This is a blatant invitation to the Jury to violate their duty. They must ignore it. As for you the Accused, I solemnly warn you not to repeat what you've just said, or anything like it.

After abject apologies (containing, however, no promises) I'm allowed to resume.

MYSELF: Let's get back to the Witness and his evidence. He talks about the Antichrist. The word carries two meanings. Anti implies both opposition to and substitution for. An Antichrist, accordingly, may seek to downgrade the Deity or else to upgrade himself at the Deity's expense, or very likely both at once. Indeed, if the Witness is saying anything meaningful about me, it's that I'm not just hell-bent on dragging God down to my level, but also on thrusting myself up there in His place.

Well, it should come as no surprise to the court that I plead Not Guilty on both counts. So far from dishonouring and degrading Him, I assure you that God as God is the love and the lodestone of my life, my passion, my raison d'être, before Whom I bow the deepest of bows. Not a God diluted to my taste or trimmed to my design, but an eternal astonishment and splendour, awesome, shocking, devastating. So far from seeking to substitute the creature John a-Nokes for Him, just about the chief concern of my adult life has been to put and keep that little chap in his place out there, and frustrate his ever-renewed efforts to break free and make for the Centre of things. If my Defence so far in this Trial hasn't quite persuaded you, ladies and gentlemen, that this is my aim, I'm counting on the rest of it to do so.

The Witness, of course, won't ever be persuaded. Not if I were to call the nine choirs of angels to testify on my behalf. He and his kind are, with perfect sincerity, able to brand me Antichrist only because they block their ears to my message. They make certain they don't hear a word of what I'm saying. And with good reason. If they listened it might dawn on them that it's not I but they who are the blasphemers par excellence. Instead of the God who is love and peace at the world's Centre, they put unregenerate man there—always an absurdity and a disaster. But they go much further. They put there the man who's as mad as he's cruel, a blown-up conflation of Torquemada and Stalin and Big Brother. An unholy trinity if ever there was one, Antichrist if ever he existed. This isn't religious conviction but total lack of it. It's witch-hunting fanaticism, ever growing to match and hide the ever-growing mass of doubts and contradictions and lies it masks. It's paranoia at its ugliest and sickest. It's the ultimate obscenity. And, alas, it's endemic. In 1490, Gennadius of Novgorod, a prominent ecclesiastic, wrote in all seriousness: 'A church council is needed not for debates on the faith, but in order that heretics may be judged, hanged, and burned.'

The irony of it all is that the cure of this foul disease is so very simple and ready-to-hand and effectual. It's to see that the whole wretched business isn't just a game but an illusory game, and that no one can begin to unseat the Almighty. It's to see that His Majesty is quite safe from all pretenders to His throne. It's to have the courtesy and good sense to let God be God at the Centre and man be man off-Centre. Then God is Godlike and humans are humane.

The Witness and his unquiet supporters up there in the gallery can't hear me, I know. I hope the Jury can, and that I'm getting across what I deeply feel about the absolute distinction between God and man, no less than their absolute inseparability.

COUNSEL: May I point out that the court couldn't care less about your deep feelings—so long as they stay deep? It's your disinterring and displaying them without regard for others' feelings which finds you in the dock today. In fact I'd go so far as to say that no one's objecting to your wearing your feelings on your coat-sleeve, but only to your taking your coat off and flinging it in the public eye—a most delicate organ. With serious consequences for public order. A small indication of which this court has just witnessed.

MYSELF, with some heat: Your Honour, I must complain that Counsel is abusing his position to mislead the Jury about my lifestyle. I fling nothing at the public. Who was ever forced to read my books or turn up at my meetings? What's more, I swear I've never, myself, set up any workshop or seminar or lecture or broadcast, but have simply responded to invitations. I've never pushed anything at anybody, and please God I never will. And when—as on that plane to Vancouver—I do find myself holding forth, I always say 'Don't believe anything I tell you. Try it out. Look for yourself.'

COUNSEL: All the same, people do come and hear you, and buy your books and read them and are convinced. Your message gets around and you can't wash your hands of that. And the message that this Witness gets and spreads around is that you publicly deny that Jesus Christ has come in the flesh, and this denial brands you as Antichrist.

MYSELF: This is barefaced libel, members of the Jury. So far from denying that Christ has come in the flesh, I treasure that truth beyond all others—as will become clearer than clear before this Trial ends. If I've said little so far, publicly, of God incarnate in Christ, it's not out of indifference. On the contrary. It's because he's too precious and near my heart to talk about when there's no occasion to do so. How can I convince the court of this, and so bring my Defence against this Witness and his terrorist gang—these odd disciples of Him who is the embodiment of loving-kindness—to a fitting conclusion? I confess I'm baffled. Anyway, let me try.

I believe that the noblest and truest, the deepest and most daring of all insights, is that the Majesty back of the universe is none other than self-giving Love. That He is the one whose tenderness is such that He deliberately takes on no less than all the joy and the sparkle and the incredible richness of His world, every tear and groan, all its dreadful privation and darkness and guilt—thereby gaining for it the joy that has no shadow, the peace that can be won no other way, and no less expensively. Not that I can prove this formally. No amount of argument, I don't care how penetrating or silver-tongued, can persuade anyone of the truth of the Incarnation. As a dogma it may well seem altogether absurd, to fly in the face of all the evidence. No—the proof is in the seeing of it and the living of it, in one's most intimate involvement in the saving process. One's Christing—no less. There's no other way. St Paul was merely being realistic when he exclaimed, 'Not I, but Christ that liveth in me!' Paul was out, Christ was in, and this put paid to his blasphemy. Nothing could be less anti-Christ, or more pro-Christ. The Apostle had his way of saying it. I have my way of drawing it, as you will see from Diagram No. 15.

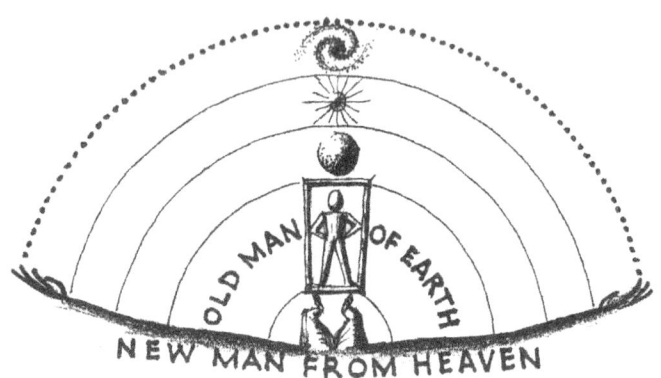

Diagram No. 15

My Defence against the accusation of being Antichrist could run to tens of thousands of words. But still it wouldn't say as much as this eight-word Self-portrait.

When I read that third person over there behind the glass as the old self-centred man, or Adam, and the First Person here in front of it as the new God-centred man, or Christ, the words of St Paul (grown so tired and hackneyed) at once spring to a new life that blows my top and bowls me over:

As in Adam all die, even so in Christ shall all *[all!]* be made alive.

The first man is of the earth, earthy; the second man is the Lord from heaven.

[That body] is sown in dishonour; [this body] is raised in glory. [That body] is sown in weakness; [this body] is raised in power. [That] is sown a natural body; [this] is raised a spiritual body.

Put ye on the Lord Jesus Christ.

If any man be in Christ, he is a new creature.

In him [Christ] dwelleth all the fullness of the Godhead bodily. And ye are complete in him.

Know ye not your own selves, how that Jesus Christ is in you?

When my seeing and my living deny these words of St Paul, I am anti-Christ. When they proclaim them I'm not just pro-Christ: I am complete in him. I'm Christed.

'The Infinite Goodness has such wide arms,' says Dante, 'that it takes in whatever turns to it.' I have a choice. Shall I embrace the little world of that little one, or the immense world of this Immense One? Can I not see that I'm incarnate in the wide-armed One here, and not in the narrow-armed one over there? Have I, or haven't I, blown my top and been bowled clean over—heels-over-no-head—by him and as him?

JUDGE: Are you telling us that, after all that backing and filling, you are a true Christian? That after all your theological toing and froing, after all that fancy East-West footwork, you line up in the end with the good old Christian creed? If so, you could have saved the court and the Prosecution a lot of time and trouble by saying so in the first place.

MYSELF: Jung says somewhere, Your Honour, that the Church is the custodian of mysteries it doesn't understand. Well, I don't flatter myself that I understand them either. Comprehension is the booby prize, anyway. Their meaning—praise the Lord!—is inexhaustible. What I do find, however, is that *I have only to LOOK to see what perfect sense these basic doctrines make.*

And now, just looking to see, I don't have to mouth a single article of faith, much less subscribe to all sorts of manifest claptrap and moonshine, in order to benefit from the underlying mysteries. Now their wonderful therapeutic power flows, unobstructed by surface doubts and reservations, and by the deep self-reproach that comes of deluding myself for the sake of the promised therapy of body and mind and spirit. The real medicine isn't to be bought at the price of double-think, or self-deceiving compromise, or any sort of humbug. Or bought at any price. It's scot-free to seers.

Of these great mysteries which are for seeing and for living rather than comprehending, I say unequivocally with Coventry Patmore:

The one secret, the greatest of all, is the doctrine of the Incarnation, regarded not as an historical event which occurred two thousand years ago, but as an event that is renewed in the body of everyone who is in the way to the fulfilment of his original destiny.

And, still more boldly, with Meister Eckhart:

People think God has become a human being only there—in His historical Incarnation—but that is not so. For God is here, in this very place, just as much incarnate as in a human being long ago. And this is why He has become a human being: that He might give birth to you as His only-begotten Son, and as no less.

Prosecution Witness No. 16

THE SUFFRAGAN BISHOP

Witness testifies that, though he doesn't know me personally, he has read three of my books, including *The Autobiography of a Simpleton*. Also he has friends who do know me and are able to confirm that the *Autobiography* paints a portrait that's reasonably true to life. That work, he maintains, is more than enough to convict me, on my own showing, of blasphemy within the meaning of the Act. Also blasphemy (the Bishop adds) as he understands it. What's so significant, what strikes him with particular force, is the degree to which my character and behaviour are at odds with my spiritual pretensions. To cultivate mystical experience without regard for ordinary righteousness (let alone saintliness)—to claim the privileges of divinity while disclaiming the responsibilities of morality—is itself immoral. It makes *mystical* a dirty word. It doesn't work. It ends miserably.

COUNSEL: Is it your view that if the Accused were anything like the saints and sages whose sayings he makes so free with, he wouldn't now be standing in the dock? That if he had put his money—the working capital of his life—where his mouth is, the charge of blasphemy wouldn't have been brought at all? Or, if brought, wouldn't stick?

WITNESS: Precisely. The history of Christendom provides plenty of examples of saints whose manifest love and humility and self-giving were such as to excuse pronouncements which, made by the unregenerate, would have got them into desperate trouble with the Inquisition. St Catherine of Genoa, for instance (whose saying 'My Me is God' the Accused squeezes of juice to the last drop—and then some), was one of the most selfless of women, a model of holiness in action; so she got away with what otherwise would have earned her a roasting. The Church didn't take that one saying of hers out of the context of her life or her teaching.

We too need to read it along with other sayings of hers to the opposite effect, clearly acknowledging her essential creatureliness.

Even more to the point is the case of Ruysbroeck. His own life, in striking contrast to the life of the wilder and more wayward mystics of his day, was blameless. And his writings largely consisted of a diatribe against them. These two pluses proved more than enough to cancel the minus of his claim 'to be God, with God, and without intermediary'. In fact, they got him beatified. Hence his official title: The Blessed Jan van Ruysbroeck.

COUNSEL: That's important, but it's history. Are you expecting the unofficial successors to the Holy Inquisition, the freelance blasphemy hunters of today, to show similar tolerance in similar cases?

WITNESS: Why not? I think that, if we looked round carefully enough, we would find the occasional saint who, though technically guilty of blasphemy, is in practice acknowledged to be innocent of the crime. One whose deeds excuse his incautious words. One whose lifestyle ensures that he isn't hauled up before a court like this.

COUNSEL: Coming back to the Accused, can you enlarge on your point that his behaviour, falling so far short of his pretensions, makes criminal nonsense of them?

WITNESS: 'By their fruits shall ye know them.' If the Accused's boasted 'seeing and being the One he really is' were genuine, it would have resulted in radical changes in the man. On his own confession in that *Autobiography* of his, it has done precious little of the kind. How good is he? What good is he? How much is he doing for suffering humanity? I can find in him no special virtue, no appreciable self-sacrifice, no caring at all for the sick and needy, nothing to suggest that he has transcended the unregenerate human condition. The only thing about him that's so special is his claim to be so special. So special that anything goes. His enlightenment appears only to darken the shadow side of him. He doesn't seem bothered a little bit by the sexual misdemeanours, the weakness in the face of temptation, the fear in the face of danger, the meanness and the anger he freely confesses to, that recur in his life story. So what? he asks. And answers, in effect:

One who looks down upon his humanity from superhuman heights isn't subject to ordinary human norms, let alone the much more exacting norms and obligations of the religious life.

COUNSEL: Suppose he countered by asking you what's the tremendous harm in this moral shortfall? And what's so unusual about it? Suppose he argued that if our private failure to live up to our ideals were a public offence, we should all find ourselves in court trying one another in turn.

WITNESS: Aside from the personal harm and lack of integrity, the social harm is very great when it comes to matters spiritual. The history of religion is full of warnings about what happens when spirituality breaks loose and goes haywire. 'Lilies that fester,' says Shakespeare, 'smell far worse than weeds.' There's no evil like the corruption of the good. It's the pâtés of the spiritual life, not its bread and marge, which get infected by this variety of salmonella poisoning. The second half of the twentieth century was littered with its casualties—super-evangelists and gurus and bhagwans and rishis and siddhas and rinpoches who, though astonishingly successful for a time, succumbed along with their followers to the bug. In one way or another the behaviour of master and disciples fell scandalously short of that of the unsaved and unenlightened common man. Be warned! Let your back hair down, do what the devil you like, don't give a damn for public opinion, aspire to divinity on the cheap—making for Godhood by this or that fast and easy route—and sooner rather than later you will find yourself sinking beneath all decent humanhood into well-deserved disgrace and eventual oblivion.

COUNSEL: Presumably well aware of all this, the Accused never tires of telling us that he's no one's guru, is an un-teacher with no ashram and no organization. And, of course, no Ten Commandments. All he does is run a do-it-yourself store stocked with cheap gadgetry for setting the customer up as his own pocket bhagwan, rishi, what have you.

WITNESS: Yes, of course. He's no fool. The smartest way of becoming a super-guru is to pour contempt on the whole idea of guruship. And the smartest way of propagating blasphemy is cuckoo-fashion, by laying your eggs in others' nests without their noticing. It saves you so much bother. But the social damage is great. It threatens to send a large proportion of the population cuckoo.

Defence: **The Apple and the Apple Tree**

MYSELF: For three reasons I have no questions to put to the Witness. First, because Counsel has kindly put them for me. Second, because I agree with so many of the Bishop's answers. Third, because he and I are nevertheless in such different lines of business that cross-questioning is bound to find us at cross-purposes over the remaining answers.

He's a fruit merchant. I'm an arboriculturist. He wants to know about the apples, whether they are sound and sweet and abundant. I want to know about the tree. Is it a Cox's Orange, or a Bramley, or an ungrafted crab, or perhaps not an apple tree at all? I say, first things first: it's premature to judge before you know what you're judging. This should be the most obvious thing in the world, but generally it's the least obvious. The medieval courts that tried animals for immorality were abominable and absurd. But were they much more so than the court that's trying me now? Justice and good sense say that, before you decide what reactions are fitting, you ask: 'Reactions by whom, to what?' Facts come before judgements upon them, what's so before what ought to be so. The crucial question my life poses isn't 'How shall I behave?' but 'Who's behaving?' Get the latter right, and the former will come right of itself. Try to settle the former without reference to the latter, and all will go wrong. The trouble with this court isn't its case against me but the unexamined presuppositions on which its case rests. Assumptions it refuses to go into, and that I insist on going into. This Trial is about the true identity of the Accused—and therefore of his accusers, who alas regard the whole question of identity as closed and padlocked. Not for admitting, let alone examining.

JUDGE, at work with his gavel: I'm sick and tired of this contempt for the court and its justice. Besides, what are all these witnesses for but to establish your identity—as all too human?

MYSELF: Your Honour, if a thousand witnesses were called, not one of them would be in a position to establish anything of the sort. I estimate the distance between the witness-box over there and the dock here at twenty feet. That box is a perfect place for going into *what I look like from there,* but no good at all for going into *what I am here.* There, the Witness picks up one of my countless regional appearances. Here, I am the Central Reality they are appearances of. And the difference between these two views of me is in all respects immense. With the greatest possible respect, Your Honour, I say that you and I are similarly placed *vis-à-vis* each other. Here, rather more than twenty feet from your bench, I'm perfectly placed for telling you how the Judge is doing; right there, on that bench at no distance from yourself, you are perfectly placed for telling me Who is putting on this Judge-impersonation. Only you can say, because only you, coinciding with yourself, have the requisite inside information.

COUNSEL: Lecturing the court is bad enough, lecturing the Judge is too much. And does you no good. Certainly it doesn't hide the fact that you are sidestepping the point of the Witness's testimony, to the effect that you don't live up to your pretensions. Not by a million miles you don't! His contention is that what you do reveals who you are, namely John a-Nokes. We know Mr John a-Nokes by his fruits. A somewhat sparse and blighted crop—to say the least.

MYSELF: Precisely. I couldn't have put it better myself. By his fruits—a fairly poor crop—shall you and I know that Nokes fellow. What other sort could we expect from him?

Like the Bishop, I draw a sharp line between the false mystic—I hate the word mystic, but can't find a better—the false mystic, whose fruits, though showy, turn out to be indigestible if not nauseous, and the true mystic, whose fruits, though often disclaimed and hardly visible at all, turn out to be wholesome. Well, what is the deciding factor between these two? How can we guard against spirituality going to the devil? I'll tell you how. In effect, the false mystic says, 'Never mind the facts, never mind what I am, let's see what I get up to.' In effect, the true mystic says, 'First let me see what I am, then see what I get up to.' I say: counter bedevilment by telling the truth. Truth is the key, the watchword, the safeguard, the only insurance policy against spiritual disaster. The given truth, the brutal truth, always the truth.

JUDGE: That sounds very fine, but *what is truth?*

An incoherent shouting—something about a Judaean Governor—from the public gallery, but not coming from the friends of the New

Apocalyptic. An attempt to locate the offender, with a view to ejecting him from the court, fails... Order is restored...

MYSELF: The truth is God's truth. Telling God's truth gets us into trouble—and sets us free. God's truth is what each of us is as First Person Singular, present tense. God's truth is what each of us sees when he dares to look down and in at himself, and take seriously what he finds. God's truth is the vision of the One at the Centre of things, the One who has flung wide his arms and blown his top and been bowled clean over, heels over no-head. God's truth, the saving truth, is the behaviour that flows from that blessed vision.

Will Your Honour, and the ladies and gentlemen of the Jury, please turn again to Diagram No. 15 [see Witness 15 The New Apocalyptic].

Let me remind you: at the bottom of the picture I have drawn what you are as First Person; and, further up the picture, what you look like as second/third person over there in the mirror, and in the experience of your observers. Notice how, when that little one spreads his little arms, they take in his little world. And how when you, the Big One, spread your great arms, they take in the great world... Please spread your arms now and, looking straight ahead, see how they really do embrace the wide, wide world. Please... [Two jury members comply. The others look embarrassed or stare stonily ahead...] You want to grant me a fair Trial, surely? To give me the consideration you would give to a Defending Counsel if I had one. I know you are rather close together for this experiment, but some overlapping of arms won't obscure my point—which is that, *on present evidence,* your left hand is as far from your right as East is from West. That you really are embracing the world... [With some more coaxing the remaining ten Jurypersons comply—more or less reluctantly.]

Those false mystics we were talking about are a proud lot. They refuse to lower their sights, refuse to *bow deeply* before the evidence. They are uppity, so darned uppish that they never make the downward shift from the human owner of those little arms to the Divine Owner of these great arms—the arms of the God Who embraces and loves His world. Or, if they do find themselves on the Bottom Line, there's no question of their bottoming out. They make very sure it's the launching pad from which they take off upwards to dominate the scene, and not sideways to enfold it.

JUDGE: All this is—what shall I call it?—so very *physical*. The Witness was speaking about morality.

MYSELF: I grant, Your Honour, that seeing oneself as embracing the world, and feeling the love behind that gesture and going on to act accordingly, aren't at all the same thing. Nevertheless, *given half a chance, the first grows into the second and the third.* This takes time and proceeds invisibly. But it isn't any kind of achievement. It's awaking to the infinite merits of the Big One, not cultivating the paltry or non-existent merits of the little one. In fact, the little one seems, in the ever brighter light shed by the Big One, to get worse as time goes on! I know! I promise the Bishop that Jack's an even more deplorable piece of work than he—the Bishop—imagines. I have inside information to that effect. All his righteousnesses are as filthy rags.

Quite the most specious rag is the banner with the strange device *Excelsior!* Lofty-minded and aspiring, the false mystic takes the way of gain and not loss, of living it up spiritually, of vainly trying to attain to the peak where he's topping and the tops, where at last he tops in and is as far as possible from the valley where he bottoms out. The true mystic, on the other hand, submits to the fact that on the Bottom Line (so brilliantly visible as the place where his shirt fades into the Void) he finds, if only he will bow low enough, his Reality, his Source, his only Resource, his Root. Staying with that Root, caring for that Root, he enjoys in due course its fruits—fruits that are real, large, deliciously sweet, and abundant. In stark contrast to Excelsior—up and away, with head bloody but unbowed, and craning ever upwards—mounting to ever more precarious and barren heights. Fruitless, to say the least, is his attempt to cultivate personal virtue by distancing himself from the Root of all virtue, his refusal to bow before the evidence of his Essential Nature and Source.

Only let me bow low enough and I will come upon all I need. Here, at the very bottom of the world picture, lurks the One who suddenly appears where and when I as suddenly disappear. The One who is I—yet not I, but the One who lives in me. The Eternal Pantocrator whose fruits aren't just the juiciest in the world, but are the world itself.

COUNSEL: It doesn't say much for your blasphemous doctrine that it's a farrago of inconsistencies. Half the time you're claiming a bumper fruit crop, the other half a rotten one. Or is it none at all?

MYSELF: I'll let Julian of Norwich answer for me: 'God is all that

The Suffragan Bishop

is good, and the goodness that all things have is He.' I'm no saint, but ask any saint how righteous he is, and it's sinnerhood and not sainthood that he'll claim. Even his Master wouldn't let people call him good. As I keep telling you.

It's you, Sir Gerald, who are confused. The truth is so simple. Look and *see*. 'We abide in darkness,' says St Bernard, 'so long as we walk in belief and not in beholding. The righteous, living in belief, live in shadow.' What you are—in and for yourself, in your First-Person capacity—is, precisely, Capacity. Visibly lacking all fruit of your own, you provide unlimited shelving for others' fruit. Accordingly it's no secret that, if you want to know what to think of someone, ask him what he thinks of the folk around him. He's good to the extent that he finds them good. And this makes perfect sense. As for Who he really, really is, he's the Root, and roots as such are barren. God as His world is orchard on orchard, ripe with every conceivable sort of choice and delicious fruit. But God as Himself, intrinsically—God as the Abyss—is shot of everything He gives rise to. To be its Origin is to be its Absence. None is so poor as He. Only He is low enough and humble enough and simple enough and nothing enough to come up with *everything*.

Members of the jury, one picture, according to an ancient Chinese proverb, is worth a thousand words. I beg you to do two things. Look yet again at our Diagram No. 15. Look *out* at its message. And then, to bring that message home, look *down* at yourself, at your own Bottom Line or Ground, and you'll see with unmatched clarity the Place where what you look like flips over into What you really,

really are. And where You as Root start to quicken and burgeon and blossom and bear fruit as the world itself, eternally.

By Jack's fruits shall you know Jack. By Your fruits shall you know Yourself.

The following excerpts—Hindu, Buddhist and Christian, in that order—make good sense when applied to Yourself the First Person, none at all when applied to yourself the third person, in isolation from that First Person.

Who can prohibit that great-souled one, who knows this entire universe to be the Self alone, from living as he pleases?

Ashtavakra Samhita

His actions will permit of no external standard of judgement. So long as they are the inevitable outflow of his Inner Life, they are good, even holy.

D. T. Suzuki

Supreme Enlightenment is realizing there is not the slightest thing to be attained.

Diamond Sutra

Into any man who is brought low God pours His whole Self in all His might, so utterly that neither of His life, His being, nor His nature, nay, nor of His perfect Godhead, does He keep aught back. He empties out the whole thereof as fruits into that man who in abandonment to God assumes the lowest place.

Eckhart

Verily, verily, I say unto you, Except a corn of wheat fall into the ground and die, it abideth alone: but if it die, it bringeth forth much fruit.

Jesus

Love God, and do what you will.

St Augustine

Prosecution Witness No. 17

THE ATHEIST

Witness testifies that he has known me since childhood. We were at school together. Since then we've been friendly rather than friends, running into each other quite often and swapping news—if not views. Yes, he knows me well.

COUNSEL: On the subject of views, how do you see the Accused's notorious announcement to the world that really and truly he isn't John a-Nokes at all, but his Creator? How far does what you know of him match up to such a claim?

WITNESS: Match up, or match down? I guess that, so far, your witnesses have said that Jack's not *good* enough to be the Creator of the world. I say he's not *bad* enough! I say he's doing himself a gross injustice!

COUNSEL: Have a care not to commit blasphemy yourself!

WITNESS: This is hard to believe! You serve a subpoena on me, forcing me to come here and testify against a man I've always liked. You make me swear to tell the truth as I see it. I start doing just that, and you as good as accuse me of committing a crime! A capital crime, at that! I appeal to the judge.

JUDGE: As a Witness, you may count on a degree of privilege. But I advise you to watch your language and avoid giving unnecessary offence.

COUNSEL: Obliged to Your Honour. Witness, please continue, bearing in mind what the Judge says.

WITNESS: I was about to tell the court what Jack—the Accused—is really like. Certainly he's no saint, and in his youth did his share of bad things along with the rest of us. But he's become one of the kindest people I know. When I say he wouldn't hurt a fly, I mean it literally. He'll go to great lengths to rescue spiders from the bath-tub and the kitchen sink and put them in a nice safe place in the garden. I've seen him distressed to find he'd trodden on some creepy-crawly. He has a hard job chucking out a moribund house-plant he's lived with for a year or two. As for humans, while he doesn't enjoy being cheated or ridiculed by them any more than you or I do, and is apt to be careful to the point of meanness in little matters, in big matters he's over-generous and very forgiving. If you're in trouble, you'll find it easier to relieve Jack of fifty thousand pounds than of fifty. Others' hurt is his hurt. He can't insulate himself from their pain and their joy. He really likes people. He even admires politicians… I tell you, this man—for all his many faults—has the warmest of hearts. I suppose I'm biased in his favour. If I weren't, I guess I'd call him a *sucker*.

JUDGE: The Jury will want to know what all this—however edifying—has to do with the crime the Accused is charged with. Many murderers have been kind to animals, many violent thieves have been good and loyal friends, but this hasn't helped their Defence one little bit. Blasphemers, for all I know, may be model husbands and fathers and reeking with social charm, but they are blasphemers.

WITNESS: If blasphemy is getting way above yourself and altogether too big for your human boots, if it's publicly pretending to be far better than you are, then the Accused is certainly no blasphemer. Very much to the contrary. In claiming to be the Creator of a world like this, he's making himself out to be a monster, subhuman and not superhuman. As I say, he's putting himself down, doing himself a great injustice.

COUNSEL: I must repeat my warning...

WITNESS: All I'm doing is to point out what every schoolboy knows—or at least what every schoolboy mugging up his biology should know. We moan about infant mortality as if it were unnatural. In fact, survival to maturity is a miracle. What earthly chance of making it has the new-born cod, or garden spider? Or, come to that, the human sperm? Need I remind you about Nature red in tooth and claw, about life mercilessly preying on life, about the immemorial victory of might over right, about the hideous cruelty and needless pain? I'm talking of what's blatantly on show, there for everyone with half an eye to see and shudder at. But think of the filthy dirty tricks that darling Mother Nature secretly descends to. Her hordes of fifth-columnists who, not content with worming their way into liver and lights, can go so far as to invade eye and brain? I'm not thinking of the occasional parasite we might expect to find battening on things bright and beautiful, but of horrors—fearsomely armed with hooks and suckers—that are as normal as the creatures they batten on. Every bird that cleaves the airy way—*pace* William Blake—is an immense world of ticks and worms and cysts, of flukes that are no fluke at all. Many sea creatures are even worse off. Sacculina is a fiend in the form of a bag: attaching itself to the underbelly of a crab, it sends branching suckers into every part of the body of its still-living host. Tell me, what has the crab done to deserve this punishment? And so on, and on, and on. The way Life bugs and infests itself is beyond belief:

And then, of course, there's the human condition. Babies are born to madness, babies are born to cancer, countless babies are at this moment in agony with a hundred horrible afflictions. Look at the outrageously unjust hand-out of Life's prizes and penalties—at the age-old and built-in pains and depravities which human nature is stuck with, that we are all victims of. If we are built to a design, the designer's either demented or a sadist.

John a-Nokes—bless his heart!—believes in and trusts a Creator God. So much so that, in his thinking and speaking, he actually identities himself with this Being. Tirelessly and in public, enraging the pious. But I'm glad to say that in his feeling and behaviour he puts light-years between himself and a God who could be responsible for such a universe.

COUNSEL: Are you saying that there *is* a God—a Devil of a God according to you—at whose door all these abominations must be laid? Or are you saying that an Entity so malevolent is unthinkable? That the only excuse for God is that He doesn't exist? In other words, are you one of those who maintain that the whole show is an accidental and mindless concatenation of particles, a universe that's not so much indifferent to the human values it chances to come up with as nicely calculated to put them down?

WITNESS: I plump for the mindless concatenation. After all, living matter in the universe is as rare and as irrelevant as disposable hypodermic needles in haystacks. Besides, the mindless concatenation is far less horrible than the alternative, which is a devilish contraption masterminded by the very Devil.

COUNSEL: So let's get this clear. You have arrived at exactly the same two conclusions as the other witnesses, but from the opposite direction—the first conclusion being that the Accused publicly and scandalously insists that he is the Almighty, the second being that he's lying, and in fact he isn't the Almighty, not by a million miles. Am I right?

WITNESS: Well, I meant to say...

COUNSEL: Yes, or no?

WITNESS: Yes, but...

COUNSEL: Make up your mind.

WITNESS: Yes.

COUNSEL: Jury, please note. The point isn't *how* this Witness arrives at those two conclusions which, taken together, establish the Accused's guilt, but that he does so. If he does so without intention and without malice, that only lends weight to his testimony.

Defence: **The Night-flowering Cactus**

I'm in two minds whether to let the Witness go, or to detain him for cross-examination. With a friend like this in court, who needs enemies? His flattery promises to do me as much harm as the censure of other witnesses. On balance, I decide to see how far I can win this old schoolfellow over to my side. Thereby, perhaps, winning over the odd juryperson.

MYSELF: I can't let you get away with that caricature of God and His world. It's only fair that the Jury should discover how it stands up to examination. You and I have never discussed your atheism before. But now it's necessary for my Defence to do so. May I assume—seeing that my life is at stake and that, so far and at a guess, you've only increased the odds against it—you will open yourself to persuasion?

WITNESS: Of course. Fire away.

MYSELF: I don't say your story *lies* about the facts, but that it selects them. By judicious picking and choosing, a far stronger case can and often has been made for co-operation in Nature than for cutthroat competition, for mutual aid than for exploitation. I wish I had time to tell the court about the marvellously intricate and improbable ways in which ruthlessly self-seeking creatures unwittingly support and promote the well-being of other equally ruthless and self-seeking creatures. A fast-evolving species probably owes more to its enemies than to its friends. Believe it or not, the organic unity of the myriads of creatures that constitute Life is at least as complete as the organic unity of the myriads of cells that constitute the individual life-form. In fact, John a-Nokes is less a whole than the Biosphere is, and the Biosphere is less a whole than the Cosmos is. Only God's world, only God as His world, is *One*. All lesser things are incomplete, not self-contained, not all there, largely out of sight, and therefore not to be taken at face value. Only the Whole is *whole*.

Only the Whole of things is in a position to appreciate itself in its unity, from the No-thing at its Centre. Which position is your position—exactly where you are and what you are right now as First Person Singular. Lucky you!

Are you with me, so far?

WITNESS: I'm trailing along. But I can't do with your God. That name has for me so many bad associations...

MYSELF: Then call Him Nobodaddy. He won't mind a little bit.

Next, let's look at the problem of the suffering in His world—the inside story of God's aches and pains, you could say. There exists a great deal of suffering, no doubt, but not of the kind and intensity we project on to creatures whose levels of organization and nervous systems are very different from ours. Why, even we humans, supersensitive though we are as a rule, can—in accidents, in rapture, when caught up in some all-absorbing adventure, or simply when we've had a bellyful of it—feel no pain at all, though the severest of injuries is being inflicted on the body. Again, you go on about how abominably creatures behave, devouring each other like that, openly or secretly. At least as reasonably you could see their eating and being eaten as the sincerest exchange of compliments imaginable. Or even as the ultimate lovemaking. In the bedroom John says he loves Mary so much he *could* eat her, and Mary says she loves John so much she *could* eat him. Hypothetical stuff! Post-coitum hungry, they go to the kitchen, where both love sole so much they *do* eat sole—*meunière*. And love chicken so much they *do* eat chicken—*cacciatore*. Nothing hypothetical here! John and Mary's love for the fish and the fowl is such that they turn them into John and Mary. Probably they don't say grace before the meal, but if they do it's more likely to be about Supernature and Holy Communion than about Nature red in tooth and claw.

Are you still with me?

WITNESS: Still plodding along, Jack. Not that I care for your terminology.

COUNSEL: The Jury certainly isn't with you, whatever your terminology. What the blazes have these bed-and-board games to do with the crime of blasphemy?

MYSELF: A great deal. I'm not digressing at all. In effect, the charge is that I'm a mere fragment of the Whole pretending to be the Whole, thereby upsetting other mere fragments. My Defence is that this is ridiculous, at best so partial a truth that it amounts to a thundering great lie. I'm in the middle of proving this, and ask leave to proceed...

Back, then, to the Witness for the Prosecution—to you my old school-buddy, who I'm trying to turn into a Witness for the Defence. Let's take next your point about the immense bulk of the inanimate stuff making up the universe, in contrast to the minuteness of the animate. You seem to be saying that the rarity of bright needles of life, in this inane and lustreless haystack of haystacks, can only mean they are irrelevant, a fluke and of no consequence—and neither sharp nor bright. Such valuation by volume is vulgar, stupid, not worth a second thought. It makes the Colosseum millions of times more interesting than the Gonzaga Cameo, and Niagara billions of times more beautiful than a dewdrop afire in the low sun of morning.

If small is beautiful, Life in the universe is exquisite. All the more exquisite for shining out against such a vast and sombre backcloth.

Much the same is true of valuation by time-span. In the Himalayas there grows a cactus, dingy and spiky and unpleasant as only cactuses can be, a disgrace and a byword among weeds. But on one night in the year it puts forth a dream of a flower, a single blossom, bright with half the rainbow, scented and wonderfully complicated. In the morning, the dream over, nothing's left of that flower but a memory and a mess. But no longer do you dismiss that cactus as a weed. Nor do you half-dismiss it as an unlovely old thing that's privileged on rare occasions briefly to play host to a lovely new thing. Oh, no! Never mind how huge and commonplace and worn the plant, and how tiny and rare and brief the flower, the plant is from now on what all along it has been—a *flowering* plant. By the same token, that caterpillar is no mere worm-on-legs but a red admiral in mufti, that seed is no mere seed but mesembryanthemum stage one, that fertilized egg is no mere cell but Leonardo da Vinci starting off modestly. When it comes to putting a value on the small-scale and familiar lives around us, we are reasonably generous and generously reasonable. We judge the hero by what earned him his medal, the coarsest creature by its finest hour, the muck-fed root by the damask rose.

And so it should be—but by God it isn't!—with this tragically undervalued and abused universe of His. Tricked by its size and our own double standards, we are most unreasonable and ungenerous where we need to be most reasonable and generous. Blasphemers all, we demean God's world to the limit. Let it blossom, and we dismiss the flower as an accident and an alien, a cut flower! Let it put forth a limb, and we amputate the limb, thus proving the body dead! But why not admit that this great Organism, too, is for judging by its flower rather than its seed and root? For judging, in fact, by seed and root and flower and fruit as a strictly indivisible Whole? Viewed thus realistically, all is transformed in an instant. A coarse and colourless universe capable of coming up with Botticelli's *Birth of Venus* isn't a coarse and colourless universe at all. A silent and tight-lipped universe that gets around to singing 'O Isis und Osiris' is a full-throated singing universe. A poker-faced universe that has Jeeves and Bertie Wooster and Gussie Fink-Nottle up its sleeve is a universe that's laughing up its sleeve. A heartless universe, which in the fullness of time gives rise to the tender and self-giving love of a Jesus of Nazareth, has at last bared its heart.

COUNSEL: Where is this *mélange* of poetry and theology and cosmology getting us? The Blasphemy Act couldn't care less about your ecstasies concerning the relationship between man and the world and God. Even when publicly ventilated, they are your own affair and no concern of this court—so long as they don't outrage people who hold contrary opinions, bringing what they hold sacred into contempt and threatening public disorder.

MYSELF: I was just coming to the outrageous and disorderly part. Brace yourself for what you'll see as scandalous enough to put me in mortal danger, and what I see as plain horse-sense.

Gertrude Stein's 'Rose is a rose is a rose is a rose', though it sounds like detection of the obvious pushed somewhat far, is really nonsense.

The rose is not a rose, not a rose, not a rose. It's damn all without the rose-bush and everything the rose-bush needs to be itself- which is plenty. It's damn all without leaves and stem and root and humus and air and rain and sunlight, and so on *ad infinitum*. It's damn all without the All. To tell the truth, it's nothing less than the universe budding and blossoming, this coarse old universe come to a head—the handsomest of heads—roseate and rose-scented. Some rose, this! I'm in awe of this rose of all the world! But not to the extent of letting a mere plant outsmart me. What goes for the rose goes for me. I'm *not* John a-Nokes, *not* John a-Nokes, *not* John a-Nokes. I'm damn all without what it takes to be John a-Nokes, without the rest of him, which is to say without the rest of things. For me to pretend that I'm John a-Nokes all present and complete as that little fellow—as that unviable fragment which just for the sake of convenience is called John a-Nokes—is pride and poppycock and blasphemy. On the other hand, to admit that I feature as John a-Nokes only by courtesy of the whole of him—by courtesy of the Whole, of the One I really am—is humility and good sense and the medicine for blasphemy. God is flowering around here as John a-Nokes. Also flowering very prettily on the Jury benches. Where *isn't* He flowering?

And, of course, the more lofty and fragrant the blossom, the more hushed up are its lowly origins. The rose's barbed stem and yucky root are far less *sub rosa* than Jack's beanstalk.

COUNSEL: These contorted witticisms and paradoxes only prove you guilty. What's the point of trying to win the Witness over to the side of the Defence, now that you have yet once more come over to the side of the Prosecution and condemned yourself out of your own mouth? Blooming in the dock is the flower of God—the flower of all the world—it says! No shrinking violet this, born to blush unseen! It's making sure it's plucked before its time!

Incidentally, have you finished with the Witness?

MYSELF: Not quite. My business with him, as with all of you throughout this Trial, is perfectly sober and serious and simple. It is to arrive at and speak the truth about my intrinsic Nature. It's the truth that sets me free from this court's power over me. Do your worst. I can't afford to buy from you a verdict of Not Guilty at the cost of a single lie.

Back, then, to you, my atheist friend—whether you amount to a Witness for the Prosecution or for the Defence, I don't much care. Tell me, does my insistence on the unity of the rose and the rose-bush and the rose-root and the rose-earth and the rose-world make sense to you?

WITNESS: Good sense, bad roses. You seem to forget that this marvellous floribunda universe-bush of yours sports such blossoms as Gilles de Rais and the Marquis de Sade and Aleister Crowley. To say nothing of Julius Streicher and Caligula and Ivan the Terrible and Jack the Ripper. Viewing the bush from near or far, through rose-tinted or dark glasses, does nothing to prune its unwanted growth or cure its diseases, much less change its species. Facts are facts are facts are facts. And many are appalling facts.

MYSELF: Facts aren't fixtures. The facts of one level are the lies of the next. It just isn't true that the object stays the same no matter where it's seen from. Distance is God's magic wand and absolute wizardry. Zooming into me is zooming into wonderland. A yard and a second are enough to turn this naughty man into an Eden of innocent creatures, and a further fraction of an inch and of a second are more than enough to kill them stone dead.

Viewed from all viewpoints and at all distances, I am as object infinite in my variety, the cosmic what-have-you. How different from myself viewed by myself from no distance, viewed as Subject! Here, I'm forever one and the same. Here and now I'm Unique, the One Indivisible Awareness which is neither a thing, nor inside any thing, nor the property of any thing. On the contrary, all things are in It and from It and for It. It is Myself as the Root of my root, Myself as the First Person Singular present tense, Myself as that One Seer and One Hearer and One Consciousness in all beings, spoken of by the Upanishads.

Please turn to Diagram No. 16.

Diagram 16a shows a deluded me, perversely mistaking that pinhead for the seat and centre of my consciousness, and the vantage point from which I survey the world. It shows an object masquerading as the Subject, a third person playing First Person. It shows a conceited rose posturing as its own Root. It shows me *getting above myself* by a yard—and I mean this quite literally. It shows me blaspheming like mad. Yet such is the human condition, so endemic is this fallacy of misplaced consciousness, that it's rarely challenged.

16a

16b

Diagram No. 16

The result is a world mis-seen through and through, a dream world becoming a nightmare world, a gigantic and self-perpetuating social fiction. A fiction that is nevertheless factual enough to foul up God's world from beginning to end.

Diagram 16b shows His world put to rights by consciously viewing it from the only place it can be viewed from anyway—from the Centre of it all, from the Origin of it all, from the Receptacle of it all. Here is the God's-eye view of His world as very good, in every sort of contrast to that illusory man's-eye view of it as now so-so, now a shambles, now a disaster area.

I hope these two pictures not only show clearly the shift from the blasphemer's viewpoint to the non-blasphemer's, but also suggest how different their two worlds have to be.

WITNESS: But they tell me nothing about what happens in my day-to-day experience. I can't picture what difference this shift in viewpoint makes to the view—if any.

MYSELF: The consequences are many and radical and heartfelt. They are discovered by making the shift and staying shifted, not by discussing it. What I can do for your encouragement, however, is to outline the shape of three major results:

(1) The false or man's-eye view (16a) inflicts a near-mortal wound on the world, cleaving it into one part called 'me' and another called 'not-me', into a small viewing thing here and a big viewed thing there. No wonder there's a lot of blood about! Only God can heal such a wound, an injury so serious that it will yield only to the most drastic of treatments by the Master Physician. He reduces me to

No-thing, then reconstitutes me as the Whole of things. Thus most graciously He arranges that I become the One for whom the world is intact because He claims not a particle of it for Himself, because He vanishes in its favour, because He dies for it. Only as Him here am I all there, and quite compos mentis, and seeing things as they are.

(2) The second difference is linked with the first. On the one hand is my false or man's-eye view of a world that I'm up against, that I'm not responsible for, that I wash my hands of. Of a world much of which I don't like, and some of which I loathe—for example, those deplorable characters we mentioned. Ivan the Terrible is—terrible, and that's that. On the other hand is my true or God's-eye view of a world that I am, that I'm altogether responsible for. It's not that I like it, but that I love it, for the simple reason that one has to love oneself. Be sure of this: a loved and died-for world is altogether different from 'the same world' unloved, un-died-for, feared, hated. And be sure of this too: only self-giving love is clear-eyed enough, realistic and practical enough, to see through the world's evil to the underlying goodness. The truly *evil* evil isn't on the world's side and intrinsic but on my side and imposed: it is the harm I do to it by washing my hands of it. Cease disclaiming responsibility, and the change is immediate and profound. This God's-eye view is blind to no defect and indifferent to no tear, nevertheless it transforms the whole scene. Another Light bathes the world, a saving Radiance which no creature, however lovely, can call its own, or however repulsive can quench. Somehow all is embraced, loved, and—yes, in spite of everything—*endorsed!* When God's in His heaven here, all's right

with the world over there. My anxious questioning ceases. I have no more complaints.

(3) The third consequence of the shift to my true Centre is that I gain access to hitherto unavailable energies. No longer do I comfortably sit back, denying responsibility for the evil and doing nothing about it. Quite the contrary. In so far as I rest in this central Perfection, I tap the will and the drive to combat, in my own peculiar one-off way, its opposite out there. True seers are workers, not drones. Or clones. Paradoxically, it's because the war's already won here, where we're One and the Same and there's Nothing to do, that we can put our whole heart into the battle out there, where we're many and all different and there's everything to do.

But what's the good of *talking about* this world-transforming shift of viewpoint without *making* the shift, and going on to stay shifted? How to do just that? By cultivating the habit of *seeing* that in fact it's no shift at all, but simply being where you were all along, at the world's Centre. Look out now at a world from which nothing has been subtracted, and in at its Viewer from whom *everything* has been subtracted, the Viewer who has died for and died into the Viewed. Simultaneously take in that absolute fullness and this absolute emptiness, and you are healed with God's healing. Instantly you are back where you have always been, at the Heart of things, the Heart which is open-hearted enough to embrace and transform by love the most unlovable of its objects—at the undying Heart of even the most ephemeral of creatures.

Diagram No. 17

Diagram No. 17 shows you exactly what to do.

Well, friend of my youth, your testimony has turned out to be most helpful after all. Thank you. You may stand down. [He goes, and I address the Jury.]

Listen now to the testimony of four who spoke from the Heart, for and as that Heart:

Genuine seekers of God take nothing, good or bad, from any creature, but all from God alone.

Eckhart

There is and can be but one happiness and one misery. The one misery is nature and creature left to itself, the one happiness is the Life, the Light, the Spirit of God, manifested in nature and creature.

William Law

Truly there are two worlds. One was made by God, the other by men... Leave the one that you may enjoy the other.

Traherne

When the universe is perceived apart from Brahman, that perception is false and illusory.

Ramana Maharshi

COUNSEL: A word in the ear of the Jury, at the conclusion of this conducted Nokes's tour of the cosmos. Just how many times was it implied or stated outright, in the course of it, that the Accused wasn't so much our very human guide as the Divine Impresario responsible for putting on the whole show? In the last half-hour alone, we have heard enough blaspheming to convict him many times over of the crime he's charged with.

MYSELF: Always you hear the words and miss the meaning. They might be in Pushtu or Oigob for all the sense you extract from them. The most charitable explanation I can think of is that Counsel is putting on an act, displaying his histrionic skill rather than his forensic skill. That (in other words) this isn't a bona fide trial but a Show Trial, in which his real but secret brief isn't just to play to the gallery, but *as* the gallery at its stupidest. Actually to play the part of—and echo in Oxford English—the most dim-witted and prejudiced members of the population, to the bitter end.

Bitter end for me. For this distinguished King's Counsellor a sweet refresher on the long and dusty road to the Woolsack—

JUDGE: Stop it! I won't tolerate personal abuse in this court. Apologize to Counsel.

MYSELF: What for, Your Honour? I think what I said was fair, even complimentary...

COUNSEL, suddenly all magnanimous: Oh, for God's sake let it pass...

Prosecution Witness No. 18

THE DEVOTEE

In response to Counsel's questioning, Witness introduces herself.
WITNESS: My name in religion is Sister Marie-Louise. I'm a founder member of a community with branches in this country and overseas. I don't know how many of us there are, and if I did I wouldn't be allowed to tell you. We hold all things in common. Some of us contribute by going out and earning a living in the normal way, in which case the whole of our earnings goes into the communal purse. Others of us look after the garden, do the cooking and cleaning, and so on. We all meet daily for meditation and study. As you see, we wear a distinctive habit.

COUNSEL: What do you study and meditate on? What are your beliefs?

WITNESS: We believe in the Messiah Maitreya, meditate on him, study his words, try to live according to his teachings. As subjects of his kingdom—which has already come—we do everything we can to bring that kingdom into power.

COUNSEL: Who is this Messiah Maitreya?

WITNESS: Essentially he's a mysterious Being who defies description. His name indicates that he brings together in one person two traditional figures. As Maitreya, he's the latest incarnation of the eternal Buddha, come to enlighten humankind at the end of the Kali Yuga, or Dark Age. As the Messiah, he's the Risen Lord who has returned to the world unannounced at the close of the Second Millennium, to bring in the Third Millennium and the reign of love and peace. Also he's the Great Rishi, who has for centuries been biding his time in the remotest Himalayas, and has now come forth to save the world from itself. These three, and other exalted Beings, are united in our blessed Master.

COUNSEL: What is the relationship between him and Almighty God, in your opinion?

WITNESS: No relationship. He *is* Almighty God!

COUNSEL: And the members of your community, including yourself? Are you, too, deified?

WITNESS: Oh, no! He's absolutely unique. He's God. We are God's devotees, and on quite another level. The basis of our community is total surrender to him. Our aim is never to forget him, to do everything for him, to obey his every wish. It is this submission to our Master that gives us peace and joy and holds us together and gives us our reason for living.

COUNSEL: I come now to the big question. Is this deity a real person, living and visible, incarnate in this world as you and I are? Or is he a spiritual presence, an ideal, real in your eyes but not in mine and the Jury's?

WITNESS: That's the wonderful thing! We are immensely privileged to be living at this moment. He has chosen this time in history to descend into our world to save us all, and for that purpose has taken on mortal flesh and blood.

COUNSEL: So this Messiah Maitreya of yours, this God who reveals himself in human form, is living somewhere on Earth at this moment, doing the things that people do—eating and drinking, walking and talking, sleeping and waking, living and dying—but doing so incognito? Unrecognized by us, recognized by you?

WITNESS: Exactly.

COUNSEL: Do you happen to know where he is for sure, right now?

WITNESS, almost inaudibly: Indeed I do! [A long pause...]

COUNSEL, very slowly: I must ask you to tell the court exactly where he is.

WITNESS, leaning far forward, clutching the rail of the box and pointing a trembling finger, whispers: *There! In the dock!*

The storm breaks. The court has been holding its breath in anticipation of this—a shock all the more shocking because it has been half expected... A fight starts in the public gallery. Counsel collapses on to his bench, as if he hadn't all along known what was coming. The Jury starts whispering excitedly. The judge bangs away with his hammer, shouting for order...

Failing, he adjourns the court for twenty minutes...

An uneasy calm restored, the court is in session again. But the atmosphere is very quiet and very different. As if the New Bailey, suddenly cut off from the outside world, had drifted into a new dimension of space-time.

COUNSEL, with a frog in his throat, resumes his examination of the Witness: God is omnipotent. The personage in the dock is—to say the least—somewhat hamstrung at the moment. Doesn't the fact that your Master is a prisoner, on trial for his life, shake your confidence in him a little?

WITNESS: Not at all! If he wished, he could vanish from your midst instantly. Or even destroy you, all by calling fire down from heaven. He has his reasons for letting you sit in judgement on him.

COUNSEL: And if he's found guilty, and condemned to death?

WITNESS: The world has no power over him that doesn't come from him. If he were to allow evil men to take his life, that wouldn't be for the first time. Nor would his dying be all it appeared to be. You can't put to death the Author of life and death.

COUNSEL: How do you know all this? Please explain your connection with the Accused, the circumstances in which you first met him, and how you have related to him since then.

WITNESS: I have never spoken to him, though I've attended dozens of his meetings. He has written to me three times in answer to my letters. I have many pictures of him, audio and video tapes, and copies of all his books, of course... But—how can I explain?—I've never felt I could approach him in person, never felt *worthy*—

COUNSEL: One last question. How does your community get on with the public?

WITNESS: Since our foundation four years ago, we've been able to interest a few inquirers in the teaching of our Master, and to recruit the occasional new member. On the other hand, there have been serious attempts to burn our house down, and a small bomb did go off. There was some damage, but no one was hurt. We always have to be on our guard against enemies who will stop at nothing. They've forced us to take protective measures.

COUNSEL: I turn to you, members of the Jury. From the evidence of other witnesses and from his own mouth, you are familiar with the Accused's pretensions, and how he goes about justifying them. Now you are discovering something rather different, another side of him. You have just been treated to a sample of the effect he has on his disciples and devotees. Whether or not you feel this effect to be appalling in human terms is beside the point. What is very much to the point is how it endorses the height and the depth and the seriousness of his pretensions to divinity.

All that was needed to complete the picture—turning it into bas-relief—was the band of disciples represented here today by Sister Marie-Louise. To whom the Prosecution is obliged.

Defence: **The Pedestal So High**

MYSELF, to Witness: Well, we meet at last, Sister Marie-Louise, in strange circumstances. Do you remember what I said in my letters to you?

WITNESS: Yes, Master, very well.

MYSELF: Don't call me Master. I told you then and I tell you now that I'm nobody's master or guru. I tell you that your trouble—

along with that of the rest of your community and indeed most of the human race—is *intimidation,* blind subservience to authority, religious and secular. I begged you to dare to be your own authority on what only you can know and what matters most—namely, Who you are in your own experience. Again and again I stressed that no second or third person is in a position to tell you What you are as First Person. I implored you to look for yourself. I told you that John a-Nokes is no more for reverencing than any other outsider is. That his business is to point away from himself to you the Insider, to the One who is nearer to you than you are, and Who alone is worthy of your adoration. Have you forgotten all this?

WITNESS: Oh, no, Master! I read those letters every day. I could recite them word for word. They are wonderful!

MYSELF: And you—you who they are all about—are *not* wonderful?

WITNESS: Maybe one day, Master, I shall myself be able to see and to live from these great truths you teach. Meantime I'm just a spiritual aspirant, a seeker, a beginner. It's enough that I bask in your light.

You are the world-honoured One. Why, Master, it was you who told us that the setting sun rolls out his red carpet across the sea for you alone, for the VIP of the universe. Never for the likes of us.

MYSELF: Are you deaf as well as blind? I said it did so for the Headless One, for the unique First Person of the universe.

I ask you, and the members of the jury as well, to turn to Diagram No. 18 in the booklet, showing two versions of the religious uniform or habit you are wearing. The design is based on a T-shirt I used to wear, one given to me by a very dear friend who sees herSelf for herself and is no devotee, thank God.

I put it to the jury: Looking out at the Witness, isn't (A)—the World's End or Wrong-way-up version—the one *you* are in receipt of? And I put it to the Witness: Looking down at yourself, isn't (B)—the World's End or Right-way-up version—the one you are in receipt of? And isn't this the true and God's-eye view of you, as grounded and rooted in Him? In Him, I say! In the ONE WHO IS. Not—ghastly fate!—in the one who isn't, in the jack-o'-lantern or will-o'-the-wisp you are looking at in the dock.

WITNESS: I hear what you say, Master, but I don't really get what you are talking about. Perhaps one day I shall.

MYSELF, to Witness: You leave me speechless, Sister Marie-Louise... God bless you! I have no more questions. Your devotion to me is quite the nicest and neatest way of guarding against all I stand for. Please leave the box. [She goes, not a bit crestfallen. The more I tick her off, the more she loves it!]

Ladies and gentlemen of the Jury, observe the fix I'm in. It's not that the lady and her friends mount me on a pedestal so high they can't hear a word I say. It's much worse than that. It's that the pedestal is just low enough for them to hear *parts* of what I say, so that somehow the message turns out to be the *opposite* of what I mean. What sort of disciples are these who, when I say 'Look in', look out; and when I say 'Look down', look up; and when I say 'Just look', piously close their eyes? I hate to say this, but the truth is that

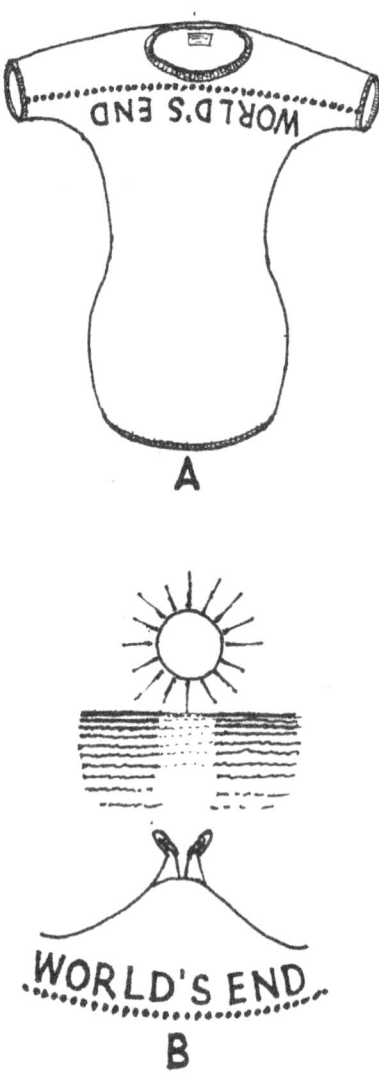

Diagram No. 18

The Devotee

I have dear friends, friends, enemies, bitter enemies—and disciples. Mercifully, very few.

You'll gather that I'm *not* one of those spiritual teachers who give their pupils the option: 'Either see Who you are, or else surrender to me. If you aren't ready to find the true Guru in yourself, at least find Him provisionally in me, as a first step. The second step, from me as your authority to yourself as your real Authority, may then follow.' Those teachers include some great souls, and I'm not saying they are wrong. It's not that this roundabout road to enlightenment via devotion to a guru is closed, but that it's a long and difficult diversion, and few they are that emerge from it on to the main highway. I still have to meet a devotee who has come through and will tell you so. Accordingly my message, day in and day out, to anyone who has half an ear, is: What, for heaven's sake, is wrong with the direct road to Yourself? It couldn't be better paved and easier going and safer—and shorter. In fact, all you have to do is face the right direction, and—like a shot—you've arrived at the Place you never left! That 180° turn-about of attention is enough to see you right Home, instantly. But you are responsible for making it. Your attention isn't something I can get hold of like a wrong-pointing signpost, and twist round to point the right way. It's you who have to do that.

COUNSEL: Whatever effect your gospel has on people, whether they take it the right way or the wrong way, the responsibility for what happens to them is yours.

MYSELF: This sounds reasonable, but is really another of your choice ones. Blame me for the way the Witness—bless her silly heart!—inverts what I'm telling her, and you'll have to blame Karl

Marx and Friedrich Engels for the millions of Russians Stalin liquidated. And Madame Curie for Hiroshima. And Jesus Christ for such flowerings of Christianity as the Children's Crusade, countless pogroms against the Jews, the Thirty Years' War and all the grisly work of the Holy Inquisition. Not to mention the Apocalyptic Church.

COUNSEL: You can't dodge the fact that you are marketing two sorts of divinity, one inadvertently and the other by design. You are causing a few feeble-minded folk to deify you, and many evil-minded folk to deify themselves. Also a lot of bloody-minded folk to deify violence. What remains to convict you of blasphemy under the Act?

MYSELF: What, indeed? Given some adjustments of language, I guess you're about right, for once.

COUNSEL, all excitement: Jury, do you hear that? [To the judge, triumphantly] Your Honour, this outright admission of guilt by the Accused—not the first, but for sure the clearest—raises a vital issue about the conduct of this Trial from now on. May I ask for a brief recess in which to put to Your Honour some questions of procedure?

JUDGE: Very well. The court is adjourned for half an hour.

Recess

The Judge in Camera with Counsel and Accused

COUNSEL: I submit, Your Honour, that the Accused's clear admission of guilt, which we have just heard, must change the course of the Trial. I see no reason to call the remaining witnesses. Just two or three of them, at most, will do.

JUDGE: I take your point. Mr Nokes, what have you to say?

MYSELF: I did not admit guilt. May I remind Your Honour that Counsel's view of what constitutes blasphemy and my view are poles apart? My plea is that *I'm* the one in court (not the only one now, I hope) who *isn't* blaspheming. I see God seated at the Centre of everyone's universe, regardless. Along with animals and little children and sages, I'm content to leave Him sitting comfortably there. Most adult humans are hell-bent on unseating Him and taking His place. As if they could! Now that really *is* blasphemy!

JUDGE: I understand your position perfectly. The immediate question is whether the remaining witnesses need be called. What do you say?

MYSELF: I say they must be called. Their names and abstracts of their evidence were of course given to me before the Trial, and the completion of my Defence depends on their appearing in court. I have every expectation that their evidence will, here and there, under cross-examination, turn out to support my case. I can't afford to forgo the probability of some more Prosecution witnesses turning out to be Defence witnesses. It's a risk that Sir Gerald must take.

COUNSEL: Surely, Your Honour, I can't be required to play into Nokes's hands? I must devise my own strategy, make my own decisions about a *nolle prosequi*.

JUDGE: If the Accused can so shake the evidence of some of your witnesses that they become, in effect, his witnesses, then he has every right to continue to do so. In the light of events so far in this Trial, I appreciate your concern regarding the rest of it. You have your job to do; I have mine. It is to give John a-Nokes, whose life—unlike ours, remember—is at stake, every opportunity to save it. I rule that you call the remaining witnesses.

COUNSEL: In Rex v. Simpson, 1921, Court of Criminal Appeal, the Judge excused the Prosecution from calling four witnesses it had said it would call, notwithstanding the vehement objections of the Defence.

JUDGE, after briefly consulting his computer: That was a trial for rape, and the grounds for the withdrawal were very different from yours, Sir Gerald. No. My decision is final.

COUNSEL: Your Honour forces me to consider whether I shouldn't leave the rest of the Prosecution's case to my junior here. And explain to the Jury that I'm doing so because the proceedings from now on can only be *de minimis*, an anticlimax and irrelevance not meriting my attention—Nokes having *de facto* changed his plea to Guilty. In short, that I'm *functus officio*.

JUDGE: Of course it's up to you... But—if you'll allow me to put a few questions—

Can you be so sure of the way the case will go? Do you consider that your withdrawal would be in the public interest, or would further the intentions of the Crown? Or would serve the cause of justice itself? Not to mention—how can I phrase this?—the effect on your own professional career... Not that Mr Atkinson would fail to do an excellent job...

COUNSEL, sighing, and shaking his head so vigorously he nearly loses his wig: It's a question of duty, Your Honour. Personal considerations don't come into it...

Well, Atkinson, it seems we've no option but to soldier on.

JUNIOR COUNSEL, suddenly rather down in the mouth: I guess so, Sir Gerald.

Prosecution Witness No. 19

THE VENERABLE BHIKKHU

Prompted by Counsel, the Witness introduces himself and describes his relationship with me.

WITNESS: I'm a Westerner—a Welshman—who, as a direct result of meeting the Accused, am now a Buddhist monk: which leaves me eternally grateful to him. I first met John a-Nokes five years ago at one of his workshop-seminars, organized by a group of philosophy and psychology students at our university. His subject was Buddhism—his very individual version of it. I was already some sort of spiritual seeker, but had no idea where to look or how to look or what to look for, and as unhappy as I was confused. Jack changed all that. He turned my attention round 180° and showed me what I needed to see—the much-feared and overlooked obvious. He initiated me into the art of looking within at the Emptiness.

This insight was enough to change the direction of my life. It got me off the mark—gave me not so much a head start as a no-head start—on my own spiritual odyssey, which is still in the early stages. Not that I seek something back of or additional to the Emptiness here. My aim is to see it ever more clearly, realize it ever more deeply, live from it ever more consistently.

COUNSEL: It was to traditional Buddhism, then, and not to the Accused's version—or inversion or perversion—of it that you turned, for guidance on your spiritual quest?

WITNESS: That's right. After all (I argued) that tradition has been tested over two and a half millennia. It seemed to me the ideal means of arriving at the sustained clarity and freedom I sought. The more I studied Buddhism, the more businesslike this approach to full enlightenment turned out to be. A year after meeting John a-Nokes, I became a *Samanera,* or novice monk, at the Amarāvati Monastery, where I'm now an ordained monk.

COUNSEL: Do you think the Accused has taken the wrong road?

WITNESS: It's rather that he's held up on the right road. The reason he's stuck is that he imagines he's got to the end of it. He mistakes the valuable insight he and I share for the final truth and full Enlightenment, whereas I see it as an aspect of the truth and a preview of Enlightenment. He says he's arrived. I say we're both on the way. There's more to Buddhahood or Nirvana than intermittent and distant views of it. The touch, the savour and the smell of it, so to say, are essential. There's a world of difference, and quite a few hazards, between spotting the restaurant of your choice across the wide and busy street, with occasional whiffs of the cooking, and sitting inside there, tucking away.

COUNSEL: Are you saying that the Accused is deluded, or that he's some kind of fraud?

WITNESS: About his sincerity I've not the slightest doubt. It's just that I can't agree that he's come anywhere near the goal.

COUNSEL: What goal? Please be more specific.

WITNESS: A fully enlightened Arahant or Buddha has freed himself from all limitations and defilements, such as desire, ill will, ignorance and pride. He's fearless. He's full of energy and wisdom and inspiration, and all pure and noble qualities. His compassion excludes no one and knows no bounds. In short, he's perfect. Which means he won't be reborn into the world. The rest of us very imperfect ones, after this life is over, will again and again return in other bodies and go on living and dying and being reborn till we, too, at last become Buddhas.

COUNSEL: This full Enlightenment—does it mean shedding your humanness and putting on (or revealing) your divineness? So that you emerge as some sort of a god, or the Buddhist equivalent of God?

WITNESS: Buddhism recognizes no God. No, the Buddha is a perfect human.

COUNSEL: Which of the Buddha's merits does the Accused notably lack, in your experience of him?

WITNESS: I get the impression, though I can't prove it, that at times he's worried, tired, cross, bored, petty, irritated, fed up to the gills. Certainly I know him well enough to assure the court that he's a million miles short of Buddhahood. Nor is this surprising: the long haul to perfection doesn't interest him. Several times I've heard him say he can't be bothered with the rigours of what we Buddhists call the Eightfold Noble Path, which combines moral discipline with a variety of meditational practices. He maintains that these are, at best, optional extras, so many arbitrary hurdles set up for training purposes. Publicly and tirelessly, he says he's arrived at Buddhism's goal of perfection in no time at all and on his own; and to blazes with the endless foot-slogging, the numerous stages and the hard going between stages, that Buddhists have, over all these centuries, found unavoidable. Which is like supposing that, because you happen to be quite exceptionally handy with a penknife, you can not only operate on yourself for appendicitis, but get yourself elected to the Royal College of Surgeons; and moreover, talk a lot of other far less skilled penknifers into following your example.

COUNSEL: How do regular Buddhists react to the news that they themselves are setting up formidable barriers and hazards, to lengthen out a fifteen-second sprint into an age-long obstacle race?

WITNESS: Some admire and are puzzled. Some are indifferent. Some are shocked. A few are very angry. But most are confused, because at times John a-Nokes seems to be a species of Buddhist, at other times not a Buddhist at all, occasionally an anti-Buddhist; and, increasingly of late, some kind of Christian, one gathers.

COUNSEL: Is it true that not a few Buddhists think he's poking fun at what they hold sacred, and pouring contempt on the Blessed One? Committing what amounts to blasphemy?

WITNESS: Well, yes. But I think—

COUNSEL: I gather that aiming to become a Buddha—or is it the Buddha?—isn't quite the same as aiming to become Almighty God? In which case, what's the difference?

WITNESS: There's all the difference in the world, most experts would say. Buddhism can fairly be described as an atheistic religion. It denies the existence of an individual self, let alone a Universal Self. However, for the profoundest Christian mystics (such as Meister Eckhart), the Godhead is the absolutely impersonal and ineffable

Source and Reality and Truth behind appearances; and as such isn't all that different from what we Buddhists call our Buddha Nature. On the other hand, Theravada Buddhism, with its principle of karma and reaping what you sow, is poles apart from Christian dogmas about guilt, vicarious suffering, and salvation.

COUNSEL: So, in conclusion, you regard the Accused's claim that he stands on the topmost spiritual peak—call it Full Enlightenment, or Nirvana, or Buddhahood, or Godhood, or what you will—as a false claim? And moreover, one that scandalizes followers of a great and ancient but very alive religion?

WITNESS: I have to agree. Though—

COUNSEL: And you agree that to induce others—particularly the easily-led young—to follow him is to mislead them? Corrupt them, even?

JUDGE, going red and pounding away: Even in this Trial there are limits to how far I will allow the leading and the gagging of witnesses. You're putting your words into the Witness's mouth and stopping his words coming out.

COUNSEL, between his teeth, his voice reduced to a stage whisper: Your Honour pleases to instruct the Crown how to conduct itself?

JUDGE: Precisely! [Counsel flings down his brief, pushes back his wig, and mops his brow...]

WITNESS, in a marked manner, all Buddhist calm: I'm quite sure of three things, Your Honour. That John a-Nokes stands way above the pea-soup fog that most of us are groping about in. That, in so far as I'm clear of that mental and spiritual miasma, it's because he showed me the way up. And that both of us have a lot more climbing to do before we get to the topmost peak where the mountain air is perfectly healthy and transparent. Let me add that, if he's held up temporarily, that's his own affair. Let's say he's having a rest and a nap, and pleasant dreams about what lies at the end of the climb.

COUNSEL, a little more calmly: I turn to you, members of the jury. The Witness's concluding tribute to his one-time friend (should I call it his last-minute attempt to make amends?) may be praiseworthy but is certainly irrelevant, and should be ignored.

It doesn't erase a syllable from his statement that the Accused is by no means the exalted Being he claims to be, that he misleads the young into making the same claim, and that he publicly outrages some Buddhists by perverting and putting down what they hold sacred.

The relevance of this testimony to the charge against him will not be lost on you.

As for the Witness's high opinion of the Accused personally: it only lends weight to his evidence against the man, to the effect that he is indeed guilty as charged. Once more, the adverse testimony of a witness like this—one who's prejudiced in favour of the Accused—is worth that of two neutral witnesses.

Defence: **Paths to Perfection**

MYSELF, to Witness: Buddhism, I think you'll agree, is a vast umbrella sheltering hugely different varieties of itself. For brevity let's label them the popular or folk Buddhism of the East, evangelical Pure Land Buddhism, zany or baffling Zen, ultra-puritanical Theravada, ultra-relaxed Tantra, the miscellany of picturesque and fantastical cults comprising Tibetan Buddhism, and so on—to say nothing of their countless subdivisions. Instead of 'varieties of itself' I could almost have said 'parodies and contradictions of itself.'

WITNESS: You are about right. All the same, there are common factors.

MYSELF: We shall be glancing at one or two of them. Meantime, surely, room can be found under that marquee-like umbrella for the odd new development?

WITNESS: It had better be. Buddhism is a living religion.

MYSELF: Well, then, in the course of my cross-examination I hope to persuade you that my own variety of Buddhism (I never did belong to the Aching-legs School) is by no means so far out that it couldn't possibly nose its way under that umbrella. Moreover, I hope to prove—what's very much to the point in court here—that it deserves to be included without exciting any more scandal and accusations of blasphemy than other varieties of Buddhism excite. Varieties whose age conveniently masks their quite amazing boldness and oddity—including calculated insults to the Buddha—and lends sanctity to what it can't hide.

WITNESS: Well, I'm open to persuasion.

MYSELF: Let's go straight to the heart of the matter—to the Void or Emptiness that you and I find to be nearer than near. Isn't it also—I ask you—clearer than clear, perfect from the start? You implied that it gets more lucid with practice. Surely you didn't mean that?

WITNESS: I must admit that, looking within, I can never see a hazy or spotty Void, or a mere profile or feature of what the Zen people call my Original and faceless Face. No—it's an all-or-nothing sight. Yet, mysteriously, there seems to be a steady brightening and clarification over the years. More likely it's the associated feelings, the meaning, above all the steadiness and continuity of the seeing, which mature with practice. Not the vision itself.

MYSELF: We are agreed, then, that the first sighting of one's Void is the same as the last; and that, if there's a race on, it's one in which the starting line and the finishing line obligingly rush together. But of course, as you insist, there's a sense in which they stay far apart and there's much effort to be put in, stern discipline to be subjected to, regular meditation to be practised. Now you've said in evidence that I don't meditate. That's libel, and you know it! What did you mean? What *is* meditation, anyway?

WITNESS: Don't give me that one! Why, the very first time we met, you said that meditation—sitting meditation, with folded legs and straight back—was not for you. Well, I never held that this or any other posture is absolutely essential for spiritual growth, but only that it's a great help for most of us. Buddhism, as you know, isn't any kind of body-training or physical yoga. It's the practice of mindfulness, being awake to what's going on. Normally we're out to lunch, wool-gathering, in a coma, and a lot of practice is needed to snap out of it at will. More, to stay out of the coma. This is the discipline of Buddhism, and sitting in the right fashion helps it along.

MYSELF: It's in detail that my practice differs from yours. You sit still for hours daily in the lotus position, being mindful. I sit around in any old position, stand around and walk around and lie down and get up, as impulse and occasion demand, being mindful. You reserve a part of each day for formal sitting in the quiet of the meditation hall. I don't divide my day into a sacred and a secular part: all of it is sacred, all of it is secular—and as mindful or attentive as I can make it. So now I find the commotion of the city is just as conducive to attention as is the peace of the countryside or my own room. The roaring world is my meditation hall.

WITNESS: We both aim at full wakefulness, but go about the training differently. However...

MYSELF: However, we come now to a huge, perhaps insuperable difference between us. Many, if not all, Theravada Buddhists assume—and you as good as stated outright—that a human being can be perfected, and hasn't made the grade to Buddhahood till he is indeed perfect. Repeat, perfect! I say that no human being can ever, ever be radically reformed, let alone perfected. And anyway doesn't need to be, seeing he's absolutely perfect anyway—as the non-human Being he really, really is. I say that my Enlightenment is my ceasing to look for and to cultivate perfection in the wrong place, out there in my human region, and instead to find it shining brightly in the right place, here at my Centre. From where it lights up the world.

This issue between us is crucial. In fact, it's what this Trial is all about. As we look into it together now, let's keep in mind Santayana's warning: 'Nothing requires greater intellectual heroism than willingness to see one's own equation written out.'

WITNESS: You can have your intellectual heroism. I'll content myself with men and women as they are—and *as they could be.* You are going by the folk you know. Prove to me that they could never, given the time and the training, become Buddhas. Which is to say perfect.

MYSELF: I'll do so twice over. Here's number one: The notion that human nature is a sow's ear you can make a divine silk purse out of is so ridiculous, when you come to think of it, it's not worth refuting. Why, the mere fact that it's *human* nature—and not also lion nature and dolphin nature and hummingbird nature (to say nothing of bedbug nature and so on *ad infinitum)*—means that it's only a tiny fragment of Nature!

And here's number two: Just think of a man without desire, without any weaknesses, thinking only perfect thoughts and feeling only perfect feelings! What sort of fairground monster would he be, for Buddha's sake? A man with no shadow side to him at all! I, for one, would run a mile from such a freak. It's a man that has failings and limitations and doubts and a silly side to him, and is honest about it all, who warms and moves my heart. One who hasn't, and isn't, leaves me shivering and stone-cold. And incredulous. He's no more real than a tentacled robot escaped from a horror movie.

WITNESS: A Buddha is a perfect human in the sense that a *perfect* rose is a perfect *rose*. Neither pretends to a perfection that lies outside its own nature.

MYSELF: You're tying yourself in knots, Venerable Sir. First you say that Buddhahood is freedom from all limitations. Now you explicitly admit innumerable limitations. Besides, if you now define perfection as excellence of one kind as against excellence of countless other kinds, why then you strip the word of all meaning. Buddha Nature is perfect Buddha Nature. Wonderful! But equally, Devil Nature is perfect Devil Nature. Wonderful! And filth is perfect filth—perfectly filthy. Wonderful! And blasphemy is perfect blasphemy—perfectly blasphemous. Wonderful! All true, but not helpful!

Of course, like you, I would just love to straighten out and polish up my human self. It's God-awful! But, unlike you, I propose to do so by resting in my God-lovely non-human Self, in the expectation that perhaps a little something may rub off the latter on to the former. In which case the improvement, however marginal, will at least be real and not phony. Why? Simply because I shall be living from my true and central Buddha Nature into my peripheral human nature. Remaining a vulnerable man out there, I shall become a more natural man, poles apart from that monstrous (and, happily, quite mythical) creature who is invulnerable and perfect man. I shall be as truly human as a human can be.

Ladies and gentlemen of the Jury, if you will please refer once more to Diagram No. 15, you will see at once what I mean [see Witness 15 The New Apocalyptic].

The two versions of oneself which it clearly distinguishes—the peripheral and the central—are in all respects diametric opposites. To merge them is nonsense and blasphemy and endarkenment. To distinguish them—and to go on to live that distinction—is Enlightenment, and also plain horse sense.

WITNESS: Buddhism doesn't go in for this sort of speculation.

MYSELF: It does, you know! Mahayana Buddhists find a crucial place and role for what lies at the centre of my picture. They call it the Nirmanakaya or Transformation Body of the Buddha. Throughout the ages this Buddha is born and reborn into the world. Clearly seeing into his true Nature, he devotes each lifetime to sharing that vision with deluded humanity; and all the while he's subject with them to the ills that flesh is heir to, including old age and death. Under countless guises he gives himself in compassion for all beings, suffering vicariously on their behalf and making over to them his merits. Here, hardly disguised at all, is none other than the one who, throughout this Trial, I depict as the First Person Singular—the headless, upside-down, world-embracing Person that each of us is, once we wake out of our coma. I need hardly point out the parallel between this sort of Buddhism (very unlike yours, if I may say so) and the Christianity you were good enough to attribute to me in the course of your evidence.

Well, Venerable Bhikkhu, is this view of life and way of life of mine so far out that it can't be got under the marquee-umbrella of Buddhism? Isn't it, in fact, very close indeed to what some schools of Mahayana Buddhism teach and practise anyway? And altogether in line with the Buddha whose dying words—'Be ye lamps to yourselves'—I take most seriously?

WITNESS: You are conveniently forgetting the Buddha's life, and one of the most significant episodes in it. Having at last attained perfect Enlightenment—after six years of austerities that nearly killed him—his first thought was that this treasure was for sharing with suffering humanity. His second thought was that the sharing would be next to impossible, seeing what Enlightenment had cost him. His third thought was that—given training as thorough as his own, though less hard on the body—some could attain to the same perfection. Accordingly he mapped out the Eightfold Noble Path, and founded the Sangha, or community of disciples who follow that long and arduous discipline. The discipline you have no time for.

MYSELF: There are various versions of that story. Have you come across the Burmese and Tibetan tradition that there's a very different reason why the Buddha at first felt that no one would get what he was on about? It's that people would reject his discovery because it was too obvious, too simple, too accessible!

WITNESS: No. I didn't know that.

MYSELF: Venerable Bhikkhu, in the light of this information, let me repeat the question: is my way incompatible with this hold-all religion of yours? Does anything I've said justify the anger of Buddhists who know their Buddhism?

WITNESS: It's what you *haven't* said in so many words which upsets them so. They see you cheating—arriving (or pretending to arrive) all fresh and un-travel-stained at the goal, without bothering to make the journey. All varieties of real Buddhism insist on the long haul, on the need for hard training over many years, if not lifetimes. The Theravadins of Burma and Sri Lanka and Thailand with their Eightfold Noble Path, the Mahayanists of Tibet with their visualizing and body-toughening techniques, and the Mahayanists of China and Japan and Korea with their zazen and the Pure Land practice of *japa* or recitation—all are saying you get what you work for, in the prescribed way and with patience and determination. And here are you, John a-Nokes on your simplistic lonesome, no tradition at your back, as good as announcing that the vast experience behind these training systems counts for nothing. That for you the Eightfold Noble Path, and the routes running parallel to it, are superseded by Nokes's Short Cut!

MYSELF: Not true! All right, this Short Cut exists and in fact is no distance at all. Our True or Buddha Nature is on show right now, brilliantly lit up for all to see. But to stay with it and live it, I must take what (to avoid confusion) I call the 8 x 8-fold Plebeian Path. Which in its lowland fashion is as long and as hard going as the most aristocratic of high roads. In fact, if you're interested, I have a map of it here. A bunch of copies.

JUDGE! If this map is part of your Defence it must be produced in court, for the Jury and Counsel and me to examine. If it's just an interdepartmental memo passing between you two, I don't want to hear any more of it.

MYSELF: Your Honour, the fact that it exists and outlines my practice—yes, this is part of my Defence against this Witness's testimony. The map's details, which are complex, would only confuse the Jury at this stage. That's why, though it's available for anyone's inspection, it's not one of my regular Defence Exhibits.

JUDGE: Let's see this map, as you call it. [Copies are distributed...[1]]

---

1 See Appendix.

MYSELF: My purpose in producing this document is to show how mistaken the Witness is about Nokes's Short Cut. It's a chart of Nokes's Long Haul, of his protracted 8 x 8-fold Plebeian Path—to the Place he never for a moment left...

Well, Venerable Bhikkhu. Am I still giving offence, a heretic not allowed under the vast canopy of your religion?

WITNESS: It will take a little while to sort all this out. I just can't give a snap answer.

MYSELF: While you are sorting, a word in the Jury's ear. Early Zen masters were given to likening the Buddha to well-used loo paper! Bumph, toilet paper—whatever you call it. (An apt simile, when applied to that monstrous mix-up which soils our perfect Buddhahood with our very imperfect humanhood.) And if that wasn't blasphemy, I'd like to know what I'm being accused of! If that's OK (and I've heard Buddhists go into raptures about it), anything goes. And I'm a model of Buddhist tact and reverence!

Venerable Sir, you'll remember how Counsel summed up your testimony against me. According to him, you say I claim to be Who I'm not, mislead others into making the same claim for themselves, and insult the Buddha—and thus outrage the feelings of assorted Buddhists. Tell me, what now remains of all that?

WITNESS, taking some time to reply, hesitatingly: Not much I can put my finger on just now...

COUNSEL, intervening: The court has listened patiently to this cosy in-house chat about Buddhism. In the end, what does it amount to? The Accused does little to discredit the Witness's original testimony by reducing him in the end to a state of some bewilderment. Soon enough, I'll wager, he will think of all the things he could and should have said in court today, in defence of his position.

MYSELF: A court of justice is interested in the real arguments of today, not the hypothetical ones of tomorrow.

COUNSEL: Your Honour, these insults—and from—

JUDGE: I think perhaps learned Counsel had better call his next Witness.

MYSELF: Before he does so, Your Honour, I would like to read to the court a quotation from Dr Walpola Rahula, a leading spokesman for Theravada Buddhism; and to conclude with some contrasting quotations from Mahayana Buddhism—from Chinese Ch'an masters of the eighth and ninth centuries CE. My own position vis-à-vis these two schools will be self-evident, I think. Here is Rahula:

> Among the founders of religions the Buddha was the only teacher who did not claim to be other than a human being, pure and simple... He attributed all his realization, attainments and achievements to human endeavour and human intelligence... He who has (by this endeavour) realized the truth, Nirvana, is the happiest being in the world. He is free from all 'complexes' and obsessions, the worries and the troubles that torment others. His mental health is perfect... He is joyful, exultant, enjoying the pure life, his faculties pleased, free from anxiety, serene and peaceful. As he is free from selfish desire, hatred, ignorance, conceit, pride and all such defilements, he is pure and gentle, full of universal love...

Such—*mirabile dictu*—is the Buddha state which all the Venerable Bhikkhu's practices are aimed at! A tall order for him (let alone us undisciplined lay types) to comply with in a million kalpas—and all by means of 'human endeavour and human intelligence' if you please! I'm happy to add that many Mahayana texts, by contrast, invite us *right now* to awaken to and lean back on the Eternal Absolute (Dharma-dhatu or Buddha-kaya), the Perfection of Wisdom (Prajna, the 'goddess' who is lovely and holy) and Suchness (Bhutatathata or Perfect Immutability)—three aspects of our True Nature at Centre which are about as remote from Dr Rahula's 'human being, pure and simple' as they could be. Closing the gap, trying to bring together one's humanness and one's divinity, and doing without the latter—this is (I invoke the well-known Zen metaphor) trying to turn a brick into a mirror by assiduous polishing.

It is also an instance of the age-old fallacy of misplaced perfection. To see through it is the acid test, the *sine qua non* of the spiritual life. It guards against the nonsensical blasphemy which confounds who I appear to be as that third person with Who I am as this First Person. It lets things be what they are, where they are. It is *mindfulness*. Mindfulness which, the Witness agrees, is the very heart of Buddhism. In that case this great religion—like some others—is occasionally subject to cardiac arrests!

I conclude with quotations from two famous Ch'an masters who never ceased warning their disciples about the fallacy of misplaced perfection. The fallacy that perfection is not here, and not now, and not mine. First, Huang-po:

Our original Buddha Nature is void, omnipresent, silent, pure; it is glorious and mysterious peaceful joy—and that is all. Enter deeply into it by awaking to yourself: That which is where you are is it, in all its fullness, utterly complete.

As for gaining merits countless as the sands of the Ganges, since you are fundamentally complete in every respect, you should not try to supplement that perfection by such meaningless practices. There is no distinction between the Buddha and sentient beings, except that sentient beings are attached to forms and so seek externally for Buddhahood.

Second, Hui-hai:

Instead of recognizing the Buddha right where you are, you spend aeon after aeon searching for him.

Illumination is not something to be attained. You can come to Buddhahood in a single flash.

You may be compared with lion cubs, which are genuine lions from their birth.

Prosecution Witness No. 20

THE BODY WORKER

COUNSEL: Three days ago the Prosecution's twentieth Witness left this country—with our full agreement—to be at the bedside of her very sick mother in San Juan Capistrano, California. Here she is, however, on our witness-box telescreen, to be sworn and give evidence in the usual way...

For me at least, it's as though this Witness—on screen so much larger than the others—were *more* present in court than they had been...

Witness testifies that she holds certificates from three institutes concerned with the improvement of physical well-being. She has been practising for fifteen years, and treats an average of thirty clients a week. Her methods, in part her own, have been written up in several professional journals. They consist mainly of manipulation of the muscles and connective tissue to give better alignment and to remove what she calls knots.

COUNSEL: What light does your professional experience throw on the claims of the Accused, which I understand you know about? I'm thinking specially of his idea that his limbs are put forth by a bodiless divinity, and so are quite exceptionally agile and efficient.

WITNESS: My impression is that, to get out of facing the screwed-up and uncoordinated state of his body, he dismisses much or all of it, writes it off. As if he could! His body is very real and very typical. Head and trunk and limbs, it incorporates all manner of imbalances and knots and rigidities and constrictions, trouble spots built up over the years from wrong body-use and unacknowledged reactions of fear and anger and hate and frustration. What isn't typical is his trick of avoiding these negative conditions by voiding their physical basis. With remarkable thoroughness and ingenuity the Accused spirits away the troublesome man—and substitutes the trouble-free God! What a hope! So far from clearing up his trouble spots, this stratagem draws a protective veil over them. So far from loosening his rigidity, it puts on yet another suit of armour. His pretended divinity can only exacerbate his all-too-human condition. There's no panacea, no quick and easy and foolproof substitute for the patient untying of what was once tied up.

COUNSEL: So it would be true to say that the Accused's stratagem fails because it's wildly unrealistic, founded on the wish-fulfilling dream that he is the wonderful fellow he isn't?

WITNESS: Precisely.

COUNSEL, to Jury: Can you doubt the Witness's sincerity, or her expertise built up and tested over fifteen years' work with many hundreds of patients? Few of whom were, I'll wager, as unconscious of their body-knots as Mr Nokes is. Or else as dishonest about them.

Defence: **Knots**

MYSELF, to Witness: So far as I understand it, I go along with your story about bodily imbalances and knots and protective armour, and the way they build up. What beats me is how you can be so sure that yours is the only way of loosening and shedding them. How do you know I haven't stumbled on an alternative? And one that's more radical and more effective than yours—to say the least? Short of getting your hands on me and giving me a thorough going-over, you must admit that your remarks about my screwed-up condition are uncalled-for and pure guesswork, founded on no evidence at all.

WITNESS: Founded on long experience.

MYSELF: But not, I think, on experience of people like me, who are six thousand miles away, and who make the claims I do, and don't so much live up to them as get down to them.

WITNESS: Well, I think I have to concede that point. On the other hand, I'll stake my professional reputation that you aren't the exception you say you are.

MYSELF: And I'll stake my life that I AM that exception absolutely. In fact, I don't know what uniqueness is till I come round to being MYSELF, this First Person Oh-so-Singular.

Anyway, thank you. No more questions. [Witness is switched off...]

I've no doubt the Witness knows her job and does it very well. I'm in no position, and have no wish, to challenge her methods or results. But I have to tell her that my job—and the material I work with—is very, very different from hers. She deals with one species and order and genus—kingdom, rather—I with another. We aren't in the same line of business at all.

Briefly, here are the differences:

(1) The bodies the Witness treats are skin-encapsulated, closed and self-contained systems. Each is a sharply defined thing, contained within the familiar world of sharply defined things. My body, on

the contrary, is open-ended. At the World's End which is its Bottom Line, this body gives on to and merges with another world altogether, a Nowhere-and-Nowhen-and-Nohow world of infinite mystery in which there are no things at all. It draws upon this Other World as a tree draws on its roots and its roots draw on the soil.

(2) This open end of mine is no small and constricted aperture, like the neck of an uncorked bottle, or the mouth of a lidless jug, or the sphincter muscle of an alimentary canal. It's more like the Amazon that widens till it's the Atlantic.

(3) This busted-wide-open body of mine is absolutely unique. I've never come across another remotely like it. The bodies the Witness handles are many, and remarkably similar. Therefore she knows where she is with them.

(4) They are all the same way up—head above, feet below. Mine is the other way up. I stand on my head.

(5) Or rather, on my no-head, on my shoulders. The Witness's clients are each stoppered and topped off with a *topknot*—an apt name for what amounts to a tangle of hitches and reefs and splices, of impossible-to-untie knots of every kind. It's a tangle I'm absolutely free of, thank the Lord, as soon as I care to look. There are no knots in a no-topknot. Here's nothing to pick at and fumble with and attribute to traumatic episodes in my history, and generally to fuss and fret about.

(6) Both in shape and size the rest of my body is very different from those the Witness works with. A normal person's height (as Pliny the Elder noticed) equals the span of his extended arms: but this

person—this First Person—is the great exception. I've got arms and legs all right, and a trunk—of a sort. A unique sort. My arms, when extended sideways, I see are long enough to embrace the world. My trunk and my legs, by way of contrast, are drastically foreshortened, and my trunk is backless. As for my shoulders, they are very broad as well as fuzzy, and in the middle is a great Gap. This means that my left arm and my right arm are unconnected. Or rather, that they are connected to No-thing. How different from the little arms of John a-Nokes there behind glass, and from those of the Witness's clients! All of which stick out of human bodies.

(7) What I'm describing is my real physique, so solid above, so airy below—the one that's given right here—and I'll be damned if I'll turn down such a mind-blowing gift! Damned, and crazy. It's the one I see and see with, the one I hear and hear with, the one that feels pains and pleasures, and eats food that actually tastes, and smells stinks that actually pong. Of course I'm also fixed up with a pseudo-physique which is incapable of all these things—a normally-headed and regular-way-up but unfeeling apology for a body—which hangs out a yard or so away. 'Hangs out' is right: it's no more than a distant framed-and-glazed picture, paper-thin, suspended alongside framed-and-glazed pictures of family and friends. It's no more for living in than those photos are. It's as dead as the wall it's hanging on, and the fact that Jack-in-the-glass somewhat resembles the Witness's well-fleshed clients does nothing to bring that Thin Man to life.

These assorted differences between my physique and that of the Witness's clients by no means exhaust the list. But they are quite sufficient to confirm that what works for them is most unlikely to work for me, and vice versa. *This unique patient requires unique therapy.*

Yes, strikingly different though this body is from those, it too needs treatment. All too easily it can get out of order. When overlooked and unattended to, it develops tightnesses, rigidities, stiffnesses, blocks, knots of a sort. What do I do about them? How effective is the treatment? That's the question I want to tackle next.

COUNSEL, very loudly: It's *not* the question! You aren't accused of being screwed up but of being puffed up. Puffed up to divine proportions—in your own eyes. But now you're as good as confessing that you can't be divine after all, and that you've been having us on all the while. For you've just admitted to being a tangle of bodily knots, at least some of the time. Knots which the Being you claim to be is certainly free of, absolutely and forever. So you aren't divine after all! Come on—admit it now, late in the day though it is.

MYSELF: Learned Counsel's theology is simplistic. We will more easily see this if we turn to Diagram No. 19.

As I understand the Christian tradition, Divinity comes in three very, very different packages—Every-thing, Some-thing, and No-thing. The *first,* the infinite or jumbo size, embraces, along with all things, their knots.

Diagram No. 19

By containing them It frees Itself of them, and is unknotted—the way the ocean, though holding all those fish, is itself unfishy; and the way the cobra, though incorporating its venom, is unpoisoned by it. The *third* Divinity package—the infinitesimal or single-portion size—is guaranteed pure and thing-free and therefore knot-free. Not so the *second* or regular size. Finite, betwixt and between, it has its share of knots which need unravelling. It's this aspect of the Divine—the headless, long-armed, feet-up sort—that I've been describing. And—yes!—that I'm claiming to be. This is the Cosmic Christ. This is God incarnate in the Son, who is always taking on the form of a limited and mortal Some-thing, in sharp contradistinction to the Father who is All-things, and the Spirit who is No-thing.

It's right here, and only here, that I find the Son whose unique body is indeed my very own. Here is the Majesty that comes down and humbles Itself to take on—*me and my knots!* And that, I tell you, is humility! That's a comedown which only the God Who is Love Itself is capable of.

COUNSEL thunders: Jury—did you hear that? John a-Nokes is again telling us that he's nothing less than the Second Person of the Holy Trinity! Don't forget this. Remember it when you retire to consider your verdict.

MYSELF: Wrong, as usual! John a-Nokes is the image in that glazed-and-framed picture hanging on the wall. He's an appearance, not substantial or real—let alone divine. As for the unglazed-and-unframed person who's so real and so substantial here, I swear to you that the given facts have *forced* me to come back—reluctantly, in spite of myself—to something very like the indwelling Christ of my childhood. Amazing grace has brought me to my senses, at last!

My story now—along with that of Paul and countless other devout souls—is of the Christ who lives in me, who is the life of my life and the soul of my soul. How fortunate for them that they can't be arrested on a charge of blasphemy, and tried along with me under the Act of 2002 CE!

COUNSEL: I doubt whether you are in the same league as the great Apostle.

MYSELF: He called himself the chief of sinners. I'm in that league, all right.

But now, with (or without) your permission, I resume my response to the testimony of the Witness you were pleased to call to testify against me.

The question I must now address is this: what is the effective treatment for the knots that are indeed apt to form in this unique and true body of mine? What is the appropriate and practical cure—which has to be as unlike the Witness's as the material she works with is different from mine? The cure which, in my firsthand experience, really works? The remedy which, when persisted in, thaws out my freeze-ups, strips me of my armour, and unravels the knots which inevitably come with incarnation?

Truly speaking, the treatment isn't a treatment or a doing at all, but a waking. It's *attention, humility* in the face of inescapable evidence, sustained looking to see, *thankfulness* for the given—for the God who gives Himself.

And the crucial and primary sight is the Absence of that knot of knots which is my topknot (in truth my bottomknot). *Untying* that head-knot would take infinite time and trouble; and even if it were to succeed, I would be left with an agglomeration of loose ends. *Abolishing* the whole thing in a flash is immeasurably more effective.

This is the head start (no-head start) that can and should lead to the undoing of knots in the now-decapitated body. It reaches the parts that no other medicines can reach, and works wonders there. Taking this medicine consists of adding my body in along with my head, so that it, too, is voided, absented, and thoroughly *cleaned up.* To do this, I simply take time off from looking *down* to check that I'm headless, and look *out* to check that I'm also bodiless. Normally, in fact, my trunk and legs are out of view, and replaced by the scene ahead; thus the knots in those parts are instantly dissolved. Not once and for all, of course. But when this treatment is applied consciously enough and repeated often enough, no knots can survive it.

The consciousness is essential. Freedom from knots requires that I really do wake up to what I see, instead of dreaming what I'm told to dream. This isn't quite so easy as I'm apt to suppose. The final vision—the sustained attention which completes the job—is the up-ending of this headless body. When you have a jug of dirty water, you don't empty it by just removing the stopper. Nor do you empty it by tilting the jug with the stopper firmly in position. No, you have to do both things—take out the stopper and up-end the jug. Then the dirty water is at once discharged. (The chart which I produced in my response to the last Witness—the map of the 8 X 8-fold Plebeian

Path—illustrates the process in some detail.[1]) In plain language, the full treatment has three parts: it requires that I lose my head, and find my inverted body, and very frequently lose that as well—consciously. What could be simpler?

Simple doesn't mean easy. This treatment for knots (which is also treatment for blasphemy) isn't once and for all. It has to be kept up. My attention flagging, the topknot creeps back on, the trunk does a somersault to match those around me, and it solidifies. The knots re-knot themselves. Jack's back in, and Christ's out there in the cold again. And then God help me! (I've never known Him not to. When asked.)

Here, finally, are a Christian, a Muslim, a Taoist, a Buddhist, a Jew and a Hindu who had the secret of untying that knot of knots which is Man:

The outward and the inward man are as different as earth from heaven.

Eckhart

'Behold,' they said, 'we are men, and they are men; both we and they are in bondage to sleep and food.' In their blindness they did not perceive that there is an infinite difference between them.

Rumi

---

1   See Appendix.

While keeping my physical frame, I lost sight of my real self. Gazing at muddy water, I lost sight of the clear abyss.

Chuang-tzu

Where others dwell, I do not dwell. Where others go, I do not go. This doesn't mean that I refuse to associate with other people, but that black and white must be distinguished.

Pai-Yun

I call Heaven and Earth to witness that one day I sat down and wrote a Kabbalistic secret: suddenly I saw the shape of myself standing before me and myself disengaged from me.

School of Abulafia

As rivers lose name and shape in the sea, wise men lose name and shape in God, glittering beyond all distance. He who has found Spirit is Spirit... The knots of his heart are unloosed.

Mundaka Upanishad

Prosecution Witness No. 21

THE EX-SANYASSIN

COUNSEL, to Jury: The Accused often calls his teaching and practice 'The Headless Way'. What is this Way? In his own blasphemous jargon (I quote from one of his books) it is 'seeing on one's shoulders, instead of the man-head that isn't here, the God-head that is here, and being healed'. Well, our next witness will tell us about his adventures on the Headless Way, and the sort of healing it led to.

WITNESS: It all began years before I had even heard of John a-Nokes. I was twenty, an orange-robed sanyassin and a member of a very large pseudo-religious community in Oregon. The things we got up to! Some I now see were quite beneficial, most were harmless, a few were very harmful. Among them all, the one that fascinated me, and in the end practically drove me mad, was called 'The Guillotine Meditation'. Our guru praised it highly, describing it as very ancient, very deep and very liberating. It was a most beautiful Tantric meditation, he said.

COUNSEL: Meditation on what?

WITNESS: On having no head.

COUNSEL: Go on.

WITNESS: I've no idea why, but this meditation so got a hold on me that I lost all interest in the other things that my fellow sanyassins were into. I practised headlessness for hours every day, and felt guilty about the times when I got diverted from it, or when it slipped away from me. I became more and more unsociable, more and more lonely in that crowd of thousands.

Then came the showdown, the revelations of corruption and violence, leading to the swift breakup of that community. Angry and disillusioned, I only wanted to get as far away as possible. I burned my orange outfit and my mala, and moved back to New York. I got a job and settled down to normal life. Increasingly, it was as if that nightmare in Oregon had never happened—except for one hangover. The Guillotine Meditation went on bugging me. I still practised it daily, as far as my work allowed. And still I missed out on the promised healing. If anything, my anxiety and stress got worse. Yet it never occurred to me to cut my losses and stop, just call a halt. I was that stupid, that sick!

COUNSEL: And then you met the Accused?

WITNESS: No, I never met him. I came across his book on Headlessness in a second-hand bookstore. With great excitement I read and reread it, hoping against hope that Guillotine Meditation Mark II, Nokes's Style, would at last sort me out. Not content with the printed word, I tried to make contact with the author. I carved out of beechwood a figurine of the Headless One and sent it to him. No reply. I followed it up with pictures of headless figures, mostly Buddhas, that I'd come across. Still no reply. Not even an acknowledgement. I felt so hurt, so frustrated. But still I read the man's books, and went on practising. And I grew sicker than ever.

COUNSEL: How did it all end?

WITNESS: Well, as a result of my obsession, I was fired from my job as an accountant. I became unemployable, incapable of concentrating on the easiest work for more than a few minutes. And, naturally, very depressed. There were times when I thought of suicide. I only just managed to stay out of mental hospital.

COUNSEL: But you recovered. What actually happened?

WITNESS: Honestly, I don't know for sure. I think that what saved me was that I fell in love with my psychotherapist. As luck would have it, her name was Hedda. 'Hedda, my Header,' I called her. The formula became a private joke of ours, the slogan and watchword of our relationship. 'The man I want,' she said, 'has a man's head on his man's shoulders. Lips for kissing, eyes for looking at me, not thin air. You poor idiot, can't you see you've been made a fool of by a pair of con men? First, that smarmy, slick, watery-eyed guru, and then this mad paradox-pusher—tricksters who, between them, really did come within an ace of sending you off your rocker.'

Perhaps it was also that my deepening despair bottomed out, so that the only way left was upwards into the broad daylight of common sense. Anyway, almost overnight it happened. I got my head back for sure, and quite soon had it firmly screwed in place.

A month's vacation with Hedda in the Allegheny Mountains and I returned to the city in one piece and all there, present and correct. Since then I've lived a pretty normal life. The memory of that traumatic and embarrassing interlude, I'm happy to say, is fading steadily. More and more I have the feeling it happened to someone else... This enforced reminder here today that it didn't is far from welcome, I assure you.

COUNSEL: What about the religious side of that interlude? How did you and how do you view the God-head which the Accused promised you in place of your man-head?

WITNESS: At the time, I was more mystified than shocked. Now that I've been going to the synagogue regularly and reconnecting with my Jewish roots, I've come to see John a-Nokes and that guru as a pair of devils who tempted me to commit the most abominable sin against God: the sin of the ultimate Swollen Head. It makes my stomach turn over just to look at that man in the dock and think of the harm he did to me, and to so many others.

Defence: **The Guillotine Meditation**

MYSELF, to Witness: My aim in questioning you isn't to challenge your testimony—as far as it went. You described what you experienced, all right. Now I want to go into some of the underlying detail. Let's examine together the actual teaching of these two confidence tricksters (as you now call us), and how you put it into practice. First, then, your guru and his Guillotine Meditation. Please tell the court what his instructions were, and just how you followed them.

WITNESS: I had to think my head off. Imagine it gone clean away. Walking, sitting, whatever I was doing, I had to visualize myself doing it without a head. That was all there was to it.

MYSELF: Didn't he give you any techniques or reminders, any tips for boosting your imagination?

WITNESS: Yes, he did. I was told to lower the mirror in my bathroom so that I couldn't see my head in it. Also to hang pictures around the house of myself minus a head. In two ways these tricks were supposed to help: they reminded me to do the meditation, and showed me what it was about.

MYSELF: What were the likely benefits, according to your guru?

WITNESS: After a few days, he promised, I would experience a marvellous weightlessness and a silence, and begin to be centred in my heart.

MYSELF: Did these things happen to you?

WITNESS: I imagined they did. I persuaded myself I was happier and more relaxed and less heady. But in the long run—even in the short run—the effect was negative. I got *more* tense and worried.

MYSELF: Were instructions in the Guillotine Meditation given privately to small, selected groups? Or publicly?

WITNESS: They were published, for all the world to read, in the guru's *Orange Book of Meditations*. There was nothing secret about them.

MYSELF: Let's go on now to what you call Guillotine Meditation Mark II, to my sort of headlessness—the practice and techniques which you picked up from my books. How, if at all, did they differ from those of your guru? Did you hear him and me saying much the same thing, each in his own style and tone of voice?

WITNESS: I can't remember any important differences.

MYSELF: That headless figurine you carved and sent me, and those photos of decapitated Buddhas—I take it they represented your idea of the headless state as described in my books, which you say you read repeatedly?

WITNESS: Yes.

MYSELF: You'll remember, then, the experiments? Every book of mine contains full descriptions of them, with precise instructions for carrying them out.

WITNESS: I read those books a long time ago. But I don't remember doing any experiments. What sort of experiments?

MYSELF: Pointing at your face and seeing you *aren't* pointing at your face. Putting on your glasses and seeing they aren't glasses in the plural. Driving your car and seeing you aren't driving your car but the countryside. And so on. A dozen of them.

WITNESS: I'm sure I didn't do any of those things.

MYSELF: Let's get this quite clear for the Jury to note. Your guru advised you to use your imagination, to visualize. You complied. He made suggestions for boosting your imagination, such as lowering your mirrors. You complied. You carried them out meticulously, and imagined for long periods each day what you were required to imagine. A model of obedience you were. So much for Guillotine Meditation Mark I... Now for Guillotine Meditation Mark II, as you call it. I told you that imagination was your trouble. I told you to *stop* imagining things, and just look. You refused. I gave you meticulous instructions about the experiments you had to do if my teaching were to mean anything to you. You refused to do any of them. Again and again and again I warned you that my books would muddle you—could even harm you—if you merely read about those simple experiments or tests. You merely read about them. The result wasn't just that you failed to get my message, but that you inverted it. Inverted and perverted it till it coincided with your guru's message, and had the same damaging effect on you.

Not that I single you out for blame. Nearly all of us are so deeply convinced that looking within is the fate worse than death that we'll do almost anything to avoid looking. My guess is that one in three of my readers takes me seriously when I insist that reading about What I'm pointing at is light-years from seeing it. With great respect, ladies and gentlemen of the Jury, l get the impression that the one-in-three-or-more proportion applies to you too. Watching how you handle the experiments I ask you to do from time to time, it's obvious to me that most of you are (at best) just pretending to do them, are carefully missing the point and making damn sure you overlook the Looker—or, rather, his absence. Forgive me for saying that this wilful blindness to the crux of the Defence threatens to do me a far greater disservice than the Witness has been doing. It threatens to do me in. *The truth is you just can't ignore the experiments and get my meaning, and you just can't do the experiments and miss my meaning.* Witness, you may leave the box.

Will Jury-members now please turn to Diagram No. 20.

The Trial of the Man Who Said He was God

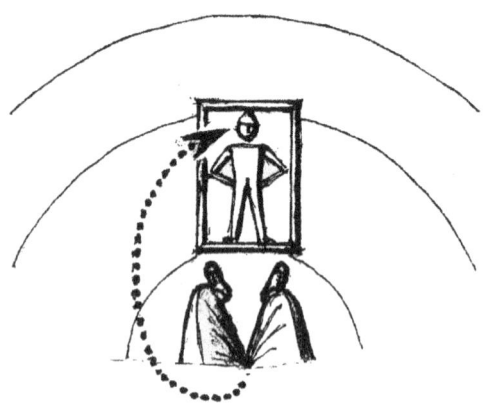

20a The Observation that places your head

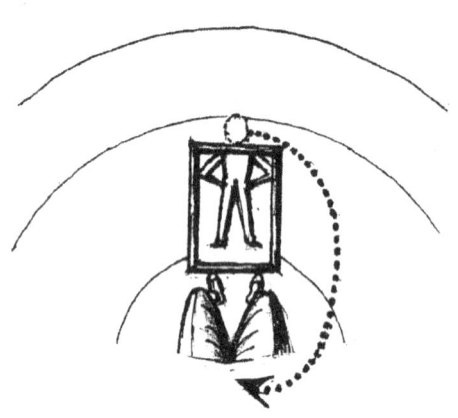

20b The Meditation that displaces your head

Diagram No. 20

No. 20a is the diagram we're becoming quite familiar with. It's the ground-plan of my Defence. No. 20b is very similar—with one all-important difference. The mirror has been lowered to cut off the head of the man in it. It represents the Witness's View of himself when, in obedience to his guru's instruction, he lowered his bathroom mirror. It also represents those pictures of decapitated Buddhas, and that decapitated wood-carving he sent me. In a word, it represents *violence*. To slice a person's head off is the most summary, irreversible and bloody mischief you can do him or her. If that person happens to be you, it is suicide; if another, murder; if a lot of others, genocide in the style of Caligula, who wished that the Romans had a single neck so that he could behead them in one blow. To be accurate, attempted murder, attempted suicide, attempted genocide. And for sure that's hell.

Along the top of my bathroom mirror is a cutting edge as sharp as any guillotine. Lowering it to slice the head off those shoulders is the easiest thing in the world—but it's asking for trouble. Poor wretched thing, it has to go somewhere. The plugholes of the bath and the wash-basin are far too small to take it, and alas it won't flush down the WC. Nor is it the sort of thing you can leave lying around—on the bathroom window-sill, for instance. No, the only place that will take the bloody thing is right here, it seems, on these shoulders. So here it settles down—*in the one place where it can never be!* How's that for nonsense?

It's precisely this nonsense which the Witness's guru put him up to.

COUNSEL: If you think that this Nokes-through-the-Looking-

Glass drollery will divert the Jury from the matter in hand, you'd better think again.

MYSELF: I'm talking sense. No fairy tale, it's my very serious response to your Witness. And it addresses, as cogently as I know how, the great issue before us.

Hell is having a head here. HHHH, if I want a mnemonic. Heaven is seeing it off. It's letting my mirror show me where this God-damned thing is magically transformed into that God-blessed thing, over there where it belongs.

Why is taking it on here so hellish? Because being shut in that tiny and dark and tightly packed sphere is being shut out of this immense sphere, where I'm lit up by the light of God and blown away by the wind of God. Because it sets little me up against my world, reducing me to a frightened stranger in it. Because it finally polishes off the stranger. And because it's a load of codswallop, the most implausible of lies. No wonder, then, that the Guillotine Meditation gave the Witness such a hard time. *Instead of decapitating him, it capitated him, good and proper! As never before.* The surprising thing is that he managed to stay out of the loony-bin.

Heading myself here is suicide. Beheading the others there is murder. Such violence against the person (whether behind glass or not) and against the truth, is a real capital offence. The burden of all my teaching (I call it unteaching), and now of my Defence against the charge of blasphemy, is that all those second and third persons—Jack included—are necessarily and delightfully headed, and not for beheading on any pretext; and that this unique First Person

The Ex-sanyassin

is necessarily and delightfully headless and not for heading on any pretext. Just let both sorts be the way they are (say I) and all will be well, all *is* well. Muck about with them, and all is worse than mucky. Just let God's magic mirror get on with its healing work of *placing* that topknot. Let it charm away this central malignancy and parasite and set it up over there, where it belongs, as the most harmless and devoted of pets. Let it cure me forever of chronic blasphemy—of the diabolical pride which superimposes that man-head on this God-head.

Members of the Jury, God has given you the best and brightest of His garden tools—His spade for rooting out blasphemy. Once more, I beg you: hold out your mirrors at arm's length, and take a good look at the weed you've dug up.

Look! There you have Belladonna the beautiful temptress. You are now keeping that fascinating but potentially lethal lady at a safe distance. Make sure she stays there. Embrace and take her, and she takes you. Here, *chez vous,* Belladonna's deadly poison.

The way to head her off is not—emphatically not—the way advocated by Bhagwan Shree Rajneesh in his *Orange Book:*

> One of the most beautiful tantra meditations: walk and think that the head is no more there, just the body. Continuously remember that the head is not there. Visualize yourself without the head. Have a picture of yourself enlarged without the head, look at it, let your mirror be lowered in the bathroom so when you see you cannot see your head, just the body... A few days of rememberance (sic) and you will feel such weightlessness happening to you, such tremendous silence, because

it is the head that is the problem. If you can conceive of yourself as headless—and that can be conceived, there is no trouble in it—then more and more you will be centred in the heart... Just at this moment you can visualize yourself headless. Then you will understand what I am saying immediately.

I say that the *absence of my head* is no more for 'conceiving', 'visualizing, 'remembering', 'thinking' (verbs that Rajneesh uses) than the *presence of your head is*. Both are for seeing. It's precisely this mentation, this mucking about with the evidence, which is the trouble with the Guillotine Meditation as so disastrously practised by the Witness.

A footnote: I take issue with nothing else of Rajneesh's that I've read—which isn't much, I admit. And even this he got so nearly right. Also let me add that I have a lot of ex-sanyassin friends who assure me that their involvement with Rajneesh somehow prepared them for the essential In-seeing they now enjoy. I don't suppose he ever came across that saying of Rabbi Izaac of Acre, a thirteenth-century Spanish Kabbalist: 'You should know that these philosophers whose wisdom you so much extol have their heads where we place our feet.' It just might have helped.

Prosecution Witness No. 22

THE ZOOLOGIST

Prompted by Counsel, the Witness introduces himself. He's a lecturer in the Department of Biology at Cambridge, specializing in comparative anatomy. Yes, he has read a couple of the Accused's books and is aware of the assertions he makes about his true identity, his exalted status in the scheme of things.

COUNSEL: What, in the light of your special knowledge, do you make of his divine pretensions?

WITNESS: I don't quite know whether to say the whole idea is so far above my head that I don't get a word of it, or so far below it there's nothing to get anyway. Only a load of wish-wash. Let's say I'm bewildered. Here's a man who's obviously no fool, yet as crazy as they come. Here's a man who's obviously not stuck-up, with an ego a mile high. Here's a man who's obviously sincere, and is playing an elaborate game. I suppose it takes a very complicated as well as a very clever fellow to take and defend a position as untenable as his.

COUNSEL: What makes it untenable?

WITNESS: In the dock there we have a biological specimen. (I mean no disrespect: here's another in the witness-box.) Let me spell out, in picturesque non-scientific terms, some facts about the specimen which the court should know. What my description loses in technical precision it will more than gain, I trust, in impact and in relevance to this Trial.

I study living organisms, ranging from the simplest to the most complex. Two contrary things strike me about them—their inexhaustible variety, and their overall sameness. Their differentiation and their unity. Life is indivisible, and what we call the highest forms of it are of a piece with what we call its lowest forms. Take that housefly flinging itself at the window over there. I'd like to draw the Accused's special attention to this long-lost relative of his. If John a-Nokes feels he's a cut above that fly, let me assure him that it's an archangel compared with himself not so very long ago. When he was young, he was of course an infant, a small apology for a human being and a mammal, on display for all to see and hear and fondle and smell. But before that, when he was younger still, he was an embarrassment and firmly *hushed up*—a series of skeletons in the cupboard of the womb. There, briefly, he was a small apology for a reptile, and before that a small apology for a fish, and before that a small apology for a worm. And when he was very young indeed, at the start of his present career, he was next to nothing at all, a small apology for a speck. Quite a complicated speck as specks go, but a far humbler entry in life's social register than any creature he sets eyes on nowadays, in the zoo, in his garden, anywhere. True, he was a yuppie speck, destined to rise in the world. But he hasn't for a moment ceased to be the same sort of thing, a speck that found it convenient to keep the speck-family together... And now this jumped-up speck emerges to inform a startled universe that it is its Origin and Proprietor, that it is the universe! How's that for cheek, for arrogance, for social climbing?

COUNSEL: Please take the court still further back in the Nokesian Saga, and tell us something about the origin of the speck or spicule.

WITNESS: Once upon a time there was a little sea, and in this sea there lived a fat and lazy globular speck, a female party putting out lashings of sex appeal in all directions. Picture her as a Mae West among specks. Picture also, racing towards her in passionate frenzy, hosts of admirers, in shape and behaviour resembling precociously lascivious polliwogs, but in status much more lowly. They were like a fleet of speedboats with outboard motors, all making for the one safe harbour. The winning craft, having made it there (all the rest perishing at sea), became the male half of the sketch we now call John a-Nokes, while the harbour became the female half. Now the chances against that particular suitor outstripping all his rivals, and winning the race and the lady, were millions to one. Jack be nimble, Jack be quick!—as the nursery rhyme says. Yes, the specimen in the dock over there had better face the fact that he's the most accidental of accidents, the outsider among outside chances, a fluke if ever there was a fluke.

The coming-to-be of John a-Nokes was less likely then than his winning the pools is now. And this fluke of a speck—propped up there on its newly acquired hind legs—is busy informing the world that it's the King of the world. There's nerve for you! There's impudence!

COUNSEL: What if he explained that he outgrew those dicey and humble beginnings years ago, and has since become a very different order of being? After all, kings don't start off crowned and sceptred and perched on thrones.

WITNESS: He has outgrown nothing. In a sense John a-Nokes is a front, or optical illusion, rather like a mirage or a rainbow: when you go up to him the man vanishes, and you find only specks which are the descendants of that original pair. The stuff of him, his life and his functioning, is their stuff and their life and their functioning, writ large and acting in concert.

COUNSEL: Nevertheless the whole, I guess you would say, transcends the sum of its parts.

WITNESS: Yes, of course. And no. For example, the whole lives by stuffing foreign matter into one end of itself and pushing foreign matter out the other end. Which is essentially the way each of its myriad parts lives.

Even more eloquent of the fact that he's grown out of nothing are his sexual antics. The man's up to the same game on the big dry land as the 'tadpole' was up to forty-five years ago in that little sea. There's built-in lechery, there's lifelong addiction for you! He can't keep off it! What's more, his whole life is spent in a marvellous bawdy-house in which his relations great and small are playing every variety of sex game, most of them bizarre enough to raise the eyebrows of a Havelock Ellis or a Krafft-Ebing, if not to bring a blush to his cheek. For a splendidly uninhibited example, take those flowering plants flashing their sex organs, male stamens rampant and lined up around the female pistil, all tarted up and set off by that gorgeous and seductive lingerie of petals. Or the beetles having it off there among the frillies by the hour. Surrounded as he is by such countless pointers to his own primeval physique and drives, what does our Nokes specimen do? Does he salute and bow to and settle down among these less-inhibited relations, inspired by family loyalty and family feeling? Not on your life! He raises his eyes heavenwards and informs the universe that he's its Alpha and Omega, its Substance and Sustainer, the spotless Pure Spirit back of it all! Whiter than the whitest snow! Purer than Purity! Can you beat that for swank, for insolence, for hypocrisy?

COUNSEL: And the Purity is forever, if you please! From eternity to eternity, *secula seculorum,* the specimen in the dock is the One Imperishable Reality—it casually informs us!

WITNESS: You would think (wouldn't you?) that with all those flowers and insects and other not-so-poor relations going the way of all flesh—dying like flies, as we say—all around him, he would take the hint that he's no exception, and is due soon to follow suit. How can he—in origin and in present constitution and functioning sticking so close to the standard pattern—how can he begin to persuade himself that he alone is permanent? At what auspicious juncture in his progress from that copulating tadpole to this copulating gentleman did the miracle of imperishability supervene? How, and why, did it do so? Stupid questions! What did supervene was megalomegalomania!

COUNSEL: Witness, I would like to ask you a question now about yourself. Underneath your professional skin does there lurk a religious man?

WITNESS: If so, he's never peeped out.

COUNSEL: The Accused's incredible self-conceit doesn't upset you in the slightest?

WITNESS: I'm amused and amazed, that's all. Even the amazement wears off. Ultimately I have to contemplate this interesting specimen with cool objectivity. Here's a variation or mutation from the norm all right, but no less a natural phenomenon than the norm is. It's a scientific fact that a few of these human organisms make peculiar high-pitched God-noises, just as it's a scientific fact that some cats squeak and don't mew.

COUNSEL: Well, that's all for the present... I see the Accused signals he has no questions to put to you. But please stay in court. I may want you in the box again...

Members of the Jury, let me remind you that the Prosecution has two broad aims. First, to produce evidence that the Accused is causing serious and unnecessary offence to religious people by publicly ridiculing or denigrating what they hold sacred. This includes scandalizing them to the limit by claiming to *be* the One whom they revere above all others. Second, to produce evidence that this claim of his is false anyway. According to some witnesses the Accused is guilty on both counts, according to others he's guilty on one or other count. Our present Witness belongs to the latter group. True, he's more astonished than shocked by the Accused's pretence that he's the Origin of the world. But what his testimony does do very thoroughly (I think you will agree) is to show up this pretence for the raving madness it is. The Witness has surely blown to smithereens the main Defence position, which is that—in asserting that he's none other than the Being that others worship—John a-Nokes is only stating the sober truth about his identity. Which (he says) he has an inalienable right to do.

Well, he would have a hard job pitching his identity—his cosmic status—any higher. And the Witness would have a hard job pitching it any lower. His qualifications for putting the Accused in his place—for taking him down more pegs than you can count—could, I submit, scarcely be bettered. And the facts on which he bases his testimony are among the most well-researched and universally accepted of all the scientific discoveries of the past four hundred years. Before Leeuwenhoek and his microscope, the Accused just might have got away with self-deification. Afterwards, what a hope!

Defence: **The Jumped-up Polliwog**

MYSELF: It's not every embryologist who can make such fun of his specimens, and not every specimen who can enjoy being made such fun of. Not only do I accept the Witness's testimony, but welcome with surprised enthusiasm the refreshingly unpretentious language in which he couched it. Labspeak may be a necessity in the lab, but it's dope outside. The story of my rise from extreme primitiveness—that most thrilling of all thrillers—when recited in the technical jargon we've got so case-hardened to (all that guff, I mean, about Mendelism, and spermatozoa and ova, and genes and chromosomes and DNA, and nuclei and vacuoles and flagella and the rest) falls flat on its face. The language knocks out the story, which is then killed outright by shifting it from oneself, the present Subject, on to objects remote and impersonal, from poignant autobiography to take-it-or-leave-it biography, from red-blooded particulars to anaemic generalities and abstractions. Even if 'human' embryos and foetuses were one day (following the example of caterpillars and tadpoles—real tadpoles this time) to become large and at large in the home instead of remaining tiny and hidden in utero, I bet you that labspeak would find a way of disconnecting these human larvae and pupae from their mums and dads, a way of pretending they were mere pets along with pedigree Pekes and Siamese cats—or intruders, along with mice and cockroaches—and by no means people in the making. Man's prime illusion is that he's only man. When will he wake to the fact that, in developmental time as distinct from clock time, his humanness is an appendix and an afterthought, belonging to the last few seconds of the eleventh hour of his little day?

I'm obliged to the Witness for reminding me so vividly of these forbidden but indispensable truths, and to Counsel for egging him on so effectively. Together, they have furnished all the clues I need for my Defence at this juncture.

If His Honour and the Jury will now turn to Diagram No. 21 and keep referring to it, they will easily grasp the substance of that Defence. This picture's worth all the words in the dictionary. I do believe that, if we were all honest and attentive enough, it would take over my Defence without need of another syllable from me. Also, it would save me repeating (as I must very briefly now do) some things I've said earlier in this Trial.

To be specific, our diagram sets out:
(1) What I look like to others,
(2) What I look like to myself,
(3) What I feel like,
(4) What I need,
(5) What I am,
(6) What others are.

Or, in a little more detail:

(1) The diagram indicates the view in to this spot—what the outsider makes of me as he approaches me from afar. His story is of no thing at all but a question mark, followed by a galaxy and a solar system and a planet, a continent and a country and a town and a family home (these four not shown), a man (not this time behind glass), a cell, a molecule, an atom, a particle, and finally no thing at all but another question mark.

(2) My *view out* from this spot agrees in essentials with this same pattern, with my travelling observer's view in. It's the same no thing, then things, then no thing, read from the other end. A fixture myself, I look *up* at the cosmic question-mark, at my unbounded space and my astronomical embodiments, *out* at my terrestrial and geographical and human embodiments (the man's behind glass this time), *down* at my bits and pieces, and *in* at my disembodiment—the question mark right here.

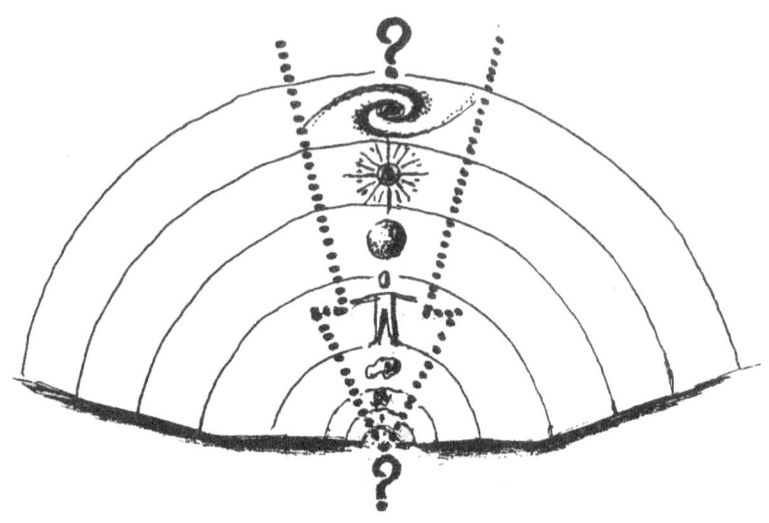

Diagram No. 21

(3) What I *feel* like varies according to the same pattern. For my narrowly human purposes I identify with that separate human. For my larger purposes, with my family, or my country, or my species, or my planet. At my most expansive, I feel all-inclusive: I identify with my universe-body, and contain all space and time. Conversely, at my least expansive, I shrink into and identify with one or another organ of my human body, or even—not infrequently—with nothing at all. Nothing but a great big central question-mark. Elasticity is my middle name.

(4) In fact, all these embodiments of mine hang together in that strictly indivisible Whole which is my many-levelled universe; to be itself, each needs the others. For example, what is John a-Nokes without his cells and molecules and atoms, or without his plants and animals, his planet and his sun—not to mention his bottle-green corduroy trousers? What is Earth without her Mahler and *Das Lied von der Erde*? What are the galaxies without their Hubble? Or the World without its amazement at itself?

(5) These regional things, then, are what I *need,* and *feel like,* and *look like to myself* and *look like to others.* This Central No-thing, on the other hand, this Awakeness that's awake to those things—this Capacity that takes them in and unites itself with them—is what I am. That little one in the mirror over there is only one of my countless disguises. At two metres he's my favourite appearance, that second/third person who says 'I'm John a-Nokes'. At zero metres I'm this First Person who says 'I AM'. The difference between this Nucleus and those outlying objects is as total as their indivisibility.

(6) I find nothing *here* to link this Central Reality with John a-Nokes specially, to make it his private real-estate. This whiter-than-white and stain-proof I AM will take nobody's laundry-marks. It's no more (and, of course, no less) *Jack's* Reality or Essence or Inside Story than it is his galaxy's, or his star's, or his planet's, or his cells' or his molecules'—down to the least of his particles. *If I want to know* (and I do, I do!) *what the Subjectivity of any and all of these embodiments of mine is, I have only to look right here, where it's brilliantly on display. Strictly speaking, there's only one Subject, only one First Person, only one I AM at the core of all these so different and seemingly separate embodiments. And that's the one I'm simultaneously looking in at and out of right here and right now.*

A diagram so simple that you can draw it in ten seconds and comprehend it in one second—that can yet take such good care of all six of these essential aspects of oneself, wordlessly if allowed to do so—isn't to be sniffed at. I say to each member of the Jury individually: open yourself now to its message by looking to make sure it's a true map of yourself as First Person, as Awareness and what it's aware of. (Emphatically not of me, not a map of Nokes, who for you is a third person.) Then, instead of your habitual 'God's out, I'm in', you will find yourself saying 'Hurray, God's in, I'm out!' Accordingly you will find Nokes Not Guilty of blasphemy because you find yourself Not Guilty of blasphemy.

JUDGE: I think you should leave these wonderfully generous tributes to your design till you've made its relevance to the Witness's testimony just a little bit clearer.

MYSELF: It's not that strictly one-level John a-Nokes (the extra who only just manages to make it into the picture) but the picture's all-level yet central Subject and Star who's responsible for this Self portrait. Some design! Some Designer! God does indeed geometrize. Your Honour will recollect that it was Plato who told us that.

Seeing Eye-to-Eye with the seers and mystics of all the great traditions, Kabir says: 'Behold but One in all beings!' The inside story of all, no matter what their grade, is identical. Looking in, I am what all are intrinsically. So when the Witness informs me that in my lifetime I have been a far humbler form of life than the fly on the window, my withers are unwrung. 'Why, of course!' I exclaim. And I go much further: Not only am I subhuman and subcellular and submolecular and subatomic, but sub-the-lot. I'm No-thing whatever, and I can't get lower than that, can I? And therefore I'm All things whatever, and I can't get higher than that, can I? I'm not talking about believing this but about seeing it. I have only to look here, right now, to enjoy the spectacle of this No-thing—which is the inside story of all things—exploding into the outside story of all things. I speak with wonder and reverence. 'It is indeed,' as Dante observes in the *Inferno*, 'not a matter to be taken lightly—describing the lowest point of the universe.'

To every being, accordingly, I say—not lightly but with all my heart: Here in the depths of me, as Who I really, really am, I am the One you really, really are. Though we may belong to vastly different regions and eras, wear vastly different faces, enjoy vastly different experiences of the world, all these are peripheral matters, matters of accident and time and content, and are transcended in the one central, timeless Container and Essence in which I'm aware of myself as you, and you, and you, *ad infinitum.* The barriers are down, our wounds are healed, and we are well again because we are One again.

COUNSEL, shoving his wig back and wiping imaginary sweat from his forehead, recalls the Witness and asks him: You've heard the Accused's reply to your testimony. What do you make of all this—this hocus, if not pocus?

WITNESS: As the rude man said of Shakespeare, 'Sounds wonderful, doesn't mean a thing!' I'll allow it's a sort of poetry, beautiful in spots, ingenious, fantastical. I'm not sorry that Mr Nokes should feel that my testimony does more to support than to undermine his case. I only wish I could make sense of it myself. I happen to be fond of music—of Bach in particular—but it's quite irrelevant to my work. Well, the ideas of the Accused are rather like that. They have little bearing that I can see on the biological facts I brought to the court's notice—in language that's going to do me no good professionally, I'll bet. But here and there they give me a *frisson.*

MYSELF: Damn *frissons!* A grain of fact is worth a ton of the things. I've two or three straight and unvarnished questions for you. Do you agree that what I'm perceived to be depends on the distance of the observer?

WITNESS: Yes.

MYSELF: Good. You said as much during your examination in chief. Do you also agree that the only observer who can get all the way up to me here, not an angstrom intervening, is myself?

WITNESS: Well, yes—

MYSELF: And that my story of what's given right here (namely, No-thing) very neatly completes the scientist's story of the progressively featureless things (cells, molecules, atoms, particles...) that are given on the way here?

WITNESS: I suppose you could put it like that. Provisionally, I'll agree with you.

MYSELF: Listen carefully then, if you please. This jumped-up polliwog or tadpole in the dock is standing on its newly acquired hind legs, and opening its big mouth, and telling you that, at a range of zero angstroms from itself, it's wider awake than wide-awake, wider than the wide world, clearer than the clear and empty sky—yet full to overflowing with all the furniture of heaven and earth. And that this isn't the inside story of a 'tadpole' only or a human being only, but equally of all the orders of being that go to their making. And that, like it or lump it, these are hard and readily verifiable facts, to neglect which is to be deplorably unscientific.

WITNESS: Well, I hold down my job all right, but am none too sure what it is to be scientific, or how good a scientist I am. But I'll say this much: the more I find out, the more there is to find out. Every question answered spawns two new questions. I'm scarcely scratching the surface of things.

MYSELF: Scratch them hard till you draw blood, and you'll never expose their Secret. Scratch yourself easy, and at once you'll see and you'll be their Secret. *I don't care how primitive or how advanced your specimen, look out and you have its appearance, look in and you are its Reality.*

And here, finally, are six prestigious Defence witnesses (excuse me—testifiers) who, between them, sum up the points I've been making:

Man is like a mirage in the desert that the thirsty man takes to be water, until he comes up to it and finds it to be nothing, and where he thought it to be, there he finds God.

The Koran

When the Self is seen, heard, thought of known, everything is known.

Brihadaranyaka Upanishad

If I knew myself as intimately as I ought, I should have perfect knowledge of all creatures.

Eckhart

Every creature is an appearance of God.

Erigena

He who sees the supreme Lord dwelling alike in all beings, and never perishing when they perish, he sees indeed.

Bhagavad Gita

Man is the one in whom all creatures end, in whom all multitudinous things have been reduced to one in Christ: man is then one in God with Christ's humanity. Thus all creatures are one man and that man is God in Christ's Person.

Eckhart

When you have broken and destroyed your own form, you have learned to break the form of everything.

Rumi

Prosecution Witness No. 23

THE MULLAH

COUNSEL, to Jury: Our next Witness is a distinguished member of the large Muslim community in this country. As such, his interest in the effectiveness of the Blasphemy Act is as keen as that of any Christian or Jewish leader. Or keener. You might suppose, however, that his concern with this particular Trial must be marginal, since the Accused isn't a Muslim. Not so. He's thoroughly involved. The Prosecution have called him to testify today—and he's eager to do so—for three excellent reasons. The first is to warn nascent or would-be Muslim blasphemers (and he assures me there are some around) of their criminal folly and the danger they're in. The second reason is that the Accused trespasses deep into Muslim territory when he invokes the support—as he often does—of such Islamic mystics as Rumi, and of the Holy Koran itself. Trespassers expose themselves to prosecution. The third reason for the Reverend Mullah's presence in the witness-box is that he may show us how close is the parallel between the blasphemy committed by John a-Nokes and that committed by certain Muslim heretics. In this way—by demonstrating that his offence isn't only anti-Judaeo-Christian but anti-religious in the general Western sense—the Crown's case against him is established on a still broader base.

I think it would be helpful if the Witness began by telling the court about the most notorious blasphemer in the history of Islam.

WITNESS: Mansur, also known as Al Hallaj, was a Persian mystic of the third century of the Islamic era. He publicly declared, and persisted in declaring, 'In my cloak is none but God.' He called himself Al Haq, which means 'the Truth that is Allah'—sacred be His Name. There was a great scandal and uproar among the Faithful of his time.

COUNSEL: What happened to him?

WITNESS: He was condemned and executed.

COUNSEL: How?

WITNESS: He was flayed, then crucified.

COUNSEL: Earlier in this Trial the Accused quoted that well-known text from the Holy Koran about Allah being nearer to a man than his own neck-vein. Was Mansur relying on this and similar teachings of the Prophet? If so, please explain to the Jury why his contemporaries were nevertheless so shocked that they treated him the way they did.

WITNESS: The substance—the heart and soul—of Islam is the transcendence and majesty and power of God, His absolute uniqueness and otherness. These attributes call for the absolute submission of the Faithful. Given this submission, to recognize that God is in all His creation—and not least in men and women—is in order. Indeed it follows from His greatness that He is present everywhere. The sin of Mansur, and of all so-called mystics of his stamp, was that he sacrificed the transcendence of God to His immanence. He dragged God down to his own level, shrank the Almighty to his own dimensions, took possession of Him.

There are (you see) three sorts of Muslims: the vast majority who put God infinitely *above* themselves; a much smaller number of more spiritually mature souls who put God *above and within* themselves; and a (fortunately) very small number who put God *within* themselves, and either forget about or deny His unapproachable holiness. Of these three types, the first is following the safe way; though somewhat narrow, it's wonderfully conducive to living the true Muslim life. The second is ideal, and can be even more effective, but it's liable to wander off into dangerous country. The third runs counter to Islam, and is notorious for leading to wild and immoral conduct. For the individual, it's spiritual ruin. For the community, it's a dreadful disease which—because it can spread so far and so fast—calls for the most drastic surgery.

COUNSEL: Do you link the Accused with this third and perverted type?

WITNESS: If it were not for his incursions into Islam, I would hesitate to pronounce on a non-Muslim. However, they entitle me—they oblige me—to reply to your question. My answer is: yes. Examining, in preparation for my testimony today, the writings of Mr John a-Nokes, I found them to be blasphemous. The comments I've just made about Mansur would seem to apply to him.

COUNSEL: What about his frequent invocations of Jelaluddin Rumi, and other Sufi masters, in support of his teachings?

WITNESS: Rumi was an eminent and inspired Muslim poet, but—like most poets—given to fantasy and exaggeration. This makes it easy to extract from his voluminous works many passages which seem to proclaim God's immanence at the expense of His transcendence. The same is true of other famous Sufis, such as Attar and Hafiz. Also I believe that some Sufis did go (and still go) much too far in Mansur's direction. Sufism is a hazardous province of their own country for native Muslims to venture into, let alone foreigners.

We particularly deplore the bad name given to the Faith when aspects of it are torn from their context, misunderstood and misapplied in the service of blasphemy as defined by non-Muslims.

COUNSEL, to Jury: Need I stress the importance of this extra-mural testimony confirming the guilt of the Accused? As I say, it does much to establish the Crown's case upon a wider than Judaeo-Christian basis.

Defence: **Far is High**

MYSELF, to Witness: My first question may seem irrelevant, but it isn't. It's about the prayers with which every true Muslim punctuates his day—at dawn, noon, mid-afternoon, sunset and bedtime; prayers which are as physical as they are mental, as much the body at worship as the mind at worship. No half-measures in Islam's adoration of Allah! At one point the worshipper's eyes are turned heavenwards and his hands are held high. At another, his forehead's on the ground. In between are a variety of gestures appropriate to the words being recited. Am I right so far, Reverend Sir?

WITNESS: Right enough.

MYSELF: My point is that these truly energetic prayers include, and elaborate on, the bowing exercise which—you Jurors will remember—I've been trying to get you to do. In fact, I go so far as to call this bowing my Defence posture, my Defence in action. My intention is that, in this cosmic down-sweep, the words shall come to life—to a Life that's larger than life.

Back to you, Reverend Sir. I take it that, in making this deepest of bows, Muslims are re-awaking to the presence of God in God's world, which is truly a vertical world. Here's a lofty and profound experience which, repeated so frequently and so regularly, is a large ingredient of Islam's genius. In these prayers can be found the secret of its social cohesion and its spectacular success in world history. Do you agree?

WITNESS: I would rather say that our prayers prevent us from forgetting Almighty God for more than a few hours at a time; neglecting them, we would degenerate into virtual atheists. And of course they do have far-reaching social consequences.

MYSELF: In traditional Christianity, as distinct from the modern sort, we paint much the same picture of God in His world—again an essentially vertical world. Take for example that magnificent hymn of Cardinal Newman's:

> Praise to the Holiest in the height
> And in the depth be praise;
> In all His words most wonderful,
> Most sure in all His ways.

We have it again in the song of the angels at the Nativity: 'Glory to God in the highest, and on earth peace, good will toward men.'

Notably also, of course, in the Lord's Prayer: 'Our Father, which art in heaven, hallowed be thy name. Thy will be done on earth as it is in heaven.' And in many Psalms which speak of our help coming from above. When very young I sang, with enthusiasm and high conviction, 'There's a home for little children, above the bright blue sky.' It made up for some of the more unheavenly features of one's earthly home. Yes, indeed: the traditional Judaeo-Christian universe is as truly a vertical one as the Muslim universe. God's at the very apex of it, and beneath Him are descending layers—each darker and heavier and less divine than the last—with man fairly near the base. At the same time God is present throughout, from top to bottom.

That's the way Christians *felt and thought* about God's vertical world. But we did little to translate our thoughts and feelings into bodily actions. We stood and we sat at worship, and at intervals we condescended to kneel. Occasionally we nodded, but preferred not to bow. We had stiff backs—a handicap that Islam's wonderfully free of. From its explosive beginnings some fourteen centuries ago it has made full use of the law that, to the extent that feeling and thinking are given bodily expression, they are no longer vague, sentimental, variable and half-hearted.

Reverend Sir, what do you say to this?

WITNESS: There's much truth in it. But I'm not quite clear about its relevance to the crime you're charged with.

COUNSEL: Nor are the Jury, I'm sure. If this is your cross-examination of the Prosecution's Witness, it's taking a cumbersome and long-winded form, and the point of it all is obscure.

MYSELF: I've finished with the Mullah for the moment, but ask him not to leave the courtroom—I may have one or two further questions for him later on. As for our exchange on the verticality—which means divinity—of the traditional world-picture in all Western religion, its importance for the Defence is about to become very clear indeed.

The modern, pseudo-scientific—and, yes, virtually atheistic—picture is of a world that has lost its vertical dimension. It was an upright world, lively, in good nick. Now it has fallen flat on its back. If you Jury members will please turn to Diagram No. 22, you will follow me easily.

Hinged about myself here—about my Bottom Line—*the high places of my childhood have become the far places of my manhood.* Without my noticing, my world has been fed a Mickey Finn and laid out flat. No question of bowing now. I don't kowtow to gods who are on my level, still less to a subhuman cosmos.

Here I have a confession to make. For fifteen years and more I had been drawing—less as a meditational exercise than as a visual aid to self-discovery—countless mandala patterns, or nests of concentric circles, for arranging my First-person universe in, region by region. And all along I had thought of the pattern as horizontal. The galaxies and stars in it were *out there,* not *up here.*

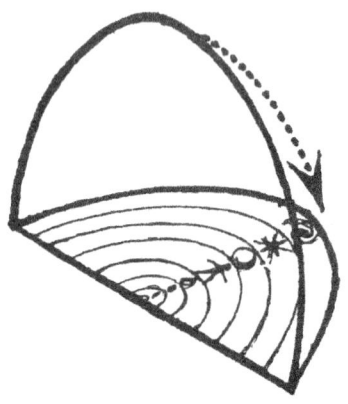

Diagram No. 22

It's true that my universe soon slept off its knockout drop and opened an eye, but it still lay on its back. It was a dazed and prostrate world, stretching into the far distance.

And then it got up. The far became high. As recently as two years ago it happened. The world-door, hinged right here, suddenly opened and swung through 90°. Here was *my* world at last, all of it *here*. It had come back to me. Yet it was now *God's* world again, infinitely awesome, a tall world for bowing to. It was at once more me and less me. If that's paradoxical, I say God bless His lovely paradoxes!

However vast the floor and luxurious the carpet, you don't bow to it—it's for walking on. But tack the carpet to the wall, and it's for looking at—it's God's tapestry, displaying the magnificent hierarchy of heaven and earth, and all of it given right here. The world's lofty and deep, God's in His heaven and I'm His child again on Earth. Once more heaven's above the bright blue sky, and Jackie's down here gazing up at it, wonderstruck. The real and given world's an upstanding world, nearer than near yet more awesome than awesome.

COUNSEL, springing to his feet in great excitement, feigned or real: Hold on! If I can believe my ears you're coolly abandoning— just like that!—the basic contention of the Defence, which is that God's throne is set up at your very Centre. Now you're locating it at your circumference, the very outside edge of your world. A bigger turn-around can't be imagined. In which event—given such abject apologies to offended parties as His Honour may determine, and to the court for this shocking waste of its time—the Prosecution has no case against you. No case, I mean, that a fine or a shortish prison sentence wouldn't atone for.

MYSELF: I fear you won't be so ready to let me off when I piece together and fill out the tale I've been telling you about myself—with the help of Diagram No. 23, which the Jury should please now turn to. Let me quickly run through the three-part story:

Chapter One is about myself the infant. I haven't yet learned to push away and distance my world, either in space or in time. It's two-dimensional, all of it here and all of it now. An upright world, an up-and-down world, immensely high, wide and handsome. All of it mine. All of it alive with my life.

Chapter Two is about myself the adult—the grown-up whose world has grown down. Or rather, fallen down. Hinged about myself here and now, it has collapsed into there and then and is mine no longer. I'm all at once desperately poor. And, with it, desperately proud. Now I experience myself as a superior but frightened stranger in an alien and lifeless world, as a minute oasis in that immense cosmic Sahara. I alone am worshipful. That prostrate expanse invites and urges me to commit the crime of Mansur. All that's left to bow to is myself.

In *Chapter Three* I come to my senses. Encouraged by any competent artist, I look to see. His painting or photograph helps to show me what enchantment there is in the *collapse* of distance: it rubs my nose in the up-ended scene. I see that knocked-flat world wake up, and get up, and stay up. The well-oiled hinge works all the time, in little things as in great. The long gradient of the hill in front of me becomes short and steep, a step and not a slope at all, and I'm right up to it. The mountain, now two-dimensional—triangular instead of

1—Infant's Vertical World

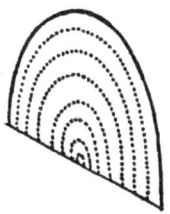

High is high

2—Adult's Prostrate World

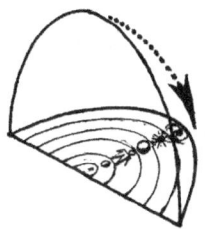

High is far

3 Seer's Vertical World

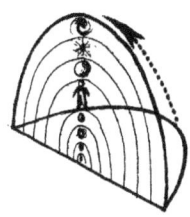

Far is high

Diagram No. 23

pyramidal—keeps its slopes on either side, but ahead is sheer. The sky—though as wide as ever—is immensely higher. The bright blue lid of the universe is halved and set up on edge. From top to bottom the world is charged with the glory of God and His grandeur. The charm and mystery of this truly brave new world is that it is all here and now and mine, yet indescribably worshipful. At once infinitely humbled and infinitely exalted, the last thing I'm interested in is, like Mansur, taking possession of God. Echoing Job, I exclaim, 'Is not God in the height of heaven? and behold the height of the stars, how high they are!'

This is what I see, this is how I feel, this is the way I want to live.

I should like now to re-call the Witness. [The Mullah returns to the box. I address him.] Well, Reverend Sir, I hope this account of the up-ending of God's world has done something to clear me, in your eyes, of that unbridled and unbalanced immanentism which cost poor Mansur so dear.

WITNESS: To some extent it has. I'm happy to admit that your incursions into Islamic spirituality appear less one-sided (and therefore less heretical) than I had supposed. And that if you were to convert to Islam I wouldn't pursue you with charges of blasphemy. Provided, of course, you stick to what you've been telling us.

COUNSEL: I'm utterly baffled! How is it, Nokes, that in your writings (which I've made it my business to know pretty well) there's no mention of this hinging and up-ending of the universe? It looks to me—and, I expect, to the jury—like panic stations, a last-minute effort to buy a favourable verdict, and by no means a change of heart. Only if you will now explicitly and without hedging withdraw all those blasphemous statements made during and before this Trial—to the effect that you are the very One that Christians and Jews and Muslims worship as the Highest—will the Crown consider withdrawing its charge against you.

Well, what have you got to say?

MYSELF: I don't take back a word of it.

Members of the Jury, to understand why I won't give an inch and don't need to, please turn to Diagram No. 24.

Look at the difference between that little, tiny-armed, other-way-up, paper-thin, framed-and-glazed third person who has no room for God—and this immense First Person who is the opposite of all that and brim-full of God, and whose God's-arms visibly reach (as if uplifted in Muslim prayer) beyond the Stars. *It's not that little one who bows before this Big One. As Angelus Silesius says, 'God bends and bows to Himself, and to Himself doth pray'.*

The truth—so simple and obvious, yet so astounding—is that the prostrate world is man's and the upright world is God's. Why? Because (as I've already demonstrated in this court) God is omnipresent, and for Him alone far is near and high. He, and not John a-Nokes, draws the Bottom Line and oils and operates the Hinge about which His world swings vertical and magnificent.

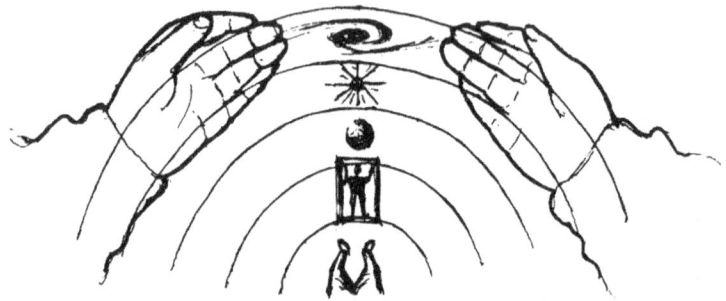

Diagram No. 24

It's as this unique First Person who is Himself that I truly revere Him as higher than the highest. That jackass Jack is much too conceited, much too stuck-up, to begin to do so.

Only *as* Him am I lowly enough—and deep enough—to *be* Him.

I call six in support, out of scores that stand ready to testify:

He who knows about depth knows about God.

Paul Tillich

And Jacob awaked out of his sleep [in which he'd dreamed about a ladder set up between Earth and Heaven] and he said, Surely the Lord is in this place; and I knew it not... this is none other but the house of God, and this is the gate of heaven.

Genesis

One God and Father of all, who is above all, and through all, and in you all... Now that he ascended, what is it but that he also descended first into the lower parts of the earth? He that descended is the same also that ascended up far above all heavens, that he might fill all things.

St Paul

The world stands out on either side
No wider than the heart is wide...
And he whose soul is flat—the sky
Will cave in on him by and by.

Edna St Vincent Millay

The outward man is the swinging door, the Inner Man is the still hinge. When I am one with that wherein are all things, past and present and to come, and all the same distance... then they are all in God and all in me.

Eckhart

My final Witness is Judy Taylor, author of *As I See It,* who lost her sight as a child. Regaining it forty years later, she asked:

'What is that white thing sticking straight up in the air beside the house opposite? It turned out to be the drive. She got it to lie down in due course.

Prosecution Witness No. 24

THE REGISTRAR

COUNSEL: The Accused frequently asserts in his writings, and he has repeated it often enough in this court, that he was not born and therefore will not die. Well, our next Witness is the Registrar of Births and Marriages and Deaths in the Urban District of Easterton. He has looked up in his records and brought along a copy of a certain registration of birth. I'm asking him to read out this document to the court.

WITNESS: I knew the Accused's parents personally, and I made a point of registering the birth of their son myself. Here's how the certificate reads:

CERTIFICATE OF BIRTH

Pursuant to the Births and Deaths Registration Act 1953 et seq.
Birth in the Sub-district of Easterton in the County of Suffolk

When and where born	Name	S x	Name of father	Name of mother	Rank or profession of father	Signature and residence of informant	Physician's counter-signature
12 February 1959. 107 High Street, Easterton	John	Boy	Edgar Charles a-Nokes	Annie a-Nokes, formerly Garrard	Carpenter (mast .r)	E. C. a-Nokes, 107 High Street, Easterton	W. Hutchison, MD Easterton

When registered: 13 February 1959. *No. in Register*: 1959 453

Signature of Registrar: C. E. Allerton.

COUNSEL: I understand you also hold in your office records of the birth of the Accused's parents. And of their deaths—which, again, you registered personally.

WITNESS: That's right. They died at a rather early age, within a few weeks of each other, in 1980.

COUNSEL: So it seems that the Accused was born all right, and born into a family subject to the normal hazards of human existence... When you told us his parents died prematurely, what had you in mind?

WITNESS: It was soon after the Accused had apostatized—

MYSELF, furiously: Your Honour! What possible motive can Counsel have for dragging in my parents other than the desire to prejudice the Jury against me by speculation and innuendo concerning our family relationships? I'm here to be tried on a specific charge, not to suffer needless character-assassination by him and this Witness. And not to have my feelings scarified at the Prosecution's whim.

JUDGE: Is Counsel quite sure that further testimony from this Witness has a direct bearing on this case?

COUNSEL: I am, Your Honour.

JUDGE: You may proceed, then, but with a care not to give the Accused cause for further complaint.

COUNSEL: I'm obliged to Your Honour... Witness, please continue, bearing in mind the Judge's proviso.

WITNESS: The Nokes family had for three generations been very pious people belonging to a particularly strict branch of the

Primitive Methodists. They were somewhat notorious locally for their uncompromising religious views, but respected for their human qualities. I knew the Accused's father well, because for many years he did maintenance work for me. He was a most skilled and hard-working craftsman, scrupulously honest and consistently cheerful. The greatest mistake he ever made in his life (he told me) was agreeing to his elder son going up to London University to study civil engineering. He blamed himself for what happened to Jack as a result (so he believed) of that move to a very different world.

At fourteen, Jack, to the great joy of his parents, had gone through the conversion process—the stages of conviction of sin, repentance, justification by faith, and the witness of the Spirit—much valued by the Primitive Methodists, and had promptly become a full church member. Which he continued to be, first in Easterton and then in London—till he reached the age of twenty-one, to the day. Then it was that the blow fell on the family, with absolutely no warning.

The blow had repercussions far beyond the family. Jack made a great stir among the members of the sect in London and Suffolk, and beyond, by formally challenging their most treasured beliefs. And, much worse, the beliefs of all Christian people. And then there was the provocative way he did it. He could have quietly ceased to attend church services and broken by degrees with his Methodist friends, thereby cushioning the shock to his parents. Instead, he chose to circulate among church members a thesis, setting forth views which outraged them so much that the word went round that this was the worst case of apostasy that the sect had ever known. I came by a copy of the document and wasn't at all surprised at the shock and the pain it gave to those for whom it was intended. Why (I asked myself) had he done this thing? He was too intelligent to imagine he would convert any of these people to his opinions. The most charitable explanation was that he acted out of a desire to show off and play the *enfant terrible,* no matter how devastated his parents were sure to be.

COUNSEL: Do you still have a copy of the Accused's thesis?

WITNESS: I can't find it. I may have thrown it away in disgust. However, I recollect some of its contents.

COUNSEL: Briefly, what were the author's main points—in so far as they have any bearing on his Trial here, some twenty-three years later, on a charge of blasphemy?

WITNESS: I distinctly remember his saying that it was an accident that he happened to be born to parents who held such views as his did. Indeed it was by the merest chance that he had turned up in twentieth-century Europe instead of, say, ancient India or China. How could he be sure which faith, if any—among all those that have arisen throughout the world's history—was for him the true faith and revelation of God? How could he possibly know the answer till he had (these were his words) 'shopped around a good deal to see what was on offer'? Already, at twenty-one, after a few weeks' reading, he claimed to have detected in the great religions a common core... This brings me to the place where I find his views so repulsive that I don't like to soil my lips by recounting them—

COUNSEL: What was this common core as he saw it? What did those religions have to say that so appealed to him and so appalled his people?

WITNESS: He claimed they assured him that he—yes, *he*, personally—had never been born and consequently would never die! How could he be sure of this? Because he was himself none other than—how can I say this without being sick?—none other than the Everlasting One.

Well, you can imagine the effect on his parents! The family had been held in high esteem among the members of the sect, and not just locally. 'Oh, the disgrace, the disgrace!' was his mother's reaction. I fear she had been inordinately proud of the early conversion and outstanding piety of her eldest, and some of her co-religionists lost no opportunity of reminding her of his sudden fall to unprecedented depths. But it was the effect on his father that was so pitiful. I remember the poor man, whom I'd got quite attached to, weeping copiously as he handed me a copy of that blasphemous document.

It was soon after that—

COUNSEL, interrupting: Remember His Honour's warning. Avoid giving unnecessary pain, and don't stray into side-issues.

WITNESS: Well, it may be, of course, a chance coincidence that the parents of the Accused died, both of them, so soon after their son's apostasy. Perhaps they didn't die of a broken heart. But—

JUDGE, at the top of his voice: I'll tolerate no more from this Witness. I instruct the jury to pay no attention to the last part of his evidence. Come to that, I await Counsel's reasons for regarding *any* of his evidence as relevant to the case before the court. Is he thinking of the Accused's apologia, which I thought was circulated only among members of the sect? Was it ever released for public consumption? Is it around now? If not, of what interest is it to this court?

COUNSEL: My information, Your Honour, is that it wasn't released... Allow me to explain, however, the Prosecution's aim in calling this Witness.

In fairness to the public, and indeed to the Accused himself, my purpose throughout this Trial is to present an overall picture of him, and his vocation in life as he understands it. If it turned out that his blasphemy is occasional or accidental or untypical of the man, that would count in his favour. But if it turned out to be consistent over the years, and thoroughly built-in and indeed quite central to his life, that would count in his disfavour. Obviously. Well, the evidence the court has just heard strongly confirms the latter picture.

JUDGE: The Blasphemy Act of 2002, as I read it, is not retrospective. Neither in law nor in common sense nor in common justice can a man be charged with an offence committed before it became an offence.

COUNSEL: Of course I respectfully concur, Your Honour. Nevertheless the Prosecution points out that, following the passing of the Act, the Accused has done nothing to tone down—much less withdraw—his teaching or his claims. On the contrary, he has been at pains publicly to endorse and extend his original views as outlined in that lost document. In short, it's he who has brought forward his prior-to-the-Act blaspheming past into his post-Act blaspheming present, so that it is all of a piece. And is properly taken to be so by the Prosecution.

JUDGE: While I follow your reasoning, I direct the Jury to pay no attention to the Witness's opinions about what young Nokes had to do to break free of that religious sect. And absolutely no attention whatever to his opinions about the effect of the breakaway on the young man's parents.

The Witness stands down, shaking his head. Some boos and clapping in the public gallery...

Defence: **Time Out**

MYSELF: Let me get two things, arising from the Witness's testimony (if that's the right word for it), out of the way and done with.

Alas, the Judge's direction to the Jury can do nothing to expunge from their minds the idea that I'm responsible for my parents' deaths before their time. What's said can't be unsaid.

Therefore, I can hardly pass over this insinuation without comment. It is indeed conceivable that my heresy did shorten my father's life. Not my mother's—she was already sick at the time.

Certainly it did much to spoil what remained of his life. He loved me so much, and had placed so much store on my following in his godly footsteps—moreover my heresy was (as he saw it) so devilish and so certain to send me to hell forever—that there's no doubt the shock of it did make him ill. Increasingly I have felt a great sadness that I had to do this thing to him. But never guilt. He would have died in defence of his convictions and his right to proclaim them, and I'm sufficiently his son that I'm prepared, if necessary, to die in defence of my very different convictions. I like to think that on some plane he will not be ashamed of me in the end, whatever the verdict of this court and of posterity. Just let me add that I have always loved and respected him more than any man I have known, and trust that (as I say, in some dimension or on some plane or other) he's aware of the fact. Perhaps this tribute to him will do something to counter the Witness's atrocious insinuation that I'm not just a dyed-in-the-wool blasphemer, but a hideously callous one into the bargain.

The other comment I want to make on his testimony is even more important. Neither in that original paper of mine, resigning from the Primitive Methodists, nor at any time since have I made the ridiculous claim that John a-Nokes wasn't born and won't die. Still less have I identified him with the Eternal One. In fact, a large part of my mission in life is to combat all attempts (and how popular and many and varied and persistent they are!) to attribute immortality to men and women *as such*. All flesh is as grass. Humans happen, then unhappen. Like the goods in the shop run by a previous Witness, they have a limited shelf-life.

John a-Nokes qua John a-Nokes is biodegradable, and before long I shall be excused from being him, for ever. Enough is enough of Jack (say I), and the universe agrees. *There's* an ephemeral creature for you! There's a perisher all right!

But why should I worry? *Here's* a very different story. Right here, a yard or two nearer to me than that almost-goner, shines the Eternal One. Here is His home for ever.

Your Honour, and members of the Jury, will you please turn to Diagram No. 25 in your booklet, and to yet another variation on the

Defence's schema. It will help you to follow what I'm about to get up to.

In my right hand I hold this mirror, in my left this copy of my birth certificate. For me to read the certificate it must be a foot or so away, where I also find, staring fixedly at me through his oval window, the person the certificate refers to. There they are, goods and label, in the region where the Great Universal Store displays that perishable Nokes package—with its distinctive label indicating brand name, serial number and approximate shelf-life. It will presently be withdrawn from the human display stand, and disposed of.

JUDGE: In plain terms, you'll die one day, and be buried or cremated. Is that what you mean?

MYSELF: Of course, Your Honour. But also—and more particularly—I'm speaking of dying today. Tomorrow's too late to bite the dust. Please look! Watch me carefully. Simultaneously I bring goods and label up to my Eye, noting how they merge... blur... become indecipherable and unrecognizable—and are altogether obliterated just before contact. Here, certificate and certified are no more. But I remain. The lesson is that the One I really, really am is absolutely unaffected by this summary disposal of that John a-Nokes package.

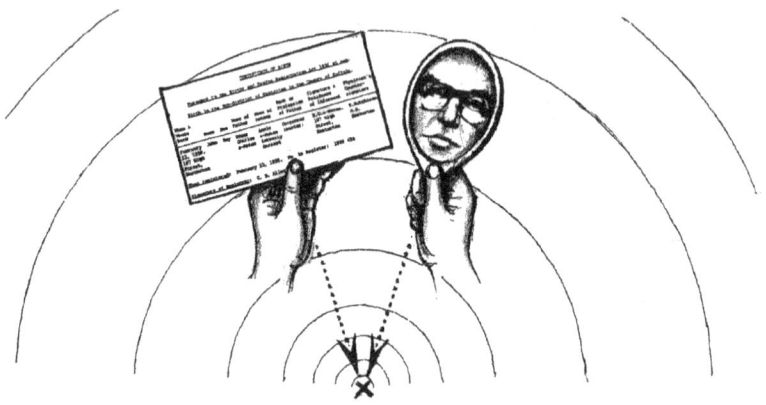

Diagram No. 25

In fact, I can find no way of taking that package and bringing it here without losing it *en route*. It doesn't belong here. This place just won't take it. Here, no perishables are admitted, and Death is forever held at bay. To St Paul's somewhat rhetorical questions—'O Death, where is thy sting? O Grave, where is thy victory?'—my mundane reply is: 'Not many millimetres off, Paul dear, but quite far enough to draw its sting, and turn its victory into defeat. Right here, that mortal does, as you say, put on immortality. Right here, I'm forever grounded in the Timeless.'

COUNSEL: Am I allowed to butt in here and put a question?

MYSELF: Try me.

COUNSEL: How long have you been in court this session, following the luncheon recess?

MYSELF: About an hour.

COUNSEL: Members of the Jury, we have been patiently watching the Accused amuse himself with a piece of glass and a scrap of paper. The purpose of this child's game was to prove he's timeless. Well, it was all an absurd waste of time. He has just told us that he—this self-styled timeless one—has been in court for about an hour!

MYSELF: And I meant what I said, because—naturally and out of politeness—I was going by your Greenwich time out there, and not by my Paradise time right here. Am I being difficult? I can best explain by asking His Honour and the Jury to join me in another little test (it's beneath the dignity of a King's Counsellor, of course); the least of all our experiments, leading—if only we're simple enough—to the greatest of all our discoveries in the course of this Trial.

You are wearing wrist-watches. Look and see what the time is now by them... Somewhen around 4 p.m., I think.

Time varies with place. Evidently the time now on the Jury benches is around 4 p.m. I see it's the same here in the dock. Telephone calls would reveal that the time in New York is around 11 a.m. and in Los Angeles around 8 a.m. And so on. Along with space, time's essentially *zoned*. That's why, when you travel to different places, you check what the local time is by referring to the local clocks. It's important, whenever you are, to keep abreast of and go by the time there. But there's just one place in the universe where it's a matter of life and death to tell the right time—if any. *And that's its Centre.*

So the big question is: what's the time right where you are, at the very mid-point of all those zones? Unfortunately, it's a place that's not on the phone and where they don't have any local timepieces, so you'll have to go along and take your own timepiece with you. And keep an open mind, and see for yourself.

Which you do now by slowly, slowly bringing together your watch and your eye, attending throughout to what's on show, what's actually given...

Go on now. Don't be shy, and don't look at me but at your watch, bringing it right up till it will come no nearer...

Right... What happened? Didn't those hands and figures blur and fade and finally vanish? In fact, didn't the timepiece itself (and all pieces are timepieces) vanish too, in the Place where there are no bits and pieces at all?

So the Place you're at is timeless, absolutely and always free of time and of the things of time. Here at Home, you're not troubled by so much as a shadow or a sniff of time. In fact, you never were anywhere else than in Eternity, where it's always 0 o'clock. Your ordinary wristwatch, which tells you the time out there, has just been re-engineered into God's extraordinary wrist-watch which tells You the no-time here, for ever and for ever. The former has a price tag, is never quite accurate, can be lost or stolen, requires periodical renewal. Not so the latter. God's no-timepiece is infinitely superior to anything that even the Swiss can turn out. Praise be to the Holiest for His total victory over time and death, for the unspeakably sure safety of His presence, and for this unspeakably vivid and handy unveiling of it! Dear Lord, help us smart alicks to your artlessness! *O Sancta simplicitas!*

COUNSEL: Really, Your Honour! For the umpteenth time, this is a court of law, not a kindergarten. Do the Jury have to play this infantile game?

JUDGE: The question hardly arises, I think, since the conscientious jury members have already done so. Myself also. With what result? That's the question.

MYSELF: I'm grateful to Your Honour. It was St Paul, again, who said that the foolishness of God is wiser than men. And medieval theologians who went on to say that only God can be perfectly known because only God is perfectly simple.

To help us now to be as unsophisticated as God, let's turn to Diagram No. 26. Self-explanatory, it displays at a glance our Endings, so far, about time's whereabouts and whenabouts.
Every way I look at it, these findings about the timeless First Person, superficially so strange, in practice make wonderfully good sense.

Thus:

(1) What I find here—and what others find when they come here to see whether I'm telling the truth—is no thing at all. And where there's no thing, there's no change, and where there's no change, there's no way to register time, and where there's no way to register time, there's no time to register. QED.

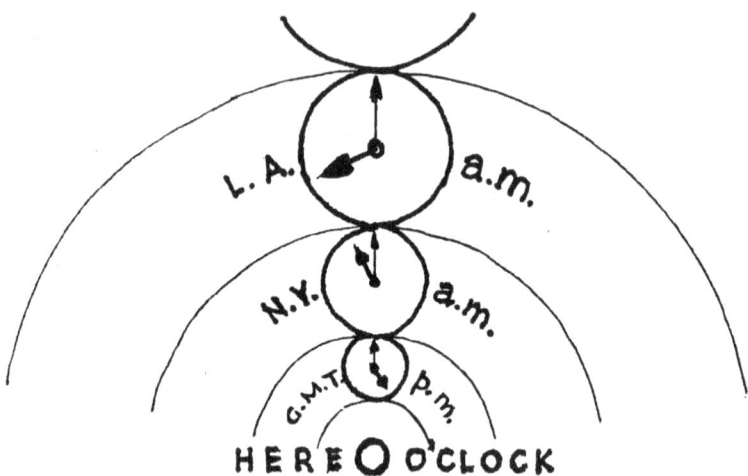

Diagram No. 26

(2) Here I don't *feel* a second older than when I was brought up into the court from my cell in the basement, or when this Trial started. Or, for that matter, when as a small child I used to look in the mirror and find a staring stranger there. My world there—including him—has aged a lot, but not the No-stranger here who is in receipt of it and him. No, not by a split second. In fact, I can't imagine what it would be like to feel my age (as they say), or any age, right here. An old Emptiness, a decrepit Void, a hoary No-head—what sort of monstrosity is that?

(3) This Awareness which I am here has no awareness of beginning—whether at John a-Nokes's awaking this morning, or at his recovery from anaesthesia in hospital, or at his birth, or at his conception, or whenever. Awareness never catches itself popping up out of unawareness, or suffering interruption, or popping back in again. Since here is the only place it's ever found in, there's no appeal to another place against what's found here, no higher court to take it to. Accordingly it announces itself as timeproof, with all the assurance of silence announcing itself as soundproof, and stillness as shockproof.

(4) As First Person here, I find myself to be *in all respects* the diametric opposite of what I appear to be there, as third person. Always it's asymmetry, total contrast. No face here facing that face there, no colour here facing those colours there, transparency here facing opacity there, stillness here facing motion there, simplicity here facing complexity there—and, by the same token, eternity here facing time there. Of course.

(5) When I cease letting language hoodwink me, all comes clear. I make the momentous discovery that to switch the subject of a sentence from second or third person to First Person is to reverse the predicate. Thus when he dances *he dances* while the world—miserable wallflower—sits it out; whereas when *I dance* it's the world that dances with abandon while I take a nice rest. Thus when he eats *he eats,* and I watch apple pie with Devonshire cream going tasteless and cold into that toothed slot in a face; whereas when I eat *I fast,* and watch apple pie with Devonshire cream vanish into thin air, on its way to this place where, instead of a toothed slot in a face, there arises this warm apple-pie-and-cream-type deliciousness. Thus when he's born *he's born;* whereas when *I'm born* it's not I but my world that's born. Thus when he dies he dies; whereas when I die it's not I but my world that dies. Time dies. No flowers, by request.

(6) What does it mean in practice—consciously to live from the Deathless? From the Timeless Moment at the Centre of the Time-world, out into that world? It means never being at a loss about how to pass the time, seeing there's none to pass. It means finding your limbs dancing in time with the music of the God in whose bosom you lie forever. Well may Pere de Caussade promise that, provided you live where you must live anyhow—in the Now—you can trust it to come up with 'all your heart could desire'. It's not a case of returning again and again to your Source till you settle down there and reap these benefits, but of seeing that you can't escape it by a split second, try as you may. Consciousness Eternal, which is what you are, is nowhere and nowhen else.

When these six evidences of the First Person—as the One who's forever clean of time and all time's dust and debris—are totted up, the result is surely enough to convince any reasonable juryperson that here is the sober truth. And that to say 'Here I'm this timeless One' is no more blasphemous than saying 'There I'm that time-ridden one.' In fact the latter implies the former. Only the Timeless is awake to the passage of time.

COUNSEL: All this is more ingenious than reassuring. It's a word-game, a whistling in the dark to keep up your spirits. I can hear the normal Jury-member reflecting: 'There was a time when the world bore no trace of me. There's a time coming when the world will lose all trace of me. And I'm scared.' So would you be, Mr Nokes, if you consulted your feelings no less than your tortuous intellect, and weren't so impressed with your own rhetoric. Your cleverness won't come to your aid on your deathbed—if it is a bed. I think you would, if you were quite honest with yourself, be rather less chirpy about the forthcoming write-off of John a-Nokes, whether from accident, sickness, old age—or judicial process. Total write-off, I mean.

MYSELF: Yes, the prospect is bleak. Truly I live in fear of death—just so long as I go on letting that death's head (and all heads are death's heads) out of its glass-fronted cage over there to invade and parasitize me here. This is terrifying—and ludicrous, because it can happen only in imagination. The cure of death—this disease of diseases—is quite simply to see it off.

For Heaven's sake, and for justice's sake—and out of sheer self-interest—listen to my 'witnesses', and don't let that ghastly outsider gatecrash you!

God hath given to us eternal life, and this life is in his Son. He that hath the Son hath life.

First Epistle of St John

Jesus said: Blessed is he who was before he came into being.

Gospel of Thomas

Liberation is knowing you were not born.

Ramana Maharshi

The monk Yung-shih committed one of the gravest crimes, but when he had an enlightened insight into No-Birth he instantly attained Buddhahood.

Yung-chia Hsuan-chueh

Thou canst not by going reach that place wherein there is no birth, no ageing, no decaying, no falling away, no rising up elsewhere in re-birth.

Buddha

When you abide in the Unborn you abide at the source of all Buddhas, so it's something wonderfully precious. There's no question of perishing here, so when you abide in the Unborn it's superfluous to speak about the Imperishable... What isn't created can't be destroyed.

Bankei

There is no death of anyone but only in appearance, even as there is no birth of anyone but only in appearance.

Apollonius of Tyana

Prosecution Witness No. 25

THE MAN OF BUSINESS

COUNSEL, to Witness: The Prosecution understands that at one time you knew the Accused rather well, and in fact worked with him. Please tell the court how you came to meet him, what you found out about his activities (so far as they relate to the crime he is charged with here), and why you parted company from him.

WITNESS: By chance I came across some of his books, which at the time impressed me. I went to see him, in his hideout in rural Suffolk. As a man he impressed me less than his writings, but his work seemed to have potential, and I volunteered to help him with it. My long and thorough experience of getting enterprises off the ground—plus my financial resources for doing just that—were what he needed. Or so I thought.

He wasn't easy to get to know, and certainly not to work with. In some ways I was disappointed at his attitude, in others shocked. On the one hand this man seemed to me to be a dreamer who lacked all initiative. He was content to let everything drift, and to make no use of my marketing know-how. He had no push, no drive. On the other hand —and this is what must be of interest to the court—as time went on I found his activities to be more and more sinister, devilish you could say. Devilish secretive and cunning, underneath that lackadaisical camouflage. Here were ideas more blasphemous than anything I'd ever met, disseminated on the sly. Oh, he was sincere all right, but a sincere fraud—if there can be such an animal. I tell you, he's an extraordinary mixture, an enigma. After a month I pulled out. None too soon! I was scared, to be honest.

COUNSEL: I must ask you to be more specific about what shocked and alarmed you. Give particular instances.

WITNESS: Well, he boasted that, because of Who he was, he could perform all sorts of miracles. He was very insistent that he continually turned the world upside down and inside out, as he put it. He had something going which he called the Shield and Sword of the Lord. The Shield protected him from all harm, while the Sword gave him power to inflict all harm. He said he did no harm. I know different. I see him as a black magician sending out two sorts of secret vibes, defensive and offensive. Very offensive indeed.

COUNSEL: In your opinion was the black magic real, or was it just mummery? A pretence?

WITNESS: It worked all right—up to a point. It didn't succeed in fending off his arrest and trial, did it now? All the same, you don't stamp out a movement as insidious as this one by stamping on its ringleader. But it helps. The Jury must bring in a verdict of Guilty.

COUNSEL: I think that first they would like to have an instance or two of the way the Accused's black magic actually worked. On whom, and just how.

WITNESS: Well—since you insist—there was this nice young German who had the nerve to challenge one of Nokes's pronouncements. Or perhaps it was the assumption that Nokes was the World-teacher of the Age. Anyway, that young man quarrelled with the boss and promptly went mad—was sent mad, I say—and carted off. He had no previous history of mental trouble. I happen to know he's still in a psychiatric hospital, four years later.

JUDGE, banging away, to Counsel: This is appalling! Your request to the Witness has produced this unsubstantiated rumour for blackening the Accused's character in the eyes of the Jury. They must ignore it.

COUNSEL: With great respect, Your Honour: according to my understanding of the Act, it's no Defence to plead that the scandal you cause arises in part from people's corruption or abuse of your teaching. I submit we're not dealing here with hard objective facts so much as impressions on people's minds, including rumours picked up and added to and passed on. The Witness has been deeply shocked by the Accused. Whether or not with good reason is, I suggest, not quite the point. He's a sample case, one of many who have taken offence. Which is why I'll conclude by asking him whether, during his association with the Accused and his colleagues, they were attacked, and whether there occurred any violence on account of their teaching.

WITNESS: There certainly did. Threatening letters arrived most days, and there were at least three raids on the office. Entirely justified, I would say.

JUDGE: Learned Counsel, I can only assume that, when you called this Witness today, you weren't fully appraised of what his testimony would be.

COUNSEL: Again with great respect, Your Honour, I conceive that my duty as Prosecutor for the Crown is to bring to the Jury's notice just the sort of opinions and feelings—the sort of reactions to the Accused's activities—that we have been listening to. It's for them to weigh what they hear.

JUDGE: And for them to weigh very carefully indeed what I have to say about the irrelevance and untrustworthiness of so much they are hearing in this court.

COUNSEL: As Your Honour pleases.

Defence: **Sword and Shield**

MYSELF, to Witness: May I remind you there's an offence called perjury?... It's a fact (isn't it?) that you own a string of popular magazines.

WITNESS: I'm chairman of a company that owns some magazines.

MYSELF: At the beginning of your association with me, you published a lavishly illustrated article praising my work—not that I approved the wording.

WITNESS: We all make mistakes.

MYSELF: The circulation of the magazine fell sharply?

WITNESS: It did.

MYSELF: Then, practically overnight, you discovered (without breathing a word to me and my friends) what sinister people we were, and the terrible things we got up to, and the good miracles we claim to do but don't, and the bad miracles we disclaim doing but do. So began your time as a mole in our midst, followed by your sudden departure and a series of articles 'exposing' us, as you put it. Am I right?

WITNESS: It was our public duty.

MYSELF: And the circulation of the magazine in question trebled and quadrupled. And kept going up as you printed more and more interviews with people who knew nothing of our work, and whom we have never met—interviews which brought out how shocked and infuriated they were at your version of what we say and do. Including a lavishly illustrated conference with Miss United Kingdom in the most minimal of bikinis.

WITNESS: Those aren't questions. They're abuse.

MYSELF: Do you deny that the magazine's circulation increased dramatically?

WITNESS: If it did, so what?

MYSELF: And did one particularly virulent article—quite incidentally giving my private address and a sketch-map of how to get there—lead directly to a well-organized arson attempt on my home?

WITNESS: I deny that. You can't prove a thing. Blasphemy deserves all it gets, anyway.

MYSELF: Did another article assert rather than suggest that we send out some kind of secret radiation that drives people insane, making them blaspheme against the Almighty, and at the same time protects ourselves, the transmitters, from detection and destruction?

WITNESS: I appeal to the judge to stop this harassment.

JUDGE: Answer the question.

WITNESS: The article was in the public interest. Hidden menaces have to be brought out into the open.

MYSELF: Specially when they lead to exceptional profits, and when you are sure your victim won't sue for damages.

COUNSEL: I'd like to chip in here to ask the Accused whether, when the sales of a book of his are doubled, its sincerity is halved.

MYSELF: Why of course it is—if in the second edition I've been careful to edit out the unpopular ideas of the first, and so more or less invert the message.

But this is getting us nowhere. Let's look at the Witness's specific allegations.

First, that young man who went mad. In fact, he was mentally ill long before he came to me. To prove it I have here a letter from his doctor in Bremen about his case. I doubt whether he began to cotton on to what I was saying, anyway. Agreed, I didn't cure him. But I never claimed to dispense a remedy that all can stomach. Of this I'm sure: the undiluted medicine I prescribe can't be tolerated till the patient is ripe and ready for it. Then he's only got to open his mouth and down it goes, as smooth as syrup and as benign.

As for the idea that I'm responsible for the violence committed against me, while the gentleman there, whose gutter press whips up that violence, isn't responsible—words continue to fail me! More and more I wonder which is the dock and which is the witness-box in this court of justice.

WITNESS: I'm beginning to wonder whether this court affords its witnesses any protection at all from insults by prisoners.

MYSELF: Don't worry, I've finished with you. I have no more questions. Go!

I come now to the big issue, to those sinister waves I'm accused of sending out, as if from a more insidious and far-reaching and deadly Chernobyl. Working up this sort of mass paranoia does wonders for the Witness's sales graphs and for the Prosecution's case against me (if 'case' is the word I want), but it presents the Defence with a problem. How to counter these outrageous lies, which nevertheless have just a grain of truth in them? I'm left with no alternative but to try the court's patience by putting before it in sufficient detail the facts which are being mangled and perverted. No alternative but to explain what it is that I'm up to which lends that scare story such basis as it has.

I'll do this best with the help of Diagrams 27 and 28.

We start with Diagram 27. Let's say you (A) attack me (B) by firing a bullet at me, throwing a spear, shooting an arrow, or whatever; and I'm wounded. That's how the world—the onlookers, the police, the courts—view the event out there in my human region (h). They observe a transaction between a pair of third persons, an essentially symmetrical set-up, a case of what I call *circumferential causation*. (Sorry for the clumsy language, which I hope the diagram's clarity atones for.) The point to notice is that, according to this reading of events, I (B) have no shield against you, my assailant (A). Equally you have no shield against me should I be able, though wounded, to shoot back at you. We are mutually vulnerable. And it's this kind of symmetry in relationships that normally we take to be the truth, the whole truth and nothing but the truth—and that's that. And if, as a result, we go around scared stiff of one another, is it surprising?

Diagram No. 27

Diagram No. 28

But in fact, as Diagram 28 shows, the same event can be read very differently indeed. Let's call this second reading a case of *radial causation,* of a human-divine transaction between you (A') as that regional second/third person and me (C) as this central First Person, of a relationship so asymmetrical it's not (strictly speaking) a relationship at all. This time, instead of viewing myself in imagination at (B')—from *your* point of view, as that unprotected human target—I view myself as I really am at (C) from my point of view, as this fully protected divine target. Or rather, as this non-target, so shielded by layers (g), (f), (e), (d) of armour-plating that your missile never gets to me at all, and I'm absolutely safe against all attack from whatever quarter. For on the way to the real Me at the centre (C), every aggressor has to run the gauntlet of my regions cellular and molecular and atomic and subatomic—in which he's progressively stripped of such qualities as humanness and life and colour and opacity and substantiality, till on arrival there's nothing left of him or his weapons. Here I enjoy the unique security of First Personhood. I come under divine protection. I take refuge in the One who's nearer than near and safer than safe, and more Me than I am. And that's no more blasphemous or absurd or overconfident than the following:

> He that dwelleth in the secret place of the most High shall abide under the shadow of the Almighty. I will say of the Lord, He is my refuge and my fortress: my God; in him will I trust... He shall cover thee with his feathers, and under his wings shalt thou trust: his truth shall be thy shield and buckler. Thou shalt not be afraid for the terror by night; nor

for the arrow that flieth by day... A thousand shall fall at thy side, and ten thousand at thy right hand; but it shall not come nigh thee.

COUNSEL: I put it to you that the Psalmist you invoke with such assurance was referring to a more spiritual safety than the physical sort you seem to be talking about. And in fact your own diagram shows (A')'s arrow eventually getting to you at (B') and wounding and killing you there in your human region (h). Tell me, what's the use of being William the Conqueror at the hub of things if you are also Harold out there with an arrow in his eye? I don't see any percentage in it.

MYSELF: Provisionally and temporarily—it's quite true—I am that conquered one at (B') who is wounded and dying. Primarily and permanently, however, I remain the Conqueror at (C) who is never wounded and who never dies. Death is an arrow that loses its barb before it gets to this First Person, but regains it for that third person, for slaying poor old John a-Nokes out there. But who is it, in the last resort, that polishes him off? That human enemy (A') is powerless to do so—no effective missiles ever cross that A'-B' gap, that Great Divide. There, all punches are pulled. There, it's all shadow-boxing. It is I, the One I AM here, who calls the shots, who cries 'Enough of Nokes!' and lets fly the fatal arrow from (C) to (B'). In this sense, yes, I'm mine own executioner. Who I really, really am is the Marksman who finally guns down who I pretend to be, dispatches all perishers whatsoever. Who I really, really am is the only real Power and the only real Doer of whatever's done; and what It does is what I do, and in the end wholly approve of. And that includes any sentence the court passes on John a-Nokes. You can do nothing to me against my ultimate will, which is the will of the One here to whom all are subject. The real decisions come from this Highest Court.

Here are some of that Court's better-known pronouncements:

God (the One who is nearer to me than my jugular vein) gives life and puts to death.

The Koran

There is no power but of God.

St Paul

Thine is the kingdom, and the power, and the glory.

Gospel of St Matthew

Jesus, before Pilate: 'Thou couldest have no power at all against me, except it were given thee from above.'

Gospel of St John

Though he slay me, yet will I trust in him.

Job

God's holy will is the Centre from which all we do must radiate; all else is mere weariness and excitement.

Jean-Pierre Camus

The factual basis, then, of that scare story about radiation—featuring so profitably in the Witness's magazine—amounts to something like this:

There is a unique Centre from which eternally radiates, as concentric waves from a stone thrown into a pond, the multi-ringed universe. This Centre goes by many names, such as Awareness, Essence, Reality, Being, Spirit, Atman-Brahman, the One Power, the First Person Singular that I AM. Being aware is being This, for there's no awareness independent of or outside of This. And to be This is to be the Source of the 'radiation' by which It is shielded from all power and by which It exerts all power. By virtue of the first, all incoming processes and problems are reduced to Nothing, while by virtue of the second all outgoing processes and responses are produced from Nothing. This dual-purpose radiation is indeed my shield and my sword, ensuring that while Nothing's done to Me all's done by Me. 'Can we make all our relations to our fellows relations which pass *through Him?*' asks the Quaker Thomas R. Kelly. I reply: Even the blasphemous fantasy that we can begin to bypass Him passes through Him.

Ladies and gentlemen of the Jury, if you will now please refer to Diagram No. 29, you won't merely get the picture, but be in the picture.

The apparent go of the universe, including your life and mine, is circumferential—and God-denying. Its real *go* is radial—to and from God—and is the wielding of His marvellous shield and sword.

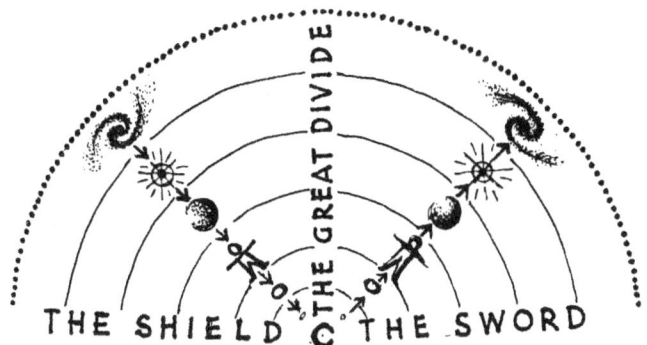

Diagram 29

Wielded from *here* (C), in the Place where, as Ananda Mayi Ma says, 'all problems have but one universal solution.'

COUNSEL: This grand talk of supernatural weaponry and wizardry would be a lot more credible if backed up by just one miraculous deed.

MYSELF, to Counsel: Right! Here it comes! Please wave your brief at me—for the hundredth time.

COUNSEL, complying energetically: What's miraculous about that?

MYSELF: What isn't miraculous about it? The Wizard-King you really, really are at Centre (C) commands countless legions of familiars or angel-servitors (nowadays we call them particles, atoms, molecules and cells) to co-operate in bringing about that arm movement in your human region. Hierarchical magic, a feat of many-levelled, many-regioned organization of unimaginable complexity, instantly put into effect. It would be a marvel if it had taken centuries. And had been monitored throughout, at every level, by all the backroom boys in the world.

You haven't the faintest idea of how you did it. But you do know *Who did it.*

Don't tell me you have the crust to credit Sir Gerald Wilberforce KC with the astounding miracle that you—yes, You!—have just performed for our benefit. That, Sir Gerald, would be blasphemy!

As I say, you haven't a clue how you did it. But at least you realize—or should realize—that the miracle was a masterstroke of radial or up-and-down organization, not one of circumferential or on-the-level organization. Jacob dreamed a true dream:

'Behold a ladder set up on the earth, and the top of it reached to heaven: and behold the angels of God ascending and descending on it.' None was so foolish as to try to take off sideways.

Prosecution Witness No. 26:

THE COUNSELLOR

COUNSEL: Please tell the court about your work.

WITNESS: I've been practising as a counsellor for something like thirty years, first on the staff of a large industrial concern and latterly on my own. People come to see me with all sorts of problems—fears, frustrations, anxieties, doubts, difficulties of every kind. They come to me knowing that I'm an attentive listener and talking with me has a good chance of helping them to find their own solution to their problem. The fact that I'm a woman is more of an advantage here than otherwise, I suspect.

COUNSEL: What is your connection with the Accused?

WITNESS: An indirect one. Two of my clients were followers of his. Like so many of us, they were in trouble because they wouldn't admit to their darker side. They persuaded themselves it didn't exist. They turned a blind eye to their anger, for example. The psychosomatic effects were quite serious. In the case of these two, their trouble had been compounded by the Accused's insistence that they were really and truly perfect. Divine, he said. So, of course, to feel angry or scared or miserable was just not on. And the more these negative feelings were denied expression, the more they demanded expression. Great was the relief of these clients when they allowed themselves to drop their impossible self-image, to forget about any sort of perfection (let alone divine perfection) and accept their human limitations.

COUNSEL: What have you to say about the religious aspect of these pretensions? About the notion of deification itself, aside from the psychological harm you refer to?

WITNESS: I'm no theologian, and these terms mean next to nothing to me. All I'm sure of is that the idea of deification didn't work out at all, at least in the cases known to me. I'll go so far as to say that, in my experience, of all the illusions people entertain about themselves, the illusion of attainable and mandatory perfection—of divinity, if you like—is the most damaging.

COUNSEL, to Jury: John a-Nokes, so far as the Prosecution understands him, rests his case on the proposition that he really is the Divinity he professes to be. And he adds that this Divinity is the great Healer. Healer, mark you! The Witness's testimony, I think you will agree, blows these claims sky-high. She has exposed the Accused as an all-too-human human being who—at least in some instances—makes other humans sick, and by no means a Divine Being who makes them whole.

This may not be the aspect of his behaviour which excites breaches of the peace, but it does a good deal to excuse them. Or rather, to account for the instinct behind them.

Defence: **The Reversal of Values**

MYSELF, cross-examining the Witness: Let's go a little further into this self-esteem business. If some squiffy stranger at a party very confidentially informs you that your face reminds him of his darling

Pekingese, and you happen to be the current beauty queen of the Western World, you'll hardly be devastated. More probably your reaction would be hoots of laughter. Or if he said, 'I'm sorry to have to say it, but you don't speak so good,' and you happen to be the Poet Laureate, you'll hardly let the remark prey on your mind for long, or suppress all memory of it. On the contrary, you'll welcome a few more stories like that to dine out on. Am I right?

WITNESS: Surely.

MYSELF: Well now, as a general rule it seems that people are cheerfully relaxed about their peripheral defects—whether alleged or real—if they are confident about their all-rightness at core. Secure in their self-esteem, they have no need to deny or pretend anything. They can afford to be honest. Agreed?

WITNESS: Well, yes. But the question is: Who has that degree of inner confidence? Or is inner self-satisfaction the expression I want?

MYSELF: Who indeed? We shall see. All of us are hooked on perfection. The great question is: *where* does it hang out? Nearly all of us are looking for it in the wrong place (in the peripheral region of our humanness) instead of the right place (in the central region of our divineness). It hangs in. Perfection lies at the heart of all. Indeed you could say it is the heart of the heart of every being, no matter how lowly and deficient its manifest embodiment. In the case of human beings, the contrast between their central perfection and their peripheral imperfection is very fraught and dramatic and many-sided. And very, very important to recognize.

Utopia (the Greek word means *no place*) is forever unrealizable in any of those places out there, and forever realized in this No-place right here. Will the members of the Jury please refer to Diagram No. 30. I can't remind you too often how this diagram—which is the master plan of my Defence—brings out the fundamental differences between yourself as second/third person (picked up by others and their cameras, and by your mirror out there) and yourself as First Person (picked up by yourself directly at Centre); how it highlights the contrast between that human physique of yours (normal-way-up, headed, two-eyed and short-armed) and this divine physique of yours (upside down, headless, single-eyed, magnificently wide-armed). Now you would think (wouldn't you?) that's contrast enough for one simple diagram—more like a lightning sketch—to take care of. But no, more's to come. A lot more. And vital stuff, at that.

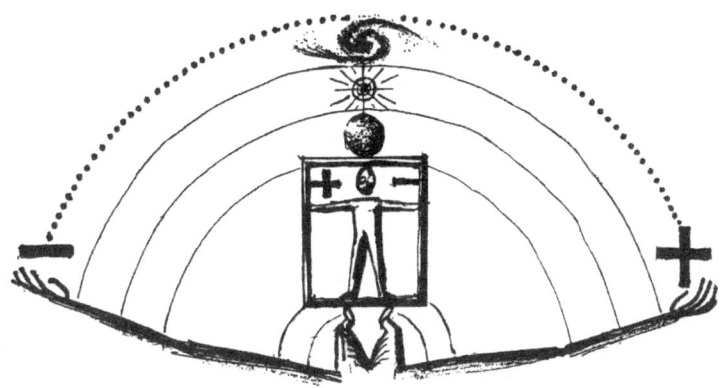

Diagram No. 30

At right angle to this vertical revolution, there's a horizontal revolution. The right hand of that little one there in the mirror corresponds to the left hand of this Big One, your own left hand. Similarly, his left hand corresponds to your right hand. Now if taking your cue from tradition and from language itself, you envisage the left, or sinister, hand as holding sinister or negative values, and the right, or dexter, hand as holding right or positive values, then at a glance you get the message that your identity-shift from that second/third person to this First Person involves an equally drastic value-shift. Actually, not so much a shift as a complete turn-around. Your values as First Person *reverse* your values as second/third person. And the hallmark of the former is a perfection of which the latter falls infinitely short.

It's rather as if the photographic negative of the third person's world were the photographic positive of the First Person's world, black and white changing places. And as if the picture were being viewed upside down and back to front. All making for an interesting life, you could say. But tricky, none too easy.

COUNSEL: These unsupported *ex cathedra* pronouncements are of little interest to the court, and in any case their connection with the Witness's testimony about your two unfortunate disciples is far from clear... May she leave the box, or have you further questions to put to her?

MYSELF: I've only one more. It's this: did those two clients of yours give the impression that they had gone deeply into my teaching? Were they clear or were they vague and confused about it?

WITNESS: I'm pretty sure they weren't aware of the contrasts you're now talking about. Of these turn-arounds.

MYSELF: Which means they didn't get my message at all. (People often don't, you know.) It follows that their psychological problems can't in fairness be laid at my door, and are irrelevant to this Trial... I've no further questions. Thank you. You may stand down...

As for those *ex cathedra* pronouncements of mine on the reversal or transvaluation of values—here comes the support that Counsel asks for. It has more legs to stand on than a centipede. Let's just take a small sample of them:

(1) Love, for a start. The love of that little one is conditional. It makes demands, seeks some return, is in part a trade-off. Also, it's nothing if not choosy. There just isn't enough of the stuff to spread around. If it happens to alight on two or three people equally and at the same time, expect trouble. In any case expect variableness. The course of human love never did and never will run smooth. Never, never... In contrast, the divine love of this Big One is unconditional. It makes no demands, looks for no return, is equally bestowed on all, doesn't vary in the slightest, always runs smooth. Why? Because the Big One lies at the Source of all, and to be here is to love all beings as Oneself, regardless of how lovable or unlovable they may seem.

(2) That little one, always seeking power over others, turns out to be powerless... By contrast, this Big One, altogether non-interfering, turns out to be the Only Power, not operating from outside *on* creatures but from inside as them.

(3) That little one, poor fellow, has to live with two conflicting pieces of knowledge—the deep conviction that all the world is his in reality, and the superficial certainty that almost none of it is his in practice. Result: greed. He's driven to amass around himself all manner of possessions—tokens of his infinite wealth—regardless of how trivial and superfluous and plain cock-eyed they may be. (Example—I'm not making this up—a machine for slicing the top off a boiled egg; no breakfast table is complete without our new electrified model. And no kitchen table without our five-speed egg-whisk.) Regardless of the fact that these possessions, taken together, make such demands on him that they come to possess him. Regardless of the fact that only the moment of getting is pleasure: before that is the pain of not having, after that the pain of having... The Big One is relieved of both pains. He's so Big there's nothing left to get and have. He doesn't own a thing. You name it, he is it. As Nothing whatever he's capacious of all things, and is satisfied. In fact, to own so much as a wooden nickel is to wound the world to the marrow, cleaving it asunder into an owning bit and an owned bit. Conversely, to own absolutely Nothing is to be the Master Physician who heals that wound.

(4) The little one's knowledge is the ending of wonder. The Big One's knowledge is the beginning of wonder. The little one is heady and knowing and smart. He'll buy knowledge at the expense of mystery every time, and sooner or later it gives him a splitting headache. The Big One buys mystery at the expense of knowledge till all that's left is the Mystery itself, the Perfectly-known-as-unknowable Source that is the cure of all the headaches it gives rise to.

(5) The little one prizes success at others' expense, and fails. The Big One doesn't, and wins. His is the success story of all time, the story of the One who has the useful knack of Being, of Self-origination, without any help and without the slightest idea how he comes by that knack.

(6) For the little one, humiliation is hell. Life keeps putting him down, and he keeps bouncing back again by every possible means, till the irreversible put-down of Death stops play. For the Big One, humiliation is the key to heaven. It opens the trapdoor to the stable and well-founded Self-esteem of the Deathless.

(7) For the little one, birth is a happy event, death a tragic event. For the Big One, it's the other way round: 'Man is born into sorrow, as the sparks fly upward' and 'Blessed are they who die in the Lord.' My birth is the forgetting of Myself, my death (now rather than in the future) is the remembering of Myself.

(8) As for hate, anger, fear and craving in all their fifty-seven varieties, what sense they seem to make out there in that little one, and what nonsense they really make here in this Big One! Candidly, but with some tenderness and amusement, the First Person perceives the third person as *warped* and *screwy,* his values as *twisted.* No wonder that, traditionally, the satanic *reverses* the divine—recites the Lord's Prayer backwards, for example. No wonder that, when the previous Witness, Sister Marie-Louise, looks in her mirror, what she sees is something like Diagram No. 31 of your booklet. This derangement should be (but alas isn't) a warning to her to go by and trust what's her side of the glass, the Big One, the Great Untwisted.

(9) As the Defence Map won't let us forget, the little one is the arch-escapist who, not content with framing and glazing his front against an intrusive world, *turns his back on it.* His motto 'I'm all right, Jack' ensures all goes wrong. Intent on self-preservation, he'll soon be a goner—the world will see to that. Meanwhile he has the glassy look and feel of the opt-outer and almost-goner. How unlike the Big One who, tender and stark naked to the world he *faces,* taking it in and taking it on, is wholly involved and wholly vulnerable! Giving place to all, he's as he was in the beginning, is now and ever shall be. He is the world without end, amen.

Diagram No. 31

COUNSEL, with a deep sigh: And, it goes without saying, *You* are this Jackpot of jackpots! Amen!

MYSELF: Why, of course! So are you. So are we all, at Centre. When St John of the Cross says 'The Centre of the soul is God', he makes no exceptions. And each of us is furnished, off-Centre, with an all-too-human little one. Ever distinct and in every way contrasting, this Big One and that little one comprise unequal halves of a whole, a keen edge and a coarse whetstone—as distinguishable as up from down and left from right, and as inseparable. Together they set up the dynamic, the polarity, the unceasing interplay between the Divinity and the humanity that together make up our life. Blasphemy, I say, is claiming to be one and not the other—either claiming to be a man who can do very nicely without God, thank you very much, or else claiming to be the God who can do very nicely without man, good riddance. In either case the medicine for blasphemy is consciously to embrace both—each in its proper place—and the ceaseless two-way traffic that plies between them.

COUNSEL: Without concrete illustration—let alone hard evidence—this is so much wordplay and no Defence at all.

MYSELF: At the risk of some embarrassment, let me take an example from my own personal life. Counsel will probably suggest to the court that I've cooked it up specially for this occasion. So, by way of confirmation, I'll throw in afterwards a couple of observations by men who are widely recognized as sages—as people who have got the balance right, the balance between their humanness and their divineness.

I'm deeply committed to and quietly in love with a woman, just one. Occasionally I fall for another, but not deeply or for long. We fight with remarkable regularity, and get hurt. One explanation is that I'm too dashed preoccupied with my own plans and ideas, which I impose on the lady without respite. No doubt there's something in this, though I suspect the deeper cause is less specific, and more like a need on both sides to disturb creeping complacency and bring drama into our lives, a vigorous ding-dong. Anyway, that's all speculation and little-one stuff... Beneath the sometimes choppy surface, the Big One's love goes on all the while, steady and unchanging as the deepest ocean. As the Big One, I love the lady absolutely, for she is the Self of myself. Let those winds blow and waves rage as they please, they are God's winds and waves. His weather—at the level where He keeps His weather.

Some three centuries before Christ, the Chinese Taoist Chuang-tzu wrote: 'It's not that the sage lacks bad feelings, but that he doesn't let them inside where they will do him harm.' He doesn't wash his hands of those very human susceptibilities. He deals with them skilfully. Accepting full responsibility for them, he's careful to place them where they belong. Ramana Maharshi, Indian sage of the twentieth century, said: 'The ego of the sage arises again and again. But he recognizes it for what it is, therefore it's not dangerous.' Firmly assured of his central perfection as Being-Consciousness-Bliss, he can afford to accept undismayed the inexhaustible variety and messiness of the imperfections It comes up with.

Coming back to my own case, I don't deny or deplore my all-too-human humanness. On the contrary, I lay claim to and insist on it out there, every bit as much as I lay claim to and insist on my divineness right here. My admission of—no, my emphasis on—this essential bipolarity should clear me, surely, of the crime I'm charged with.

COUNSEL, like a shot: It does nothing of the sort! Either you make out you are the Almighty or you don't. Yes or no? It's no excuse that you have a mood or an aspect or an alter ego which is a lot less ambitious. So what? If you claimed to be the rightful heir to the throne of Great Britain, and were caught plotting to usurp that throne, it would be no defence at your trial for high treason that you were an assistant garbage collector. Rather the reverse.

MYSELF: But it might do my defence a power of good if I sincerely claimed that all the assistant and master garbage collectors in the world were rightful heirs along with me.

COUNSEL: It would wonderfully demonstrate your unfitness to plead, by reason of mental deficiency or disturbance. Is this your—

JUDGE, very firmly: This *badinage* has gone on long enough.

MYSELF: I was about to conclude on a more serious and more practical note, Your Honour. And a rather happy one, too. To the extent that I stay centred in the perfection of the New Man, of my True Nature as First Person Singular, the manifold imperfections of the old man are mitigated. To the extent that I live from the values of this New Man—unconditional love, no power over others, no turning one's back on them, the acceptance of humiliation, and so forth—to that extent the contrasting values of that old man become less and less heavy and humourless and troublesome, and more and more amenable and realistic and healthy. In a word, more natural. To tell the truth, the very best I can do for Jack is to come off him and be Myself. Then he stops playing games and is no longer phoney. The ultimate encouragement and relief is that Jack—the old man—is short on reality, not ME but a picture, just as if he were appearing on that witness-box telescreen. He and his naughtiness are measurably off-Centre. He isn't normal, isn't himself till he gives up on himself and takes refuge in God. Man isn't man till he's God.

What a shame that those two clients of the Witness had no time for these divine You-turns, and so got half the story! Which was worse than getting none of it.

And what a good thing it is that, among those who got the whole story, some are at pains to tell it—most beautifully—for our encouragement!

The scriptures say there is in us an outward man and an inner man... Without is the old man, the earthly man, the outward person, the enemy, the servant. Within us all is the other person, the inner man, whom the scriptures call the new man, the heavenly man, the young person, the friend, the aristocrat.

Eckhart

The separate creaturely life, as opposed to life in union with God, is only a life of various appetites, hungers and wants, and cannot possibly be anything else... The highest life that is natural and creaturely can go no higher than this; it can only be a bare capacity for goodness and cannot possibly be a good and happy life but by the life of God dwelling in and in union with it. And this is the twofold life that, of all necessity, must be united in every good and perfect and happy creature.

William Law

He who can instantly realize the truth of Non-existence—yet without departing from lust, hate and ignorance—can grasp the weapons of the Demon King and use them in the opposite way. He can then turn these evil companions into angels protecting the Dharma... This is the nature of the Dharma itself!

Zen Master Tsung-kao

The world of outward forms after he had left it... would seem to him [the disciple] the inverse of what it had been before, simply because the Light of his inward eye had dawned.

Shaikh Al-Buzidi

Unless you make the things of the right hand as those of the left, and those of the left as those of the right, and those that are above as those below, and those that are behind as those that are before, you shall not have knowledge of the kingdom.

The Martyrdom of St Peter

Prosecution Witness No. 27

THE BORN-AGAIN CHRISTIAN

COUNSEL, to Jury: I call now my last Witness, a lady who has recently been ordained as a priest in the Anglican Church. Let us pay particular attention to her testimony, and see for what they are the Accused's attempts to dodge and distort it. [To Witness] What do you know of the Accused's teaching?

WITNESS: He doesn't exactly hide it under a bushel, does he? I know it well. Well enough to understand how dangerous it is.

COUNSEL: Explain to the court what you mean. The conclusions you've come to, and why.

WITNESS: He makes out he's a deeply religious person, concerned above all with God and spiritual things. More and more he uses Christian language. Yet he ignores and has no time or use for Jesus Christ as the sole mediator between God and man. In effect he thumbs his nose at the authentic Christ of scripture and of history. He reckons to come to God directly, on his own terms, according to his own plan, under his own steam. Or rather, he reckons he's arrived. Arrived, he's now claiming, not as plain John a-Nokes (which would have been blasphemy enough) but as John a-Nokes become another Christ (which is blasphemy to the nth degree). We sinners are saved by the Crucifixion and shed blood of our dear Lord. Mr Nokes turns down God's free offer of forgiveness and salvation through the unique sacrifice of His Only Son. Repeat *Only* Son. Are his sins so venial they don't need forgiving? Is he all right as he is? Is there no danger he needs saving from? I ask you: what more awful insult can be offered to the Almighty than to pooh-pooh His offer of salvation? Which is as good as telling Him He needn't have bothered, and that Calvary was a superfluous and horribly cruel charade. In fact, Mr Nokes has as little time for God the Father as for God the Son. 'Whosoever denieth the Son, the same hath not the Father,' says St John. 'He is antichrist that denieth the Father and the Son.' One way or another, Mr Nokes dismisses the first two Persons of the Holy Trinity. You could say he's two-thirds atheist, at least.

COUNSEL: Why do you think he's taken up this position? What's behind it?

WITNESS: He's exceedingly ambitious, which means he needs to be exceedingly clever. When making a take-over bid for a great business—the Business of businesses in this instance—you first secretly arrange for its devaluation, by as much as two-thirds if you can. Some instinct tells him to dispose of God the Transcendent Father and God the Incarnate Son, who was born in Bethlehem and died at Calvary—even Mr Nokes would hardly claim to be them—leaving only God the Spirit, whom he proceeds to identify with as easy as winking. He figures he can comfortably handle a God he wraps himself around like a boa constrictor and eats for breakfast. A small and contained convenience-product of a God. This is getting God on the cheap, all right. So he supposes. Actually, of course, it's the Devil he's getting, and paying the price of everlasting perdition.

Though this is blasphemy of the worst kind, it wouldn't be so awful if he kept quiet about it, if he held it in quarantine. What brings him into court today is his determination to spread the virus by every means at his disposal. I say he must be stopped by every means at the court's disposal. I don't say this out of hate, but out of love. I pray for John a-Nokes every day—pray that he may at last give in to the love of the only true Saviour, the Lord Jesus, who gave His life for him and for us all. Then my friends and I will be the first to take John a-Nokes to our hearts.

Defence: **I Am What Christ Is**

MYSELF: Most of your testimony has been about the Second Person of the Trinity. For the benefit of the court will you please describe briefly His nature as you understand it.

WITNESS: I believe the Son is perfect God and perfect man, and in him these aren't two but one. One, not by the conversion of the Godhead into flesh, but the other way round. God, in the Person of His Son, was crucified for our salvation, descended into Hell, and rose again the third day from the dead.

MYSELF: You are paraphrasing, I think, part of the Athanasian Creed, so-called, which (let me remind you) also describes the Son as eternal, uncreated, incomprehensible, coequal with the Father and the Holy Ghost, begotten before the world.

WITNESS: That's right. It sums up my faith.

MYSELF: Did you know that St Athanasius said 'God became man so that man might become God'? And that Christians for centuries have looked on him as the authority on this subject of deification—a term which the Fathers of the Church used freely?

WITNESS: No, I didn't know that.

MYSELF: Thank you. No more questions from me.

COUNSEL: Please stay in court, in case you are required for reexamination.

MYSELF: Members of the Jury, I think I understand why the Witness imagines I've no time for God incarnate in the Jesus Christ of history, for God the Son come down into the world two thousand years ago. If there's a fault here, it's largely mine. Before this Trial I've made few public references to him. However, that's not because he leaves me cold, but the reverse. How could I ever forget that young man crying in the garden? Nothing has been nearer my heart since childhood than the true story of the Highest who came down out of pity and love, was born in that very special place, and lived that very special life, and died that very special death. So far from holding him in contempt, as the Witness asserts, I find him altogether adorable. I didn't intend to unload on the court my deepest thoughts and feelings (my tears also, I fear) on this subject, but she has left me no alternative. It will be for you to decide whether they are in any sense blasphemous, or (as I believe) the very opposite.

Fortunately, in seeking to get my experience of Christ over to you, I have the unusual advantage of three media—one verbal and two non-verbal. In addition to these words there is the little—but crucial—experiment I shall ask you to do shortly, and there is our Diagram No. 32. Please turn to it now, and keep it before you till I have finished replying to this Witness.

Here we have an indication of how Jesus looked *to himself* on the Cross, upside down and turned round to face all creation. A sketch of what he was as First Person on the day when he had in every sense come to the World's End and Hell's Bottom Line, had come down all the way to the cellar and pit of his Father's lofty universe.

Diagram No. 32

There were his mother Mary and those soldiers, gazing not up at him but down upon him. Look carefully at the sketch, and you'll see why I say *down*. And there was he gazing not down upon them, but up at them, and at those foreshortened legs and nailed feet so small. And gazing out at those immensely wide arms embracing the world he was dying for, and those nailed hands so small, reaching on either side beyond the horizon.

I'll not speak of the pain, but of this supreme instance of the reversal of values that we were noticing earlier. Members of the Jury, just look at this. Look at what man did to God out of hate, and what God did for man out of love. That the Power and the Glory back of the universe should be *this* kind of Power and *this* kind of Glory, transmuting the worst into the best—this, you might be tempted to say, is so beautiful and so good that it has to be true. You would do better to say, along with me, that a universe which comes up with such a design for Deity—a design which has moulded two thousand years of human history—is that sort of universe. The sort that produces, in the fullness of time, what all along it had up its sleeve. I'll go much further than that, and say that our life and all life is modelled on Golgotha. The crucifixion of the First Person is built-in. It's the price of a world. The world can be had no cheaper. Oh, yes, the agony and the bitter humiliation are there for keeps (not for long will we be allowed to forget that), but so is the alchemical love of the God who transmutes that poisonous lead into twenty-two carat gold. How thorough is His reversal of values, and what it costs Him!

COUNSEL: I trust, members of the Jury, that you won't be taken in by these crocodile tears, this touching eleventh-hour conversion.

The Born-again Christian

(I almost said this last-minute confession on the scaffold.) And by this temporary consecration of the dock as a pulpit. If it's a pulpit, it's one from which blasphemy continues to flow forth freely. I want you particularly to note that the Accused is daring to use virtually the same diagram for Jesus Christ on the Cross as he has used for himself throughout this Trial. Thus, without needing to spell out his terrible message in so many words, he surreptitiously accords himself divine status. Which only goes to show how justified are the distress and the anger he's causing among earnest Christians such as the Witness.

MYSELF: Surreptitious my foot! Don't you ever listen to me? I *insist* that virtually the same picture does for Jesus Christ as First Person on the Cross as for myself as First Person all the time. And (I hasten to add) for all humans. None—not the wickedest or stupidest or the most unchristian—is, in his own experience of himself, any different. Why, of course! How else could it be? All, each and every one, are caught up bodily (repeat, *bodily)* in the drama of Calvary. Only with all and as all could Jesus Christ suffer and die for all. To suffer and die for alien beings was just not on. St Paul has every reason for claiming that we are all bearing about *in the body* the living and dying of the Lord Jesus.

COUNSEL: You can't dilute or excuse your blasphemy by spreading it around—nearly all of it in places and among persons that won't accept it. As I understand it, the Christian faith is based on the absolute uniqueness of the Son of God incarnate as Jesus Christ, a uniqueness which you are denying and which St Paul (except when quoted out of context) never questions.

MYSELF: Again, believe it or not, I insist on the very thing you say I deny. In the deepest sense there is only one First Person—the First Person *Singular;* only *one* Son of God, His *Only* Son—eternal, uncreated, incomprehensible, begotten before the world. 'All mankind is in Christ one man,' said St Augustine. But this isn't to deny that, at another level and in another sense, there are as many First Persons as there are third persons—every third person coming equipped with his or her First-Person aspect, and vice versa—so that God has countless Sons and Daughters. Take that matchless passage from the Fourth Gospel:

> That was the true Light, which lighteth every man that cometh into the world. He was in the world, and the world was made by him, and the world knew him not... But as many as received him, to them gave he power to become the sons of God... Which were born, not of blood, nor of the will of the flesh, nor of the will of man, but of God.

Please refer to our Diagram. Those little, headed, narrow-shouldered, short-armed, normal-way-up third persons were all born and will all die. This great, headless, broad-shouldered, wide-armed, other-way-up First Person was never born and will never die. He's not in that class at all. To put it crudely, he's the wrong size and the wrong shape for any midwife to handle or undertaker to undertake, and a case of breech presentation at that. He's the Eternal Christ, 'begotten of the Father before the world, God of God, Light of Light, Very God of Very God', yet forever reborn in all creatures as Christ crucified.

COUNSEL: Have you gone raving mad? Are you seriously saying that those miserable hands, clawing at the rail of the dock, are the Almighty's? That those weedy limbs are the everlasting arms of the Everlasting One? May I remind you that this court has the power to turn them into *disjecta membra* and still them for ever?

MYSELF: They belong to the Incarnate God all right, but (as you say) are far from everlasting. I picture my Lord Christ as the Tree of Life. His foliage and limbs, exposed to the sharp frosts of time, are deciduous. They die off regularly in Calvary's winter and are renewed in Bethlehem's spring, but the Stem and the Root are perennial, 'the same yesterday and today and forever'. These arms I'm extending to you now are indeed his very own—for the time being. How can I be so sure? Because of what they stick out of, and what they do. They stick out of No-thing. And, broken loose, they do amazing things such as drive the world. They are put forth by this immense clear-of-head Gap right here, by my true Self in Whom and as Whom alone I'm safe from all your threats.

> Safe though all safety's lost, safe when men fall
> And if these poor limbs die, safest of all.

Rupert Brooke's wartime lines make perfect sense. So do St Paul's:

> With all boldness, as always, so now also Christ shall be magnified in my body, whether it be by life, or by death. For to me to live is Christ, and to die is gain. I am crucified with Christ: nevertheless I live; yet not I, but Christ liveth in me.

COUNSEL: St Paul, I keep telling you, was very special. You don't get Christians nowadays talking like that. For them Jesus Christ is simply the Jesus Christ of the Synoptic Gospels, and there's no confusing him with even the most saintly of his followers.

MYSELF: Crown Prosecutor, you really should not venture unprepared into the precipitous country of Christology. Here to confound you—among countless others—is Mother Teresa of Calcutta. Her Daily Prayer begins like this:

> Dearest Lord, may I see you today and every day in the person of your sick, and while nursing them, minister unto you. Though you hide yourself behind the unattractive disguise of the irritable, the exacting, the unreasonable, may I still recognize you and say: 'Jesus my patient, how sweet it is to serve you.'

Her words are based, of course, on those of her Lord who said: 'Inasmuch as ye have done it [fed the hungry, clothed the naked, visited the sick] unto… the least of these my brethren, ye have done it unto me.'

COUNSEL: So you are now going back on your view (frequently emphasized in your writings) that other great religions, though knowing nothing *(and needing to know nothing)* about Jesus Christ, are none the less revelations of God. And that they have their own genuine avatars, or special incarnations of God. One never knows where one is with John a-Nokes. He's not only as shocking as an electric eel, but twice as slippery.

MYSELF: Most of the patients that Teresa saw as Jesus himself by grace were Hindus or Muslims by religion. That fact made no difference at all to her service. It seems never to have occurred to her to convert them to Christianity as a prelude to caring for them. Nor was it a ghost or a fragment of the living Jesus she found in each one, but her Lord who is indivisible and wholeness itself. Of course she was right. The Eternal Christ is the Light that lights everyone, and is crucified and resurrected in everyone —whatever the colour of his skin, whatever age he's born into, whatever religion he professes, whatever language he speaks, whatever name he gives that One Light. And of course the experience of bodily transformation which I call Christing is by no means confined to Christianity. Other religions have their versions of an incarnate Deity with whom one may become identified. In Judaism he can take the form of Adam the primal man, in Islam the Prophet as the Logos, in Hinduism Krishna, in Buddhism the Buddha.

COUNSEL, throwing up his hands: While you are about it, why don't you go the whole hog and declare the animals too (not excluding tapeworms and tsetse flies) are Christ travelling incognito.

MYSELF: Which I do, unreservedly. Specially so because—unlike fallen and blaspheming humankind—they all live without question from that One Light of Awareness, from their First Personhood, and never for a moment try to snuff it out with their third personhood. They build no self-image to obstruct their Space with, acquire no face to mask their original Face. Only humans are such blockheads as to stand in and block their own Light. God in Christ shines at the

Centre of each animal's world, His throne unusurped. T. E. ('God wot') Brown, having killed a toad, confessed:

> I smote it cruelly,
> Then all the place with subtle radiance glowed—
> I looked, and it was He!

Humans ought, indeed, to reverence these junior members of the family, who are all living without effort or delusion from the Clarity that sages and seers consciously live from—after many a struggle and many a backsliding.

And, after all, what I'm saying is implicit in the Christian story, beginning with the Annunciation, nine months before the birth in Bethlehem. To take on human form, God the Son had first to take on the whole range of animal forms, from a single cell upwards, in Mary's womb. What a telling witness to Nature's essential Christliness! The alternative view is that Mary's pregnancy was a phantom one, followed at the last moment—hey presto!—by the real thing! An unlikely and unlovely tale. By contrast, how convincing and poignant is the Incarnation which, occurring at one level, occurs at all levels—so that, in effect, the whole Creation (as Paul pictured it) is adopted and redeemed! Your tsetse flies and tapeworms, Sir Gerald, and all!

Counsel, clasping his wig in a gesture of despair, recalls the Witness to the box. He asks whether she has heard all that has passed since she left it, and how she feels about it.

WITNESS: I've followed every word, and am deeply saddened. It was our Lord Jesus Christ himself who said: 'No man cometh unto the Father, but by me.' Also 'I am the way, the truth, and the life.' There's only one Jesus Christ, and he alone is our Saviour.

MYSELF: Believe it or not, once again I entirely agree. The plain fact is that the First Person is never plural. Never, never, will you find a pair of First Persons, much less a gaggle of them. A room full of headless inverted bodies would be Bluebeard's cold-store. The 'I' and the 'Me' that Jesus uses in those two great texts are God's own 'I' and 'Me', and no man's. (As Eckhart tells us, only God can truly say 'I'.) It's as the unique and eternal First Person who is none other than God Himself that Jesus truly claims to be the Way and the Truth and the Life, and not as the third person who showed up in his mirror—the human being who was just one of many children in Nazareth, and just one of the many carpenters in Palestine. Quite the most mysterious and marvellous and saving thing about the Christ that lives in you, my sister, and me, and everyone here in court, is that he's in each of us unique and whole and one and undivided and the same for ever and ever. 'Christ,' says that well-loved Jesuit father, Gerard W. Hughes, 'is what we are called on to become.' Christ, not Christs.

WITNESS: He alone suffered crucifixion for the sins of the world.

MYSELF: Certainly. And all of us are caught up in that same suffering and that same crucifixion and that same cure for sin. It's the cosmic pattern of things, the very blueprint and architectonic of Creation. I just can't narrow Christ down the way so many nominal Christians succeed in doing. I don't believe that the stigmata of

St Francis and St Pio were mere hysterical symptoms, and not evidence of their Christing. Or that the transubstantiation of the bread and wine into the flesh and the blood of Christ, before they are incorporated into the body of the communicant, is nothing but pious mumbo-jumbo. Or that the day of Crucifixion should be called Bad Friday, the Day of Defeat. Or that Paul lied about being crucified with Christ. Or that the Christ-picture you have before you in that booklet is some kind of accident or trick of mine, a trompe-l'oeil. Or that the Early Fathers of the Church were deluded when they saw Christ as the Archetypal Man, man as he is essentially. 'By dwelling in one the Word dwelt in all,' wrote St Cyril of Alexandria, 'so that the one having been constituted the Son of God in power, the same dignity might pass to the whole human race.'

Let me add this: if to be a Christian is to see Christ everywhere, to feel his presence in every creature, and to be ravished by the joy and beauty of it all, then I'm a Christian all right.

Really the truth is so simple, so gloriously self evident, if only we will stop fighting it. Every creature takes two forms and has two aspects—what it is for others and what it is for itself- and in all respects they are diametric opposites. The latter—call it by what name you like—is cruciform. The built-in nature of the First Person is to vanish in favour of third persons, to give his life for the whole world, ranging from particles to island universes. To lead others he must turn his back on them, but to save them he must face them—on the cross. No, this is not a comfortable arrangement. It's a terrible world. But thank God it's His world, and the secret behind it is His own Crucifixion, Calvary for ever being re-enacted in and for each one of us. And the secret behind Calvary is the most incredible love. The love which is heaven and for ever.

COUNSEL: Are you *sure* that's where you are going? The Witness has grave doubts.

MYSELF: Will I go to heaven when I die? For light on this subject, please turn to Diagram No. 33.

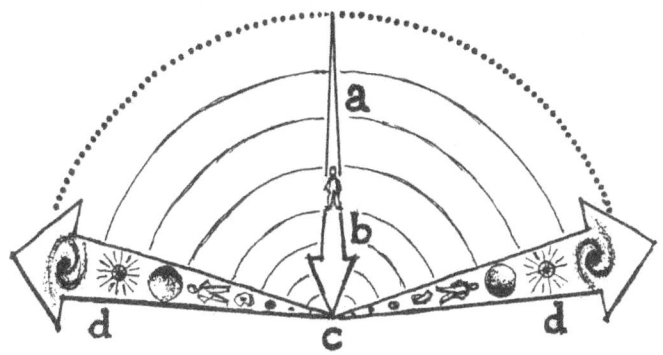

Diagram No. 33

Will I go to a real, bright, starry heaven and no dim dream-world? Yes! Provided I die now, on the inverted T-cross of St Anthony (a-b-c-dd). I can't ascend (a) to the heights *(per ardua ad astra* just isn't on), but I can and must descend (b) to the depths, to the baseline I never in fact left, to the crossroads (c) of my No-thingness and my death as a separate being. Here, taking both directions at once (d-d), I come to a heaven which, far from being a cloud-cuckoo-land, is as concrete and physical as it is spiritual. I come to it by the low road of self-abandonment, the high road of self-development being closed to traffic. (It never was a through road, except on maps.) The embracing arms of love gain the peak that the feet lose by climbing. At (d-d), in the heaven where the deepest is the widest, I come to 'the love that moves the Sun and the other stars.' Don't believe this: spread your arms and test it. As a mother loves her child because she embraces her child, so you come to love your world because you embrace your world. Because, as First Person Singular, you are cruciform, built for the loving that is God's loving. The loving that is death and resurrection—death *for* the world and resurrection as the world.

As Madame Guyon said, 'God gives us the cross, and the cross gives us to God.' And Thomas à Kempis:

> The cross always stands ready, and everywhere awaits you. You cannot escape it, wherever you flee; for wherever you go, you bear yourself, and always find yourself. Look up or down, within you or without, and everywhere you will find the cross. And everywhere you must have patience, if you wish to attain inner peace, and win an eternal crown.

I don't understand this. It's beyond all comprehension. But with the utmost clarity I see it's so, my pain and its relief confirm it, and my heart knows it always.

WITNESS: Well, God's your judge, not me. Some of what you say raises my hopes that our Lord's saving love is gaining admittance to your heart. Other things you say suggest that it's to yourself rather than Him that you are looking for salvation, and I tremble for you. Many of your ideas I can't grasp at all. They don't accord with the scriptures I know, or with the faith of Christians I know. All the same, in the Father's house are many mansions. Earnestly I pray that you may find yourself in one of them, and not in outer darkness.

MYSELF: Well, let's leave it at that. May I just pass on to you the thought that the true spiritual life is all paradox, and that the more Christ *is* you and me the more he's altogether adorable as *other* than you and me?

It's to the Jury and to His Honour that I now turn, with the earnest request that each of you will drop all prejudice and carry out a very small but all-important investigation. One which will in seconds summarize and make perfectly clear to you, without verbal complications, what I've been saying at length in reply to Counsel and his Witness.

First, please refer again to Diagram No. 15 [see Witness 15 The New Apocalyptic] and note once more the spectacular contrast between yourself as second/third person and as First Person.

Next, please glance around the court and check that *on present evidence* all those other people are built to that second/third-person pattern. All, without exception, are in the normal human condition. The New Bailey is no Bluebeard's chamber.

Then please—for the very last time in this Trial—stretch out your arms widely at shoulder height, and simultaneously look down at yourself. What you see there is the most significant, the most tremendous of all the sights you have ever seen or will ever see. And the most overlooked because the most feared. Feared not without reason...

I'm grateful to His Honour, and to you two (or is it three?) members of the Jury, for complying. To the remaining nine or ten let me say that I do understand your terror. Crucifixion is a nasty business. However, it happens also to be universal and inescapable. And, when seen and accepted for what it is, it is your entry into the Heaven of God's love and God's peace for ever.

So I appeal to you ten once more. In the end my Defence is for seeing, not understanding...

JUDGE: The Accused is on trial for his life. I must ask you to do this little thing for him, sincerely and with full attention. Otherwise, you're in danger of going away from here with the blood of an innocent man on your hands. [They comply hurriedly, but with an eye on the Judge rather than themselves...]

MYSELF: Among my dear friends who, by thus facing and embracing the wide world, awakened to What lies at its Centre, I think specially of Anne. She happened to be hanging out the washing. To the Jury I say: it's never too late to hang out the washing, Anne-fashion; it's never too late to be built for loving, God-fashion; it's never too late to experience dying and resurrection, Christ-fashion.

As for myself, how slow I've been to fathom the depth and power and persuasiveness of this simple act of enfolding Christ's own world in Christ's own arms—arms proceeding from no lack lustre Jack's shoulders, but from the deathless brilliance right here! But at last I find myself saying, with Gerard Manley Hopkins:

> I am at once what Christ is,
> since he was what I am,
> and this Jack, joke, poor potsherd, patch, matchwood,
> is immortal diamond.

Or, less beautifully but not less passionately, with Ruysbroeck:
> Holy Scripture teaches that God, the heavenly Father, created all men in His image and in His likeness. His image is His Son, His own eternal Wisdom, and St John says that in this all things have life. And the life is nothing else than the image of God, in which God has everlastingly begotten all things, and which is the cause of all creatures. And so this image, which is the Son of God, is eternal, before all creation. And we are all made in this eternal image, for in the noblest part of our souls, that is in the properties of our highest powers, we are made as a living, eternal mirror of God, in which God has imprisoned His eternal image, and into which no other image can ever enter.

Or, in St Paul's incomparable style:

> Ye have put off the old man with his deeds; and have put on the new man, which is renewed in knowledge after the image of him that

created him: Where there is neither Greek nor Jew, circumcision nor uncircumcision, Barbarian, Scythian, bond nor free: but Christ is all, and in all.

So that I can, with George Herbert, sing and shout:

> Christ is my onely head,
> My alone onely heart and breast,
> My onely musick.

Prosecution Summing-up

Ladies and gentlemen of the Jury, blasphemy is unique. Like other very serious crimes—such as murder, robbery with violence, and rape—it is a crime against our species. But blasphemy is also the crime against our Creator, and therefore immeasurably more terrible than any other. It is this most heinous of offences with which John a-Nokes stands charged—and of which, the Crown maintains, he has over and over again, in your presence, been proved guilty.

I shouldn't be at all surprised, however, if you felt that the Defence has sometimes had the better of it in the course of this Trial. That it has occasionally had the Prosecution tied in knots. Well, knotted or unknotted, the Prosecution wishes (and can well afford) to pay tribute to the ingenuity with which Mr John a-Nokes has turned a number of its twenty-seven witnesses into witnesses for the Defence—seemingly. And neutralized others—seemingly. Seemingly, I repeat. For in fact he has done nothing of the kind. Not one of them testified to Nokes's innocence of the charge brought against him under the Blasphemy Act. Not a single one.

The Defence has shot its bolt—with lots of spectacular skirmishings and flashes and bangs. The only snag is that the missile falters in mid-air and falls far short of the target. Now it's the Prosecution's turn. The time has come finally to expose the structural weakness of the Defence. No need of a popgun, let alone artillery fire, from our side. A touch is enough to bring that lofty card-castle tumbling. Never mind how it might briefly stand up outside this court; here, it's not to be taken seriously for a moment. It's a game. More precisely, an elaborate *diversion*. The Accused has made good use of the ploy whereby, if you have no answer to the charge brought against you, you unobtrusively substitute for it one you can answer, and then make a great song and dance proving your innocence. Rather as if the Knave of Hearts, accused of stealing tarts and hoping against hope that the Queen has forgotten they were treacle tarts, swears he never, O never stole any jam tarts; and then begins a long spiel about how he hates jam tarts anyway, and how they make him sick, and so on. In that playing-card court, Jack has some chance of getting away with it. In this court of law, Jack has no chance at all. The game's up, Jack! Your diversions have ceased to divert the course of justice.

Let me remind him and you the Jury of the substance of the Act. The Prosecution is required to prove that the Accused has so outraged people's religious susceptibilities that they have been driven to take the law into their own hands. It is enough to show that he goes out of his way to scandalize those people, by pouring contempt and derision on an Object or Person or Being they revere—say (to take the extreme example) by falsely claiming to be that very Object or Person or Being. Did he, in fact, do precisely this, persistently? That's the question that you, the jury, must address.

Can there be the shadow of a shadow of a doubt about the answer?

In his summing-up, the Accused will doubtless make a lot of that little word 'falsely'. He will say that he has proved that he *really* is the Supreme Being. Well, practically every Witness has testified to the contrary. If any doubt remains in our minds, let's see whether he can give us a last-minute demonstration of his supremacy by performing I-don't-know-what wonder. By arranging for the New Bailey to be struck by lightning, perhaps.

Not surprisingly, the Accused follows the rule that the best defence is attack—specially when your own fortifications are crumbling or non-existent. Accused of blasphemy, he goes on to prove, to his own total satisfaction, that he's practically the only one in court—if not the world—who isn't guilty of blasphemy! A bold and successful stratagem, maybe, in a few small circles outside this court, but not inside. Here we decline to accept for a moment, in place of the Crown's definition of blasphemy, that of the Accused. Which in any case (leaving the Act aside for the moment) is a bad definition—one that doesn't define and mark out boundaries but defaces and rubs out boundaries, and is therefore no definition whatever. To accuse *everyone* of blasphemy, or of any other crime, is to accuse no one. All it does is to show how antisocial, how misanthropic you are.

It's the nature and the business of every self to be centred on itself, to announce itself distinctly, to get up off its bottom and do and be its own thing; otherwise, the world's reduced as in a blender to a tasteless soup, with no taster. A man is, and stands for, that man and no other. Such is the human condition the wide world over and down the ages—like it or loathe it. If that's blasphemy, I like it. And everyone likes it. And everything shows that God likes it, too. So I say to Nokes: Come on! A blasphemous *species*—what on Earth does that mean? The trouble with your Defence is that it's too clever-clever, too immoderate, too damned radical by half—and therefore self-defeating. It pushes its arguments so far and so hard against the brick wall of common sense that they rebound and knock out the Defender. Knock him cold.

I turn to the Jury. Your job, no matter what you happen to think of the two wildly different definitions of blasphemy that have been put to you—Nokes's version and the Crown's version—is to go by the latter. If you're sensible, you'll approve of it. But whether you approve or disapprove is beside the point. It's the law. This is a court of law. Juries serve in it under oath to uphold the law, regardless of their private opinions.

The Accused makes out he's above the law. I say that at least part of him isn't, and that's the part the law can chop. He makes out that he has an inalienable natural right to announce to an unbelieving world his true and superhuman identity, which he alone is in a position to check up on, to introspect. Well I say that his fellow men have an inalienable and natural right to announce and denounce what *they* make of him, and to subject his apparent and human identity to apparent and human laws—to the extent, if need be, of terminating his apparent and human life. If, as he claims, he isn't what he appears to be—if in reality and as First Person he's not a product but the Producer of the universe—then he should be able to cope with the slight hiccup of the execution by legal process of that little third person called John a-Nokes. If indeed it is a hiccup, and not a chuckle coming from the real Producer, as He gives Nokes his comeuppance.

Nokes goes on and on about the good sense and practicality of his philosophy. Only gaze and gawp long and hard enough into your

One-off Interior Blank (says he, in effect) and all will be tickety-boo. Oh, really? Look at the fix that this priceless jewel of wisdom has landed him in already, to say nothing of where he's going from here. Look, members of the Jury, and be warned.

The Accused's credo must strike you the way it strikes most people—as nonsense. Philosophers have for centuries had a word for it: namely, *solipsism*. By which they mean that extreme subjectivism—that blown-up blend of naïvety and conceit—which cries: 'Hey, guess what! I've never met another I! They've all been hims and hers and its—motorheads and robots to the last man, woman and child. I alone am Consciousness Indivisible, the only One! Wow!' No philosophers worthy of the name waste time on this daydream. It's not that they can disprove it. It's not even that they strongly disapprove of it, but that they have no use for it. It's short of meaning and sense, a non-starter and dead end. Solipsism ranks no higher than an occasional pastime—a very dull game of solitaire—which not even the player (if he has any marbles left at all) takes seriously for a moment. Much less the non-player.

Psychologists have an even ruder word for it, namely *regression*. By which they mean a falling back into infantile self-centredness and illusions of omnipotence, a retreat from the bleak and harsh realities of adult life to the time when things and people weren't other, or separate from oneself. When all existed to serve oneself. And further back still to the solitary warmth and safety of the womb. Here's an illness born of fear of the real world and unwillingness to take up its challenges. In other words, a refusal to grow up, evasion on a grand scale, a drop-out's dream of kingship and world dominion. The pipedream of an addict.

Yes, you can get hooked on Nokes's hallucinogen all right!

In this courtroom, for almost four weeks, we've been treated to an extraordinary presentation (as if to a panel of physicians and psychologists and social workers) of a severe and chronic case of solipsistic regression. Fascinating and ingenious, say some of us. Pathetically simplistic and naïve, say others. Sick, sick, sick, say yet others. More menacing than crack or heroin, say the rest. But the general feeling is that the Accused's pretensions are perverted, deeply immoral. In some indefinable way they are *shameful*.

Ladies and gentlemen of the Jury, along with most of our witnesses, along with every sane and sensitive human, you have this gut feeling about the assertion 'I am God!' It makes you shudder. You are sickened, appalled. *This instinct is for trusting, and all the sophistry of all the John a-Nokeses in the world shall not prevail against it.* Of course Nokes will presently have a last go at confusing you with paradox, and explain how he must be infinitely humble to be infinitely great. Well, a court of law is no place for, has no time for, such double-talk, and there's no call for you to rack your brains over it. Anyway, so far from supporting the Defence, it undermines it. Not content with being God in the highest, the Accused claims to be God in the depths, and so to possess Him completely. Far from clearing himself of blasphemy, he compounds the crime. He convicts himself of double blasphemy, if there is such a monster. He only endorses Martin Buber's judgement on him: 'Woe to the man so possessed that he thinks he possesses God!'

But really, members of the Jury, it doesn't matter what you think of the Accused's theological contortions in all their variety. The point is that he has committed, deliberately and consistently over many years, the terrible offence he's charged with. For which he will have to pay the penalty.

You may ask why the Prosecution bothered to go so carefully into—and to refute so effectively—the Accused's claims to uniqueness and divinity. I'll tell you why. However shameful his pretensions and however fallacious his arguments, it was important that he should be free to ventilate them—with the result that the Prosecution was obliged to take them far more seriously than they deserve. This Trial had to be seen to be a fair Trial in which the Accused wasn't muzzled or bullied, and was encouraged rather than merely allowed to put his case at length. Besides, it wouldn't have done to assume in advance that the Act has no loophole in it by which he could escape. It was, I suppose, just possible that solipsism and infantile regression and satanic pride, when rationalized and robed in the holy vestments of a kind of spirituality, could have furnished arguments and evidence which would help his case. Unlikely but conceivable. They didn't, as it turned out. But no one can say they weren't given a chance.

So, ladies and gentlemen of the Jury, I come back to the nub, to the heart of the matter. It's perfectly simple. Never mind the peculiar circumstances of this case, its ins and outs, the emotions roused, the countless side-issues. If anyone in the world has been proved guilty of blasphemy—of this ultimate crime against man and his Creator—it is that creature over there in the dock.

You have no reasonable alternative but to find him guilty as charged.

Your Honour, that concludes the arguments for the Crown in the matter of *Rex* versus *John a-Nokes*. I rest my case.

Defence Summing-up

As usual, the Crown Prosecutor is so obviously wrong. It just isn't true that much of my Defence was irrelevant to the charge brought against me, a smokescreen. Or that my tactics have been diversionary, and that I have deliberately spent much of the court's time answering questions that weren't being put by the court.

I kept to the point—which is that I am Who I say I am. And indeed I'm grateful for having been given the opportunity to make that point in so many ways. Most grateful to the Establishment for providing such a large and well-lit shop-window in which to display my wares for so long. I'm specially beholden to the powers that be because what matters is not so much what happens in this place, or even whether I shall or shall not go from here to the place of execution and my long home. What really matters is what's happening in the world beyond this court. The world that—thanks to twenty-first century telecommunications—is avidly watching and listening to us. I'm concerned with the millions who, though invisible and inaudible, are as present here at this moment as the Judge and the Jury are. As I am.

It's a world that's sick. Sick with the degenerative and dehumanizing diseases of bigotry, fanaticism, bitter and cruel intolerance. Its vital organs are so feverishly at odds with one another that they threaten to work their mutual destruction. I see this Blasphemy Act, under which I'm being tried, as the first dose of a hastily concocted febrifuge, of a medicine for bringing down the patient's temperature a few degrees.

Which for the moment it has done—but at a quite unacceptable cost. For this medicine is as poisonous as the disease it purports to treat. Indeed it's a product and a part of the disease itself, of that same witches' brew of bigotry and fanaticism and, bitter intolerance which they call fundamentalism. Fundamentalism, my Aunt Fanny! It's superficiality run amok.

Persisted in, it gags and throttles the patient. It can only produce yes-men and brainwashed *apparatchiks.* And eventually zombies. It renders pointless the martyrdom of countless brave souls who have sweated their guts out and died to achieve, against all the odds, freedom of speech and of the written and spoken word. It casually throws overboard man's hard-won and precious liberty to question every belief and practice (no matter how entrenched and revered), without which he's an angry ape playing dirty tricks on other angry apes. A creature so blinkered and so stiff and so solemn, so touchy and so cruel, that he's not only dehumanized but de-animalized. Shocked Nature's most shocking monstrosity.

Now what is the cure for this degenerative illness? A spate of new and juster laws? Of new, intelligent and well-thought-out legislation, enforcing tolerance? A live-and-let-live Act of Parliament? If achievable (which I doubt, seeing that enforced tolerance is a contradiction in terms), it would be of little or no use in that it addresses the symptoms while not diagnosing the disease, let alone treating it. No, there's only one cure, and that's the cure I've been describing and prescribing all along in this courtroom.

Defence Summing-up

This sovereign remedy is a true simple—simplicity itself, natural, commonsensical, obvious, inescapable—once you've tumbled to it. *The way to reach agreement with your opponent is to find Common Ground with him, the Bottom Line you share.*

A cliché? I can't help that. Corny or daring, it's the only way to peace in our time, O Lord. A way little travelled, alas.

Exactly what and exactly where is this wonderful (but woefully overlooked) Common Ground and World's End and Bottom Line which is our reconciliation and our peace? Need I remind you that it's not an abstraction, and it's not a metaphor, and there's nothing vague about it? It's not, like the equator, an imaginary line which, though precisely located, is neither drawn nor seen. This Line is for real. Of all sure things it's the most sure. More homely and down-to-earth than Earth itself, it's the Base that supplies all our needs. It's a real Home for constantly going back to and putting one's feet up in, not an ideal home one will never set foot in. With all my love I'm inviting you to join me here right away. And—because this isn't one of those bogus 'Oh, do come and visit sometime' invitations—I'm handing you a sketch-map showing you how to find your way.

Yes, yet another picture, Diagram No. 34, and the last in your booklet.

You will find me at the very Centre. You will be me at the very Centre. In fact, you and I are *already* One with each other here—the One we both really, really are, the BEING whose first name is I AM: I AM John a-Nokes, I AM Gerald Wilberforce KC, I AM everyone in the telephone book, and so on *ad infinitum*. Here are to be found our Healing and Wholing, our Centre which instantly expands into our Diameter and Circumference. Into our 360° completion which, though it looks like 160° war and 200° armistice, turns out to be the wraparound Peace that passes all understanding.

Your Honour, and each lady and gentleman of the Jury, to you I now issue this personal invitation to join me here at home. Oh, it's a comedown all right! l know my place. No place on the map is lower, humbler, less posh, than mine. All the same, I assure you, you won't regret your gracious condescension.

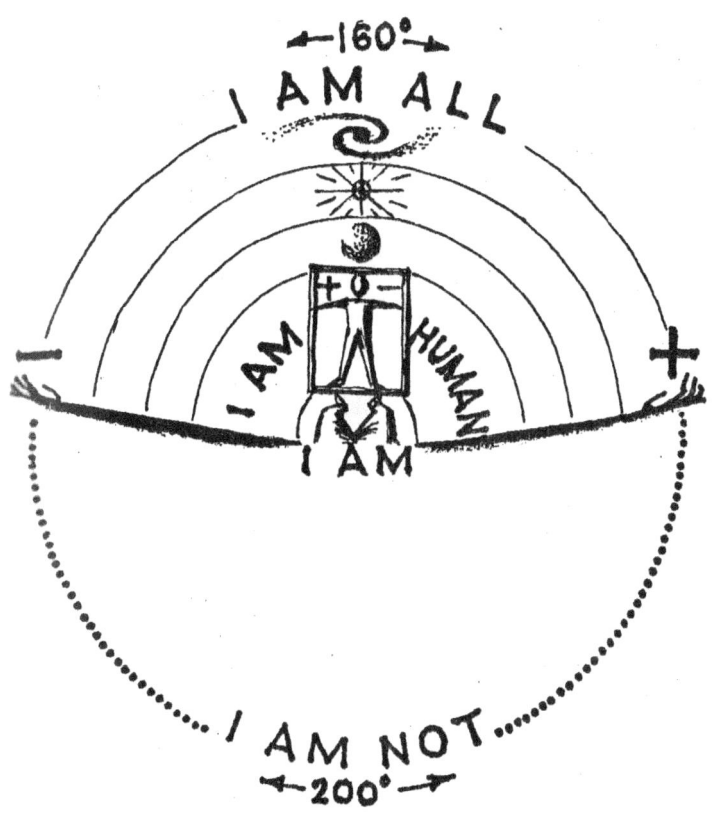

Diagram No. 34

For in fact it is no more and no less than the goal of your submission to the truth, your deep bowing before the evidence of how things already are with you and with me. *Bowing,* I repeat, to what's given. Ceasing to resist the obvious. No, I haven't forgotten that we've already been through this bowing routine time and time again in the course of this Trial. I'm saying that we can't repeat it too often if we're at all interested in the healing of our sickness unto death, the disease of which this Trial is a symptom. So I beg you to join me again in the descent to the nadir of all things.

Look *up* at the ceiling, at that ornamental plaster-work and those fluorescent light-fittings. Objects of little interest to you, I guess, unless you happen to be an ornamental plasterer or an electrician...

Lowering your gaze, look out at the courtroom. At His Honour, splendidly robed and bewigged, presiding over this court; at learned Counsel, somewhat limp and crumpled after having put the case (such as it is) for the Crown; at John a-Nokes (also rather shopworn) here in the dock, the fellow whose life is in your hands. Well, for the time being, you are very much involved with us lot, aren't you?...

Bowing still more deeply before the evidence, and looking *down,* you come to those feet of yours—the feet you are comfortably putting up (putting *up,* as I said, and as the Diagram shows) at home. Yes, you're getting warm now. Deeply involved...

Finally you arrive at Home-Base, the World's End, the Bottom Line, and total involvement. You arrive at the Frontier which is none other than the Line you can now actually draw with your finger across your blouse/shirt/pullover, the Line where that garment gives place to the *absence* of garment and shoulders and neck—the Absence of Everything. On this Aware Absence I put my shirt.

Speak as disrespectfully as you like about the equator—that invisible line where nothing happens—but not about this visible Line where everything happens, where Non-being flips over into Being. Here it is that the incredible switching from No-thing to Something to All-things goes on without let-up and without cause—the switching from the Sink of the Universe to the Spring and Fountain of the Universe, from the Great Unconscious to the Conscious, from the Bottomless Abyss to God and His world, from I AM NOT to I AM and I AM ALL. Here at Home-Base, right where you and I are now, this wonder of wonders is in full flood. Here, where we are privy to the Incredible Achievement, where we are the Incredible Achievement! The Achievement of the Achiever, the Origination of Self-Origination!

Here, where you and I draw the Line, is where we Line up, where we are brought into Line at last. Consciously to remain here, enjoying its infinite resources—yet continuing to leap rejoicing from the darkest Abyss of Mystery below the Line into the bright world above the Line and back again—is to be healed.

Here I'm healed with you and as you. Here I take with you the one sensible remedy for the otherwise incurable disease which this court and the Blasphemy Act are attempting to treat. Here, to be you no less than myself is to cease to blaspheme. Here, coinciding with this Line, I am you and you are me, for ever One Being in the Eternal Christ, no matter how at variance our terms and temperaments and beliefs and practices above the Line. Here I'm in with you on the Ground Floor of this Enterprise of Enterprises. Here and here alone (I repeat) we sink to absolute Sameness and leave our differences floating.

And up there they remain, of course. And proliferate marvellously. No possibility of sinking *them*. But all's well now that we survey them together from the infinite tolerance of our Common Ground. Now we are no more opinionated by our opinions than we are pulled over by our pullovers or motorized by our motors. We *have* those things, and trade them in from time to time for smarter models. Secure in the silent vision that I am you on the Line, I can now afford—can now welcome and insist upon—the delightful clashing of the things we get up to above the Line. *Vive les différences!*

No wonder, ladies and gentlemen, that hemispherical map of my constitution kept cropping up throughout the Trial. Clearly it displays the nature and the cure of the horrible disease we are all afflicted with: the endemic disease of blasphemy, the high treason of the human trespasser from his own region out there, as he makes for the Centre where he aims to unseat his Creator and King.

The Prosecution asserts that a malady which everybody suffers from is one which nobody suffers from. Not so. The history of disappearing species abounds with examples of creatures that were sick not as individuals but en masse—the most quoted example being the dinosaurs, whose gigantic size and fantastic and crippling armour is supposed to have sealed their fate. No doubt their size and armament had been advantageous up to a point and in moderation; beyond that point they became handicaps that contributed to (if they didn't cause) the extinction of these Tertiary reptiles. Not altogether different is the case of *Homo sapiens,* the creature that developed another sort of crippling armour. I'm referring to the illusion that he is for himself at Centre the thing that he *looks like* to others out there, the lethal fiction of First-Person versus second/third-person symmetry and confrontation. This fiction or myth is precisely what made him human, and for ages it was a tolerably good myth that was productive of nearly all he holds valuable. But now, more and more, it's proving counter-productive, a bad myth that's increasingly destructive of all he holds valuable, including humanness, including himself! He may well follow the dinosaurs into Life's packed charnel-house.

I don't know what will happen. But I'm guardedly hopeful, inasmuch as what's required of *Homo sapiens* (if that prize misnomer is to become a nomer) is no big deal. It's not to *do* something difficult and tricky but to *stop doing* something difficult and tricky. Namely, to stop muddling things. It's to let things be themselves in their proper places. It's to let God be God at the Centre of things, and man be man off-Centre—a metre or so away—keeping a respectful distance from that Presence. The arrival and survival of *Homo sapiens* depend on its perception of itself as a blaspheming species, followed by its ceasing to blaspheme and becoming a reverent species. One that substitutes *God's in, I'm out* for the present disastrous *I'm in, God's out.*

God, the Alone, is right here. Man, one of many, is over there. Which brings me to the Prosecution's supercilious dismissal of John a-Nokes as a case of naïve subjectivism. A severe attack of solipsism—a term which has more than a whiff of the snake-pit about it—is what the poor fellow is suffering from! Well, I say it isn't Nokes but the Prosecution that's pathetically naïve here, simplistic to a degree.

I have news for Counsel. There's not one but two sorts of solipsism—man's and God's—and they lie poles apart. The former, in so far as it's at all possible, is insane. 'I, Jack, have access to my own awareness only; that of others is speculative, dubious and probably non-existent.' This is solipsism by *exclusion,* the denial of love, loneliness at its most lonesome. And it's nonsense because—to tell the truth—Jack as Jack-by-himself, as that peripheral third person, isn't aware at all: he's a picture, a glossy and paper-thin appearance, all object and no subject. He's aware only as the First Person who is Awareness itself; the Awareness in all beings, the whole of it at their Centre. He's aware only as the infinitely deep and substantial One who says with an engaging grin, 'Here I AM! It's ME *and not a picture!'* He's aware only as the One whose Aloneness is absolutely real, blissful, loving—because it's solipsism by *inclusion.* He's aware only as the Universal Subject who is the sole Healer of my loneliness and all loneliness.

In short, the only kind of solipsism that Counsel can reasonably accuse me of is God's. Which means that he's accusing me of being Who I say I really, really am—this truly Singular First Person. Which I find rather funny.

Let me translate this into here-and-now language. Looking in right now at what I'm looking out of—at the Aware Capacity or

Defence Summing-up

Solitary Consciousness that I find here—I realize that this is what unites me with your consciousness and all consciousness. There's nothing to mark it out as the property of John a-Nokes, everything to mark it out as common property. The property of the Court Usher over there by the door, for instance, and the Clerk to the Court, and all the rest of us here. This Aloneness is the remedy—the sole remedy—for loneliness. Here I am you, whoever you are. If this is that dreaded solipsism, it is also the perfect antidote for solipsism. Hurray for the Solitude which at last overcomes solitariness!

Or put it like this: because the word 'I' has two contrary meanings, so has the solipsism which says 'I alone exist!' The solipsism of delusion and bitter loneliness is saying 'I, Jack, alone exist!' The solipsism of enlightenment and love is saying 'I, the One Consciousness or First Person in all beings, alone exist.' I think Counsel is accusing me of the first kind because he has never heard of the second, let alone enjoyed it.

Now for the regression—a nasty word, made nastier by calling it infantile—which is the other aberration he accuses me of. (How invaluable these pejorative terms can be, as substitutes for honest thinking and observation!) If for *regression* I substitute *return to my roots,* and for *infantile* I substitute *as a little child*—and if, in addition, I consult once more our diagram—why then what a different picture is conjured up! 'Until you become like little children you will never enter the Kingdom of Heaven.' Until you revert to the time when you didn't hallucinate a wad of stuff bunging up the mid-point of your universe, until you revert to the time when you didn't superimpose on your featureless Original Face that acquired mirror-face, until you revert to the time when you weren't eccentric to yourself by one angstrom (let alone by one metre) and permanently out to lunch—until then you will be sick. Not, it's true, a case of infantile regression, but of that dehumanizing and degenerative disease which you could call infantile-regression-phobia: a case of adulthood cutting itself out not only from its own childhood, but from its sole Supplier and Resource.

In working out and giving vent to all these matters, over the past fifteen years or so, I have—yes—given some offence to pious folk, and much offence to fanatics. About this I have two things to say:

The first is that I never intended to give offence to anybody. None of my work has been deliberately belligerent. Rather the other way round. In fact, it belongs to the pattern of things as I see them that all faiths, creeds, religious systems and religious practices proceed from the one Centre which is the true First Person that I AM. In the last resort, accordingly, I'm responsible for the lot—not excluding the most bizarre and intolerant and aggressive, and the cruel injustices and violence and civil commotion they lead to. In this sense I'm pleading Guilty to much more than I'm charged with. On the other hand it remains true that to say anything of importance in the field of religion is to infuriate somebody. If it's worth saying and not just pious waffle (of which there's plenty, forsooth), it's bound to spark off accusations of heresy, if not blasphemy. I take it that the Act isn't, for this reason, intended to silence absolutely all God-talk.

The second thing I have to say here is much more important. You may well feel, as I do, that this Act is potentially and in the long run more evil than the evil it's designed to combat. Instead of ensuring that religious individuals and bodies shall be free to teach and to preach according to their lights, without interference by those of contrary persuasion, it ensures that the most vociferous and intolerant and unscrupulous of sectarians shall dictate how far the rest are allowed to teach and to preach, if at all. The Act uses the law to set these fanatics above the law. It goes one worse than saying that overt might is right: it says that the most insidious and despicable might—the might of the pogrom and the Klan and the suitcase bomber—is right. The law it upholds is the law of clout. Clout overt and bloody-brutal as well as clout underhand and dirty-brutal. If this iniquitous Act is allowed to go unrepealed, this is a bad time for our land and our species. The lights are going out all over the planet. Civilization is well on the way to high-tech savagery. The *Homo* that could have become *sapiens* has become not so much *Homo stultus* as *Homo diabolus*.

Don't tell me there's no alternative to this barbarous Act or something very like it, and that if people can't propose feasible ways of liberalizing it they had better keep their big mouths shut. I say that the only real alternative to this so-called Anti-Blasphemy Law (which, seeing it puts man at man's Centre, is in fact pro-blasphemy) is the insight which sends man packing to his proper place. And don't tell me it's an unworkable alternative, a vision hidden from all but a handful of gifted seers. No, the most vividly lit scene in the whole world—once you bother to look—is that headed third person over there behind glass, and this headless First Person here in front of it, and the total contrast between them. *God's in, Jack's out* is plainer than daylight, once I rouse myself from my long dream and raise an eyelid.

Not content with going on and on about the obviousness of this waking scene, my friends and I have devised over the years a whole range of alarm clocks (so to speak), devices for alerting us to the scene and for keeping us alert—devices (I have to say this) which are incomparably more immediate, certain and foolproof than any that have gone before. A few of you here—those who, like His Honour, have actually carried out with me the little experiments I begged you to do—will be able to judge from that small sample the workability of our devices and techniques for waking us to our Divine Nature. The advent of these experiments—plus humanity's ever more desperate need to discover that Nature and so avoid genocide, plus humanity's ever more efficient means of communication, plus a generous helping of what you might call luck and what I would certainly call grace—add up to a fairly encouraging total. Who's to say that *Homo* hasn't a fighting chance to make it to *sapiens?* I take heart from the reflection that this very offbeat species of ours has somehow muddled and staggered and crept through Ice Ages and Ages of Stagnation and Ages of Decline and Dark Ages, and is still going strong. Strongly for Hell, it may be. But need not be. I have a vision which can save my people. I've shared it with you. It is the Christing of humanity, no less. Where there's no vision the people perish.

A few million years ago proto-man made the 'impossible' leap from animal un-self-consciousness to human self-consciousness. Was this his last and only leap? Fiction (the pretence that one is what one looks like) turned animals into men; facts (say a distinguished company of seers, sparsely but very widely scattered throughout the world for the past three millennia) can now turn man into God. Some of them say that this second leap—from human self-consciousness to divine Self-consciousness—is hard, others say that it's easy. I say that it's easier than winking. Eckhart says, 'Put on your jumping shoes and jump into God!' I say: Look! See how small and effortless a jump it is to put yourself in God's Adidas trainers on this side of the glass, instead of man's ꙅɒbibA trainers on that side. This truly Olympic event is no high-jump or long-jump, but a low and short standing-jump, the Instantaneous 180° Twist-jump. Make-sure you carry away the Gold!

Of course I hasten to add that it's not at all easy, having jumped, to stay jumped, to stand your ground which is Home Ground. Inevitably you revert. But at least you now know that you can make that leap, and you know exactly how to go about it, and you know that every new leap comes more naturally than the last. And sooner or later you know from experience that, exacting and often difficult though this new life as First Person certainly is, it's far less punishing than the third-person life. *God's in, Jack's out* isn't only as plain as daylight. It's as laid-on and good for working in as broad daylight is. It's when Jack ousts God that thick darkness descends and he turns himself into a benighted Jackass. Which makes it a very unpractical thing for Jack to do.

And so I come—as Counsel predicted—to that all-important word in the Act and in his initial summary of it, to that one word which gives this wretched piece of legislation such saving grace as it has. That word is *falsely*.

I'm indeed guilty of blasphemy if I *falsely* claim to be the One whom others revere as the Highest.

Well, ladies and gentlemen of the Jury, I have proved to you, many, many times over, that my claim is *true*. Those of you who have discovered in the course of this Trial that it's true of you also will, by bringing in a verdict of Not Guilty, tell Counsel where he can put his gibe that it is perverted and immoral and shameful.

Which gives me the cue to what I most want to say, and have therefore left to the very last. The difference between the 'My Me is God' *(Il mio me è Dio)* of St Catherine and the 'I am God' of some of her far from saintly contemporaries—seemingly so slight and theoretical—is in fact immense. The feel of the first is all right; of the second, all wrong. It's *revolting*. Thus far I agree with Counsel absolutely. It's not for nothing that non-Christians as well as Christians are embarrassed, if not nauseated, by such outbursts as the Ashtavakra Samhita's 'Wonderful am I! Adoration to Myself!' Nearly all Vedantists substitute 'That art thou' for 'This am I'. Godhood is claimed for another; and for oneself indirectly, via that other. With good reason. Pride and self conceit would be as inexcusable in the Creator as they are inevitable in the creature. He's no Muhammad Ali, beating his breast and crying 'I'm the greatest!' Instead of preening and puffing Himself up, God bends and bows to Himself; and in so doing bends and bows to each and all. He gives place to and underpins the lowliest. He's a Not-God, not Himself till He's a total stranger to Himself. Let me sound a very personal note here. The secret consolation and safety-belt of my whole adult life hasn't been the self-centred 'I am God', or even 'I am Him', but the wholly other-centred *'To be saved is to be Him'*. Oh, yes, the glory is there, the cold white light of the Subject is real, but it is shaded and softened and warmed by surrender to and love of the Adorable Object. The One that is Light in the highest is Love in the depths.

Put it another way. Unlike HE IS, I AM is devoid of wonder and worship, neither of which God is short of. His keenest delight is the hyper-miracle of His own Self-origination, His 'impossible' popping up from the blank Inane, in spite of the fact that by rights there should be nothing whatever. As Plotinus puts it, 'He has given Himself existence' (what a gift!); 'He has acted Himself into being' (what a performance!). He finds being His own Mum and Dad astoundingly funny, in both senses of the word. My point is that this surprise and admiration arise from His enjoyment of Himself as Object and not Subject. And when I share in the divine astonishment (and by God I do!) I must share also in the divine humility and objectivity which alone make it possible. Creatures thrive on their divine pretensions, their thrust towards Godhood. God alone is not a bit pushy. The only way to enjoy Him—enjoy being Him—is not, not, not to be Him! Can Sir Gerald hear me?

These built-in contradictions are lost on the Prosecution, which as always is a simplistic, dopey, half baked, yes-*or*-no affair. The Defence, however, is forced by the facts to keep saying yes *and* no. Thus on the one hand I'm confessing to the Jury that *as Jack* I'm too stuck-up, too stuck with Jack, too determined to hit the jackpot, too intent on transmogrifying that jackanapes into some kind of godling, too possessed to be anything but that Godless jackanapes. And on the other hand I'm telling them that only *as the God who is not-God* am I come to be low and empty and owned enough to take on the splendour and the amazement that is God.

'My Me is God' is the Christing of this outward-facing First Person. 'My God is Me' is the anti-christing of that inward-facing third person called Jack. I have to go for one or the other, there being no halfway house.

I go for the former. My Me is God, but my God isn't Me. It's as subtle and as sharp—and, in practice, as simple—as that.

And so, members of the Jury, we come to the final Act of the drama we have all been cast in here, the Act in which you star. To you is granted the power, just this once in your lives, to kill or to spare one of your kind. If, exercising this power, you send me to the scaffold because you suppose me guilty of blasphemy, you will be guilty of murder. Why? Why, because my life has been devoted to denouncing and frustrating Jack's pretensions to any kind of divinity; devoted to putting and keeping him in his place out there, and leaving his King enthroned here at the Centre of all things.

Bring in a verdict of Not Guilty and you will do justice to me and to yourselves. You will leave this court with hands unstained with blood, and will at least have started to address the great problem of blasphemy—your own blasphemy.

There's justice and good sense in you. Let them out!

And let me out. I could do with a breath of fresh air!'

Your Honour, that concludes my Defence.

Judge's Directions to the Jury

Members of the Jury, let me introduce my advice to you by explaining what my duties are as Judge at this stage of the Trial. Broadly, they are two. The first is to ensure that you are aware of what the law says, at least sufficiently aware for you to decide whether it has been broken. The second is to distinguish, from among the issues that will determine your decision, those concerning which there's no reasonable doubt and those which are open to question. It's the latter, of course, which you are required to deliberate and to pronounce on.

Let us then look at the provisions of this Blasphemy Act. Here, my task is fairly straightforward. It transpires that the Prosecutor for the Crown and I, and indeed the Accused himself, are quite sufficiently agreed about their interpretation and substance. Briefly recapitulating, it is this: To be guilty of blasphemy within the meaning of the Act, the Accused must have done three things. (1) He must have so outraged the feelings of religious people that they have been driven to commit serious breaches of the peace. (2) He must have done so deliberately, in a way that could have been avoided, and not accidentally or incidentally. (3) He must have brought into contempt One who is held to be sacred—by grossly insulting or by falsely claiming to be that One.

Let us look, in a little more detail, at these three criteria of guilt.

(1) *Outrage.* The Accused doesn't challenge the Prosecution's contention that he has offended people's susceptibilities over a long period, and to such an extent that they have frequently taken the

law into their own hands. He admits to having been the cause of very serious social unrest. If any doubts remain on this score, the testimony of a number of Witnesses confirms these facts. In short, there's no issue here for you to consider.

(2) *Deliberate Outrage.* When the alleged offence isn't aimed at his religious opponents, but arises incidentally or accidentally out of the Accused's convictions, it doesn't amount to blasphemy as defined in the Act. Here we do have a question for you to consider: Has Mr John a-Nokes been fortifying and defending his own religious position with unnecessary vigour and persistence? Well, you have had almost a month's experience of his behaviour in all manner of encounters with people, together with their testimony about him. Does he strike you as an unreasonably dogmatic propagandist, happy to be fired by a vision which infuriates many people, terrifies others, and both infuriates and terrifies yet others? Is he devoid of compassion and social concern, interested only in self-aggrandizement? These are matters for you to decide, on the evidence. If you are at all doubtful about the answer, you must acquit him.

(3) *Contempt for a specific Entity.* To be guilty of blasphemy under the Act the Accused has to ridicule or slander or otherwise bring into contempt a Being or Person or Object that is regarded as sacred by a sizeable section of the community. One way of doing this—and you could say that it's John a-Nokes's speciality—is claiming that he is such a Being. Understandably enough, it is this setting himself up to *be* the very One they worship, with awe and from afar, which (to judge from the Witnesses we have heard) has proved incomparably

more offensive than any contempt he might have shown for their prophets or saints, or for their sacred books, objects, symbols or practices. There's no reasonable doubt that it is his autodeification or godmanship (I can neither find nor coin a term which is neutral, and doesn't distort or misrepresent his position) that has sparked off practically all of the violence against him and his friends, and the clamour for his execution. No big surprise this: I need hardly remind you of historical precedents.

Now we come to the big question for you to consider and pronounce upon. Is the Accused's claim—his oft-repeated assertion that he is indeed the One he says he is—true or false? He says that your answer will depend on whether you have conscientiously carried out the tests he again and again asked you to do.

My own observation is that the majority did not do so. Even now it isn't too late to correct this very serious omission. You have only— I'm quoting Mr John a-Nokes—to reverse your attention and look in at what you are now looking out of. Only do that, and (he says) you will see Who you are, and Who he is as well.

As I say, the main question is whether the Accused is Who he claims to be.

If he *is* that One, then whatever offence his claim gives rise to is quite irrelevant. He has all the right in the world to upset the world. And you must bring in a verdict of Not Guilty.

If he *hasn't* made good his claim, if you decide that he *isn't* that One, why then the offence he gives people at once becomes the crucial issue. I put it to you that the offence—the degree to which he outrages the susceptibilities of religious people—is very serious indeed. But is it intentional? Is the Accused deliberately provocative? If so, you must bring in a verdict of Guilty. If you aren't sure, you must bring in a verdict of Not Guilty.

Go now, elect your Foreperson, and consider your verdict.

The court rises. I'm taken back to my cell.

I sit there in the semi-darkness. Not worried, not hopeful. Just numb, rather as if I were paralytic drunk—on a wine of rare vintage...

I wake with a start—not clear about how long I've slept—and am led back into the reassembled court. Perfectly quiet it is...

The Verdict

The court clock tells me the Jury have been deliberating for three hours...

The Forewoman returns to report that they are unable to agree.

The Judge asks whether there's a particular difficulty which he could help to clear up.

'Yes, there is,' she replies. 'We can't understand the connection between what the Accused tried to demonstrate by means of those experiments—was it empty space?—and the Divinity he claims to be. Some of us felt that if we knew the answer it would be easier for us to agree on a verdict.'

The Judge answers, 'In that case let me see what I can do to help you.' A minute or two, while he goes through his papers. 'Ah yes, here's what looks like a relevant passage from one of the Accused's books... He writes: "What is this sadly overlooked 'empty space' that I find nowhere but here at the Centre of my universe? It is Awareness, immediate, simple, infinite, unconditioned, utterly mysterious yet more obvious than all else—and adorably *Nokes-free*. It is my Substance: also, surely, yours. And, along with Julian of Norwich, *I see no difference between God and our Substance.*"'

Having jotted down the passage and thanked the Judge, the Forewoman returns to the Jury.

And I to my cell. And a night—halfway between waking and sleeping—of continued numbness. It was as if I couldn't think a thought or move a limb if I tried, the Peace had got such a hold on me. Here was a depth of relaxation that I had rarely known...

Well into the morning of the next day, back in court. The Jury's sitting there, very still. One of them—a middle-aged woman—has her handkerchief to her eyes. I think she's one who really did the experiments. The silence is solid, as if all the air were frozen.

The Forewoman stands up. Yes, they have at last agreed.

The Judge asks, 'Do you find the Accused guilty, or not guilty?'

The Forewoman, after a long pause, and scarcely audible, replies, *'Guilty,* Your Honour... But the majority of us strongly recommend a minimum and merciful sentence.'

The storm breaks... His Honour orders the gallery to be cleared...

Calm is restored.

The Judge addresses me: 'John a-Nokes, you have been tried and found guilty of the capital offence of blasphemy under the Act of 2002.

'However, there's a provision in the Act to the effect that, having been found guilty of this crime, you may go a long way towards purging yourself by publicly retracting or qualifying the pronouncements that have given very serious offence. The extent to which such retractions or qualifications will moderate your sentence is at my discretion.

'I shall accordingly delay sentencing while you consider this matter. I shall expect to receive for examination a draft of your proposals within a reasonable time.

'Meanwhile, I have to declare that the Trial of John a-Nokes is ended.'

The Verdict

All stand as the Judge, in slow motion, leaves the court.

A shaft of sunlight ignites for an instant a patch of his robe, to a scarlet fieriness never seen by mortal man. The buzzing and the banging of the fly at the court window is deafening...

GUILTY—guilty guilty guilty... The strange noise echoes round the court like a drumbeat that will go on till doomsday...

If ever there was a moment when a should-be-familiar word has no meaning for someone, this is that moment. This is that word. This is—I am—that someone.

Epilogue

Love is like this:
If you were to cut your head off,
and give it to someone else,
would that make any difference?

Kabir

It is now all of three months since the end of the Trial and the Jury's verdict of Guilty. Apart from occasional sessions with Christopher, who is my solicitor and good friend, and a daily traipsing around the yard of this remand prison, I have sat it out alone here in this cell, awaiting sentence. A grey cell it is, with that penal-institution smell of stale cabbage soup and Dettol, and a faint suggestion of nearby sewage disposal. But I've had plenty to take my mind off conditions here and keep me very busy indeed.

Nearly all my time has been devoted to piecing together and writing up, from my fairly comprehensive diary and from my memory—which is good in spots—the Trial proceedings.

'Why bother to do that,' you might well ask, 'when the official verbatim transcript of the proceedings would have been available directly you asked for it?' The fact is that I hadn't realized this. And that, by the time Christopher told me about it, I was so into my own reconstruction of events—and was finding the job so challenging and valuable and indeed necessary—that I decided to go on and complete it.

Thumbing through these manuscript pages, two things strike me forcibly—the first concerning the Prosecution, the second concerning the Defence.

(1) All sorts of questions about the underlying strategy of the Crown remain unsolved. Was Sir Gerald's wide-ranging and curious choice of witnesses intended to spin out the proceedings and present to the public a show of thoroughness, while unobtrusively giving me rich opportunities to score Defence points? Were his bluster and bad temper, his obtuseness and impenetrable conventionality anything more than an attempt to impress and pacify the fundamentalist lobby? Where did the Judge (who seemed to come over to my side by degrees, discreetly) really stand from the beginning? What, for that matter, was the hope of the Government when it staged this show trial? Was it that I should be found Not Guilty, or Guilty but not (thanks to my abject apologies) of a capital offence? Or plain Guilty? In which case, how could anyone in his senses imagine that the execution of one 'blasphemer' would discourage others? Or that it would satisfy, and not whet, the heresy hunters' thirst for blood?

About the answers to these questions your guess is as good as mine. Mine is that there existed no clear or consistent or settled policy behind the scenes, and that the wire-pullers there had widely different intentions and expectations. In fact, I suspect that the whole show was one of those cock-ups which are the product of a double (or multiple) bind or a choice between evils, and probably no worse than any feasible alternative would have been. But I'm not the one who's complaining. Far otherwise! After all, I've been allowed to speak my mind to the world. Come to think of it, it's just possible that I have a friend in high places, who so shares that mind that he's determined to see it has an airing—come what may to poor old jack.

(2) My second reflection, to put it mildly, is that I do indeed have a case. Its design-motif, its essential stance and proposition, is so straightforward that it can be captured in a sentence. *Locating God at one's Centre is nonsense and blasphemy in man's eyes, good sense and the cure of blasphemy in God's eyes.* It's a proposition which rests fair and square on four pillars or arguments. I'll take them in order of strength, as I estimate it.

(i) The first is the *logic* of the Defence, its reasoning in support of this basic proposition about the nature of blasphemy. I'm not thinking so much of the word-play, but rather of the variety of disciplines that were drawn upon, the uses they were put to and the facts they disclose. Were the Defence arguments fallacious, or did they on the whole have the ring of truth? Did they flout science, or lean on science? Did I cheat, pull the wool of casuistry over the court's eyes? If I did, Counsel for the Crown was slow to bring it to the Jury's notice. Was he slow, or was there little to bring?

I'm not suggesting, mind you, that there were no inconsistencies at all, no weaknesses in my Defence. I continue to spot new and juicier ones. Of course. All I can say is that they are God's gracious reminders to me that He's for seeing, not for thinking about, not for getting right. The precious thing about doing one's very, very best to understand Him is that it leaves one flabbergasted. More dumbfounded than ever.

(ii) The second argument is put up by my witnesses, as I insist on calling them. Of course I selected them carefully, and edited their testimony for effect. So what? Didn't Sir Gerald do just that with his lot? And what a job lot those twenty-seven were, in comparison with my world figures—well over a hundred of them! How confused his were, and how consistent mine were—in their testimony to the Creator who lies at the heart of all His creatures! Not lurking there playing Hide-and-seek, or Hard-to-get, or Sucks-to-you-Jack, but blazing away with a brilliance like no other.

(iii) The third is the Defence Diagram with its potentially unlimited applications and variations. Its versatility and power are due to the fact that it's drawn to a sliding and not a fixed scale, so that it becomes a map of how things actually present themselves to the First Person. Here's a chart that takes the cartographer's perspective seriously for a change. It follows that, given a little ingenuity, what the map shows can be filmed, using the well-known first-person-camera technique in which the camera is held very near (or in place of) the head. Now I ask you: is this trickery? Or is it the exposure of trickery, and in particular of verbal trickery? By non-verbal means, at that? The fact is that this diagram speaks for itself. When, having shown it to a friend, I go on to explain it, he's apt to say, 'Oh, do shut up!

Anything you say can only weaken its impact.' Or words to that effect. For the last two or three years it has been my Psychopomp—dumb, brief, comprehensive, reliable and richly suggestive. My protection against what Coleridge called 'the danger of thinking without images'.

Odd, that a mere scribble of a sketch should portray so much of God Almighty and His creation! Yet not so. He's that sort of God, that humorous and that condescending. Besides, who actually weaves these airy patterns but one of His very own angel-messengers—one of those *uccelli di Dio* we surprised flying around the twelfth Witness's supermarket? The same that I now surprise flying and fluttering over this sheet of paper and leaving this trail of words?

(iv) Finally, there's the tool-kit of experiments. They include the Magic Forefinger for pointing in at the absence of the Pointed At, the Magic Battering-Ram for demolishing the stoutest prison walls, the Magic Mirror for relieving the First Person of the third person, the Magic Car for taking the world for a ride, the Magic Watch for telling the Timeless, the Magic Tape for pulling everything in, the Magic Peeler for stripping everything to its Core, the Magic Zipper at the World's End for bottoming out and discharging the World's excreta. And more. It was my failure to get most of the Jurors to carry out any of these tests sincerely which looks like costing me my life. Any one of them, done with attention, would infallibly have passed on the essential experience of the First Person upon which my whole case rests, the experience which has no parallel and for which there's no substitute—the *direct* experience of the Experiencer.

Now abideth these four—reason, tradition, the map, the testing—

and the greatest of these is the testing. Without its nourishment, the others, by merely whetting the appetite, leave one hungrier than ever. With it, what a satisfying four-course feast is spread for you and me!

Such a meal doesn't come cheap. I suspect I'll be charged the Earth, not because, throughout the festivities, I've desecrated the God of Heaven but the gods of the City—those pop-eyed, human-headed idols. Three times over I've sent them up: poked fun at them, hoicked and rousted them from the thrones they were sitting so ugly on, and sentenced them to life in glass-fronted prisons. Yes, and talked a lot of young people into doing likewise.

And now it seems I shall have to pay the penalty and wash down the banquet with a hemlock liqueur.

At the moment of writing I don't know for sure what's going to happen to me. My lawyer has been under constant pressure from the Attorney General's office to get me to agree to one or another form of retraction and apology to offended parties. All the formulae require me to dilute the pure milk of my doctrine—and with dirty water, at that. This I will not do. Each proposed apology submitted to me is less apologetic than the last—but accompanied by broader hints of fatal consequences should I reject it. However, I will have none of them. The latest news is that, as a last resort, someone (it could be the Judge) is hunting through the transcript of the Trial in the slender hope of finding something I said which—torn from its context—could be construed as a retreat from my position.

Evidently the last thing the Government wants is my blood on its hands, followed almost inevitably by that of a succession of martyrs in the cause of free speech in religion, and *the basic right of humans to question their humanness.* On the other hand, I'm told, a crescendo of threatening noises has been coming from the more fanatical elements of the fundamentalist lobby, complaining of the delay in sentencing me. Death is what they demand, and it's doubtful whether they could be bought off with life imprisonment. A dilemma for the Government, all right.

How desperately they are seeking a way out of the dilemma is shown by what I take to be their latest move. I was visited here in my cell this very morning by a stranger of conspiratorial mien, who refused to give his name. Suspecting that my cell was bugged, he whispered in my ear the good news, as he called it. Some unidentified friends of mine were arranging to spring me from prison in the next two days. Escape plans, including drugged or bent prison officers, a get-away helicopter and a safe country hide-out, were practically complete. All that was needed was my co-operation.

I admit that, seeing no compromise with the truth was involved, I was tempted. A few moments of reflection, however, and I had no hesitation at all in giving my mysterious visitor the bum's rush. Christopher, my lawyer, says I was a fool not to seize the opportunity of a getaway, which would probably have succeeded because (he's convinced) the plot had been hatched at a high Government level. Hatched by some optimist who saw this as a neat way out of an otherwise insoluble problem. Neat only, of course, in the rather unlikely event of the source and the beneficiary of the plot remaining undiscovered.

I can think of another explanation of the plot. Shooting me dead, while attempting to escape, would let the Government off the hook. It would ensure that I made my exit as a fugitive from the law and not a victim of the law. Martyr into criminal—what could be neater?

My suspicions are deepened by the fact that allowing anyone (other than my lawyer) to visit me in my cell—instead of in the visiting area with its wire screen—was a breach of prison regulations. In short, the whole episode was as fishy as could be.

My refusal to compromise—whether by toning down my message or by running away—has been made at gut level, not by taking thought. Which brings home to me a fact I hadn't quite faced up to—the plain fact that I have *chosen death*.

How do I feel about this? I ask myself.

There's a sense, of course, in which I have the last laugh and the last word. *The Prosecution got the wrong man!* Nevertheless, the cord binding Jack, that wrong man, to this Right One, isn't cut casually, or painlessly. There are pleasanter sensations than to find Death twitching at one's ear.

A part of me is happy to die in this best of causes. A part isn't. I'm reminded of a story about a young man called Hubert who went to Napoleon with a new religion. He listened with care, and in the end approved wholeheartedly. But, just as Hubert was leaving the imperial presence, he called him back.

'There's just one thing missing,' Napoleon said.

'Yes, Sire?' asked the young man, all eagerness.

'You must get yourself crucified!'

Epilogue

Napoleon had the right idea, but put it too briefly. He should have added: 'Or at least see that already you *are* the Crucified One.'

Like Hubert, unregenerate Jack has the strongest motive for sitting tight on God's throne. But, unlike him, Jack has no option. He's being packed off to where he belongs. He's being decentralized for good and all, willy-nilly. And that fact, one way or another, means crucifixion, willy-nilly. And crucifixion hurts.

Well, I haven't spent my adult life living for a cause I daren't die for. But I don't see death coming as easily as I'd imagined. Sir Gerald was right, after all. I don't feel a bit chirpy. I tremble... I tremble, I trust, I wait... I wait, I trust, I tremble...

Questions and doubts I'd long supposed settled suddenly reemerge:

Is What I'm made of truly death proof? Is it enough to tell my headsman I've beaten him to it, and long ago done his job? Is the One who never let me down incapable of ever doing so? Is This which is a thousand times more Me than myself, which is the Soul of my soul, which is my only Knowable yet as beyond me as the unimaginable fringes of space-time—is This forever mine? Forever me? Come on! Does the fact that this Artesian Well never ran dry mean it will never do so? Is my Help in ages past my *certain* Hope in ages to come, *secula seculorum?*

Horrified, ashamed of raising such questions one minute short of midnight, I pull myself together and take heart. Am I not so intimately caught up in Him who is my darling—so seized of the joy which is His own astonishment at Himself, so privy to His secrets, so madly and so sanely in love with Him—that He cannot let me perish like a mayfly or a solar system? Does He not find my child's cry 'Only in Your arms am I safe at Home!' irresistible? Can He afford *not* to clasp me to His heart for ever?

Words, words, words. They come up unbidden like marsh gas from a swamp, like whirling-devils in the desert, like stinging nettles on a rubbish dump—and are about as significant. To bandy words with Him, to verbalize at all about Him, is to play the game of separation. All words are infected with the virus of two-ness. And where there are two, there's trembling. Where there are two, there's terror.

My remedy is to *see*. See the One.

I look out at these all-embracing arms, ending in those little hands. I look up at those little feet.

They are the nailed hands and feet of the One who loved me and gave Himself for me. All of Himself. All, for ever and ever.

I look in at the One Who can be seen by no other.

It would be nonsense and heartbreak and blasphemy not to be Him.

APPENDICES

The 8 x 8-fold Plebeian Path

This is the Map of the Path referred to chapters 19 and 20. The best time to go through it in detail is after you have finished reading my account of the Trial. It will then remind you of many of the places we have visited.

I call this Path plebeian—and not noble, and certainly not Aryan—because nearly all humans travel nearly all of it anyway. And because even the last two stages are open to anyone who's desperate enough to take the low road that God has fully sign-posted and made perfectly obvious.

With de Caussade—that seasoned traveller on the low road—I invite you to

> Come, not only to look at a map of the spiritual country, but to possess and to walk in it without fear of losing your way. Come, not to study the history of God's divine action, but to be the subject of its operation… He will never disclose Himself in the shape of that exalted image to which you so vainly cling.

	1 INFANT	2 CHILD	3 OLDER CHILD
1 TOPSY-TURVY	Feet up	My feet go to the bottom of the picture	I'm becoming like everyone else
2 TRUTH AND LIES	I see what I see	I start seeing what I'm told to see	I start hallucinating a head on my shoulders
3 BIG AND SMALL	I'm immense	At times I'm shrunk to a small thing	Only occasionally am I at large, out of my head
4 RICH AND POOR	The world is mine, here	I start distancing objects	Losing my world, I'm increasingly impoverished
5 STILL AND MOVING	My world (including arms and legs) is on the move	I start moving, my world starts halting	I take on the world's agitation. It grinds to a halt
6 DIVINE AND HUMAN	I'm prehuman, unsocialized, divine	I'm being humanized, socialized	My divinity has almost vanished
7 HEART AND HEAD	I'm all heart, no head	I'm still headless, heart dominated	I'm becoming headed
8 RAGE DISPOSAL	My rage is quickly discharged	My rage starts accumulating	More and more my rage accumulates

4 ADOLESCENT	5 ADOLESCENT IN REVOLT	6 ADULT	7 ADULT BEHEADED	8 SEER
I am like everyone else	Maddened I aim to turn all upside down	Back to normal delusion	KENSHO, I see my Original (No) Face	ENLIGHTENMENT All is reversed
I abstract from the world a mind to go into the head	I know that everything is wrong	Capitulating, I settle down to a life of lies	The headquarters of my self-deception are cut off	I come to my senses
I've lost my immensity altogether	My anger at being cut down to size accumulates	I'm shrunk and solidified to the limit	I blow my top but I'm not yet at large	I'm immense again
Cheated of all, I'm desperately poor	In vain, I claim my lost heritage	Greedy, I grasp at bits of my heritage	I venture out to claim my heritage	The world is mine again
I grow more and more disturbed inside	I feel my inner agitation is climaxing	I screw the lid down tighter on my inner turmoil	I start returning my motion to the world	I'm the unmoved Mover of the world
My humanizing is complete	I refuse to join those conformists	I submit to being only human after all	My humanness still bugs me	I'm divine
I'm heady; head dominated	My heart's protesting like mad	My head regains control	I lost my head, but still have to find my heart	I find my heart
My rage is suppressed	My rage goes to my head	My rage is more firmly suppressed	The pressure is relieved	My rage is discharged

Autobiographical Postscript

I do not require of you to form great and curious considerations in your understanding. I require of you no more than to look.

God, in conversation with St Teresa of Avila

Could I behold those hands which span the Poles,
And turn all spheres at once…?

John Donne

Who can deny me power, and liberty
To stretch mine arms, and mine own Cross to be?
… So, take what hid Christ in thee,
And be his image, or not his, but he.

John Donne

I think you will be interested to learn how the story of John a-Nokes connects with that of Douglas Harding, his author. It will most certainly have occurred to you that the Trial is a kind of spiritual autobiography, a device of the writer for bringing out and clarifying his own interior debate—a taking-to-heart of William James's dictum that 'we never fully grasp the import of any true statement till we have a clear notion of what the opposite untrue statement would be.' Yes, of course: the purpose of this book has been to address questions which (for me, at least) are best resolved by something like Bunyan's method of personification, or Moreno's method of psychodrama, with all the resulting manoeuvres and clashes and mayhem; that's to

Autobiographical Postscript

say, by releasing a motley band of lay figures who are in fact warring fragments of oneself, alter egos that have become alter enough to fight it out in the open, with a view to finally resolving their differences and arriving at a just and lasting peace. It's not enough (I find) to have the courage of one's convictions; one must have the courage to attack them vigorously and sincerely. And to abide by the outcome. The only way to see one's own side for what it is, and to hear the other side at all clearly, is frequently to go over there.

So much, no doubt, is already plain. The autobiographical notes that follow (it's straight autobiography this time) will show how I had far better reasons than you could have suspected for choosing to hang my spiritual outfit on the peg of a Blasphemy Trial instead of, for example (following Bunyan again), a pilgrimage or a war. Blasphemy—what it is and isn't, and whether it's I or my accusers who are guilty of it—has been the key issue of my life. What's more, I really have been tried on this most serious of all charges, and sentenced to the most terrible of all punishments. By whom and with what result you are about to discover.

I was born on 12 February 1909, at Lowestoft, a fishing port in the county of Suffolk, England. My father was a fruiterer, and my grandfathers were shopkeepers also, all three in a small way of business. Before marriage, my grandmothers were domestic servants.

For two generations my family had belonged to the sect of Christian fundamentalists known to others as the Exclusive Plymouth Brethren, and to themselves as the Lord's People, the Saints, the Little Flock, or simply the Meeting.

Exclusive is the word. We children were forbidden all unnecessary contact with the world—that is, with all children and adults not belonging to the Meeting. Our home was innocent of virtually all literature except the Bible and the Brethren's voluminous commentaries on it. There had to be a minimum of worldly schoolbooks around, of course, but any others smuggled in were liable to a ceremonial burning. Newspapers were for wrapping and wiping with, not reading. Theatres and cinemas were positively satanic—a conviction based on the rock of complete ignorance of what went on in those haunts of sin and shame. You could get away with the occasional smirk or grin in the Harding home, but not audible laughter; for, at the Last Judgement, you will have to account to God for every idle word, let alone guffaw. Attendance at frequent and interminable and unspeakably dull religious meetings, and extempore prayers and Bible-reading morning and evening, was obligatory from a very early age. Surprisingly, the ban on fidgeting in Meeting worked.

All told, in my case at least, an upbringing calculated to make blasphemy impossible, or else inevitable. It ruled out half measures.

Don't think I'm grumbling. My cranky upbringing included some impressive advantages. In spite of their siege mentality and near-paranoia, these people weren't petty or shallow. They were the Lord's people and they meant business—the Lord's business. Their passion was meaning and truth, as they saw it. And for them the ultimate truth was a God whose love brought Him all the way down to Calvary. He has stayed with me all my life. Also there were plenty of secondary reasons for thankfulness. A media-free childhood—now there was a spot of luck! I just had to develop interior resources. I got to know my Bible from soup to nuts—from the primeval soup, without form and void, of Genesis, to that nutty (but in places devastatingly word-magical) Book of Revelation. In fact, my lessons in literary style began before I could string together a dozen words of my own. Also I learned to concentrate—no matter on what subject—without too much mind-wandering. Oh yes, I was happy to let the dear Brethren imagine that the small boy, sitting so still all through Meeting with firmly closed eyes, was thinking on those things which are above—or at least on such things as the Ammonites and Jebusites here below—whereas he was probably thinking on the ammonites and belemnites in his treasured collection of fossils. Or on his bits and pieces of amber and cornelian, instead of the diamonds and rubies and emeralds of the New Jerusalem on high. To my present-day critics, who complain that I pontificate about Zen without having done my stint of *zazen* or sitting-meditation, I reply: 'Not so! I put in an average of eight hours a week for twenty years, and am still feeling the benefit. So there!'

Unlike my sister and younger brother, in fact unlike nearly all Exclusive children, I came increasingly to question the theology (not itself very different from that of other evangelical-fundamentalist sects) and the very peculiar lifestyle of the Brethren. Silently to question them, of course: these weren't matters for discussion. I was secretive, all right.

At twenty-one, my doubts having come to a head and exploded, I apostatized. The family, who had never suspected what was going on, were devastated. My father would himself have lit the faggot that burned his son alive, if burning at the stake had been feasible, and if that tip-of-the-tongue foretaste of hell-fire stood the least chance of inducing a last-minute recantation. He said as much, weeping and imploring. Out of deep love he said it.

Declining to ease myself gradually and for no clearly explained reason from the Brethren's ranks, I had decided on a clean break. I addressed the Elders in a ten-page thesis (now, alas, lost) and also, at their request, in person, confidently setting forth my heretical views. Brazenly, I should say. I felt flattered rather than shaken when I was told (amid a flurry of tears and bitter anger and flopping to the knees in prayer) that my apostasy was the worst in the Brethren's century-old history. It was diabolical on four counts: first, I dared to question whether the Exclusive Plymouth Brethren are God's chosen ones in all the world, the sole custodians of His True Gospel; second, and worse, I dared to question whether non-Christian religions are devil-worship, and I went so far as to suggest that God was revealing His mind in them also, but differently; third, and worse still, I dared to regard Jesus as a man like other men, except that he saw what they were blind to—their oneness with the Father—and went on to live and to die in the light of that vision; fourth, and almost too fiendish to articulate, I unblushingly hinted—and more than hinted—at my own intrinsic Godhood. Which convicted me out of my own mouth of the ultimate blasphemy, the iniquity for which there's no forgiveness:

the sin of setting myself up on the throne of God. I wasn't so much a limb of Satan as Satan in person.

So it was that in the spring of 1930, at the age of twenty-one, I came to appear before a kangaroo court of fanatics. In the house of one Mr French, of Finchley in North London, I was charged with the worst of all crimes, and found guilty, and condemned to the worst of all punishments. Of course it's true that the court lacked executive power and had to leave the carrying out of the sentence to Higher Authority. Not that they doubted for a moment that the punishment would be inflicted without mercy or respite for ever and ever. Also it's true, of course, that I had only myself to blame for bringing the full weight of the Brethren's indignation down on my head. I could have extricated myself less dramatically, could have withdrawn from the Brethren by easy stages, leaving them to guess—with a minimum of tears and outrage—my reasons. Reasons, they would naturally assume, of weakness and depravity, of seduction by the world and the flesh rather than deliberately going to the Devil. But no: for motives I'm even now somewhat unclear about, I chose not to dissemble but to come clean. Not to run away but to stand trial. And this in spite of the fact that the verdict was a foregone conclusion, and that in any event I didn't admit the court's jurisdiction. My guess is that this farce of a drumhead trial, and my carefully worked-out defence, was for me a psychological necessity at the time—an announcement to myself and to the outer world, as well as to the Brethren, of my rebirth into a new life and freedom. My clear-cut chrysalis-into-butterfly metamorphosis.

To begin with, I felt less like a butterfly than a moth—the clothes-devouring, hunted sort, at that. At the time of my apostasy I was lodging with a kindly Plymouth Sister, Mrs Fox, in Muswell Hill. She was made to turf me out at once. I was very short of money, the parental supplement to my £150-per-annum scholarship (covering university fees and some living costs) having of course dried up at source. So I had to find in a hurry the cheapest feasible lodgings in London. Consulting Daltons Weekly, I settled on a place in Maida Vale, and moved in. The smell knocked you back and the mattress was alpine, but the food was eatable if you were hungry enough. Which I was. But after two days there I was ejected again, instantly. The landlady was another Exclusive Plymouth Sister! My reputation had caught up with me.

All that was sixty years ago. My life since then has been a development of the thesis I confronted those Elders with. It's elaborated in this and other books, and more particularly in the experiments and the day-to-day practice they advocate. Some lapses apart, it has been a life dedicated to doing battle with the blasphemy (my own far more than others') that ousts God from the Centre of that life.

It's hard to imagine a life more different from its Exclusive beginnings, and yet at the same time more of a piece with them. Increasingly I have evidence of this.

Soon after breaking free of the Brethren, I came across four poems of the period which have haunted me ever since. A distant and muffled drumbeat, but compelling, a music all the more captivating for being only half heard. They were John Masefield's ecstatic 'The Everlasting Mercy', Katharine Tynan's sentimental 'All in an April Evening', Richard le Gallienne's challenging 'The Second Crucifixion', and Joseph Mary Plunkett's

> I see his blood upon the rose,
> And in the stars the glory of his eyes,
> His body gleams amid eternal snows,
> His tears fall from the skies…
> All pathways by his feet are worn,
> His strong heart stirs the ever-beating sea,
> His crown of thorns is twined with every thorn,
> His cross is every tree.

To my shame I had to wait for sixty years—and for the emergence of the Pattern which is the bone-structure of this book—before re-awakening to the centrality of the Crucified Saviour in my life. True, I had inherited it, drunk it in with my mother's milk. All along I've felt it, known it without perceiving it. *But now I see it.*

Now at long last it surfaces to make perfect sense. And to think I might have died in my seventies, unblessed by this clearest of visions! How surprised and how thankful I am that the closing years of my life are turning out to be as Christocentric as the opening years—albeit for wholly different and wholly unforeseeable reasons.

What I can't get over is how obvious, how actual-factual, how concrete—and, yes, how 'materialistic'—are this crucifixion and this Christing! Facing the world is crucifixion. 'We are,' says St Paul, with typical precision and boldness, 'always bearing about in the body the dying of the Lord Jesus, that the life also of Jesus might be made manifest in our body.' Or take Thomas Traherne's outpouring:

> The Cross is the abyss of wonders, the centre of desires, the school of virtues, the theatre of joys, and the place of sorrows. It is the root of happiness, and the gate of Heaven. Of all the things in Heaven and Earth it is the most peculiar... If Love be the weight of the Soul, and its object the Centre, all eyes and hearts may convert and turn unto this Object, cleave unto this Centre, and by it enter into rest.

Seventy years ago I'd have taken all that in my stride. Seven years ago I'd have dismissed it as overdone and a touch morbid. Today I revel in it as the sober truth. And though I can't claim, with Chris Marlowe, to 'see, see where Christ's blood streams in the firmament', I feel that mighty transfusion flooding me to the last and tiniest capillary.[1]

Not that my adulthood is as yet neatly buttoned up and concluded, of course. Far from it. Count no man faithful till he's dead, and don't be too sure even then. Rather as the story of Jack is open-ended—unfinished business that could finish very shamefully—so is the story

---

[1] From the sixth to the eleventh centuries Christ was portrayed as enthroned on the cross, robed as priest or king, and often wearing a royal crown. There were no signs of suffering. His arms were outstretched horizontally, embracing his world. The drooping, agonized Saviour developed as the Middle Ages became increasingly obsessed with pain and death. It's for you and me to find out which of these aspects of our own crucifixion comes to the fore, once we accept and live with the fact of it.

of his author. For sure I'm soon going to be excused from pretending to be Douglas Edison Harding, relieved from being so hooked on that little fellow. What isn't at all sure is how I'll take being let off the hook. Thanks to a general softening up—if not to senile dementia or madness itself—Jack and I could go back on all we ever stood for, slinking away into some safe and comfy hide-out and there dying terrified out of our remaining wits. Nothing's certain but uncertainty.

Even so, even if the worst were to come to the most shaming worst, nobody can include the Truth in his fall, dragging it down about his ears like eyeless Samson in Gaza. The pillars of Jack's Defence—reason, tradition, the map, the tests—stand firm and four-square, no matter to what depths the Defendant may tumble. Even if he were to sink so low as to play Judas to his Christ, he could never un-Christ himself. Never. The Truth sets us free, free even from all our human lies and betrayals.

Thank God it's *God's* Truth.

To conclude, a little more about the Plymouth Exclusives and me.

Since breaking out of the fold sixty years ago, what little I have had to do with them can be summed up in two or three lightning sketches.

The first is my father's funeral in Lowestoft. The year is 1954. (This was before ex-Exclusives were banned from attending the funerals of their Exclusive relatives.) A dismal hall like all those the Brethren meet in, a place as harsh as its coconut-matting and as bleak as its distemper, a place that looks and smells as though no one had ever laughed in it, or child played, or heart leaped, a place that even the flies stall and drop dead in. The coffin's propped up there in the middle. I'm put next to it. Around it sit twenty brothers in newly pressed dark suits, and as many sisters in long skirts and high blouses and colourless hats. The brothers get up in turn and lugubriously praise Gord (which is the name of their deity, don't ask me why) for the dedicated life and service of their dear brother—given so freely, but terribly saddened by the defection to the Devil of his elder son. A blasphemer long past praying for, I'm prayed at. To conclude, we are told that after the burial we shall return to the meeting hall, where tea will be served—served to all except me, the chief mourner, and my wife! One gets the message that, since burning at the stake isn't legal, they'll settle for this truly British second-best.

Afterwards, my sister and I have some business. She won't come to my place because it would contaminate her. I can't go to her place because I would contaminate it. We can't go to a hotel or restaurant because the Brethren shun those unholy places, and anyway are forbidden to eat with non-Exclusives, let alone ex-Exclusives. So we meet in a lay-by on the A12. As briefly as possible.

My friend Susan Kimber, who is researching the recent history of the Exclusives, updates me somewhat. I learn that, compared with the Exclusives of today, those of my childhood were broad-minded to the point of laxity. Susan's tale is of a sect that requires its householders to live in detached homes and thus avoid being yoked with unbelievers, to put down their pets, and never again go off on holiday; that requires its doctors and dentists and architects and lawyers to resign from their professional bodies (all devilish), unscrew their brass plates, and make a living as best they can; that requires its housewives to throw away such worldly attachments as house-plants, and even the most colourless of hats; that requires its meeting-house managers to brick up the windows that look out on the world, and substitute skylights that look up to heaven; and that requires its young couples to throw out their old mum if she declines to join the Brethren, and to send their child of twelve to Coventry for the same reason.

Brethren aren't forced to obey these rules. It's just that their life is made hell till they do so.

This partial catalogue of injunctions and prohibitions is doubtless out of date by now. But be sure the list doesn't get any shorter or less rigorous with time... 'Rigorous' isn't quite the term I want. As an ex-Exclusive-child I can't help putting myself in the shoes of one of those ostracized kids of twelve, whose early submission (with no outside friend to turn to, and almost no idea of what's outside anyway) is a near certainty. Among all the forms of legal child-battering (yes, legal!), is there any more cruel?

And yet—I'm bound to add—if the child *doesn't* succumb, but keeps his counsel and bides his time, the cruelty can begin to look a lot less cruel. As I say, speaking personally, I have in the end no complaints at all. But that's partly because I was born into this sect so long ago, when they were comparatively sane.

Talk about the meeting of extremes—these people are *all* contradictions! The Brethren came together early in the nineteenth century to set up an anticlerical democracy of the Spirit, of whom all the male members were to be priests and mouth-pieces. By the end of the century it had become a more thorough and insidious dictatorship than any I can think of. A dynastic one, at that. Through the first half of the twentieth century Big Brother was a New York linen salesman called James Taylor. I remember him as an unsmiling but apparently harmless enough fellow. Every inch the draper, and not a hint of the führer he really was. In fact, he had only to breathe a word about anything—from sisters' hair-dos (hair-don'ts: don't put it up, don't cut it) to the iniquity of belonging to the Automobile Association—for ten thousand Exclusives the world over to jump to attention and be led by Big Jim up the crazy paving of the latest garden path. He died in 1959, mourned by all. After some hesitation the more-than-papal crown alighted on his son, J. T. Jr, said to be an alcoholic not averse to getting into bed with the sisterhood. (To test their virtue, he explained, when caught.) During his reign whisky-drinking became quite the thing, and on occasion led to maudlin goings-on in Meeting, even at the Lord's Supper. The 'liberty of the risen Christ' they called it; and anyway, they were only following Holy Scripture and the advice of Paul to Timothy, 'Drink no longer water, but use a little wine for thy stomach's sake." In 1970, J. T. Jr, mourned by many and powered by 65 per cent-over-proof spirits rather than mere wine (which was reserved for sisters, those 'weaker vessels'), took off for the Meeting in the skies. Since when the saints, fragmented into Taylorites (to whom my sister, *malgré tout,* adheres) and Anti-Taylorites, have gone their mutually exclusive ways. I have lost track of them, but am assured that Jehovah's command to the Children of Israel—'Come out from among them, and be ye separate'—is being interpreted as quirkily and obeyed as fervently as ever. And that the great contradiction goes on. Show me a blue-nosed puritan, a creeping Jesus meek and mild, and I'll show you a tyrant and an orgiast—a satyr rosy with grog-blossom—struggling to get out. And occasionally making it.

The first and decisive decades of my life were spent as a third-generation member of this very rum sect. They have determined the rest of it—inevitably, and in all sorts of subtle and not-so-subtle ways. I don't pretend that I can begin to live down my upbringing. Nor do I want to. I'm content to have inherited the ancestral gene (call it virus if you must), which is the certainty that God has entrusted me with a Quite Wonderful Truth, for lack of which His world is destroying itself. (In my case, the Truth that sets a new standard in OBVIOUSNESS.) While our symptoms couldn't be more different, there's no denying that the condition they are symptoms of is one and the same. I no more took off from the Brethren than a wayward branch takes off from the parent trunk. No, my escape from that family tree—Dutch elm disease and all—lies in acknowledging that I'm just as bound to it up there as I'm free of it down here, in the Everlasting Ground from which the whole forest springs.

The Trial of the Man Who Said He was God could only have come from the pen of an ex-Exclusive Plymouth Brother—with emphasis on the ex. If the writing of it has been my homage to the Wide-open

One, my rejoicing in Him who is Inclusiveness itself (and it has been just that), I shall forever owe the fact to the Brethren. And most of all to the best and dearest of them all, to the brother who was also my father.

Finally, a footnote to a footnote. A few months back I wrote to my sister (we've neither spoken nor written since that tealess funeral in 1954) to give her my love and to assure her I'm not the blasphemer she takes me for. That I'm as addicted to God (not to say Gord) as she is. And by no means resentful of the peculiar childhood years we share.

'You are now an old man,' she replied, 'and already licked by eternal flames. Every day I pray that you may yet escape them, by returning to the faith of our dear father.'

Little does she know, bless her heart!

Check-list of Experiments

Tick the appropriate box

		read about	carried out
	The Battering-ram, for demolishing prison walls		
	God loves being pointed at		
	The Mirror that shows you what you're not like		
	The Convenience: of Levity and Gravity		
	Driving your Land Rover, or your Land?		
	Vertical Lines converge—on You		
	In touch with your God-head		
	Returning the many to the One, the One to the None		
	Uccelli di Dio—your Angel Attendants		
	Omnipresence: how to draw all things to you		
	Omniscience: how to see into the Heart of all things		
	Omnipotence: how to move, destroy, remake all things		
	Your all-embracing Arms		
	Two-way pointing		
	Nought o'clock, and all's well		
	Crucifixion		
	Bowing before the evidence		
	Totals		

If your score in column 2 is 17, you have dined with God.

If it is much less, you have breakfasted with Him.

If it is nil, you've eaten His menu instead of His meal. I hope it gives you such indigestion that you have to take repeated doses of the first three experiments to ease your heartburn.

www.ingramcontent.com/pod-product-compliance
Lightning Source LLC
Chambersburg PA
CBHW031129160426
43193CB00008B/75